The
MODERN
GUIDE TO
Witchcraft

The
MODERN
GUIDE TO
Witchcraft

Your Complete Guide to

WITCHES, COVENS,
& SPELLS

Skye Alexander

Adams Media
New York   London   Toronto   Sydney   New Delhi

▲adamsmedia

Adams Media
An Imprint of Simon & Schuster, Inc.
100 Technology Center Drive
Stoughton, MA 02072

For information about special discounts for bulk purchases, please contact Simon & Schuster Special Sales at 1-866-506-1949 or business@simonand-schuster.com.

The Simon & Schuster Speakers Bureau can bring authors to your live event. For more information or to book an event contact the Simon & Schuster Speakers Bureau at 1-866-248-3049 or visit our website at www.simonspeak-ers.com.

Manufactured in the United States of America

23 2022

Library of Congress Cataloging-in-Publication Data has been applied for.

ISBN 978-1-4405-8002-4
ISBN 978-1-4405-8003-1 (ebook)

To Ron, always

Acknowledgments

I wish to thank my editors Tom Hardej and Peter Archer, and all the other talented folks at Adams Media for making this book possible.

CONTENTS

PART II
AN OPEN GRIMOIRE 155

SO YOU WANT TO BE A WITCH

You've picked up this book because you're interested in witches. You wonder about who they are and what they believe. You know being a witch has something to do with finding a deeper connection to nature and to the entire cosmos. With finding an inner power and beauty that can help you accomplish what you want in life. In the back of your mind flits the image of an ugly old woman dressed in black, riding a broomstick, but you know that's wrong—and you want to find out more.

What does it mean to be a witch?

Witches come in all sizes, ages, colors, and personalities. They're doctors, computer programmers, teachers, landscapers, bartenders, and flight attendants. The person who cuts your hair or repairs your car might be a witch. Witches can be male or female—no, a male witch is *not* a warlock, and he might get angry if you call him that, for good reason. *Warlock* comes from an Old English word meaning "oath breaker" or "liar."

The simple fact that you're reading this book suggests that you think you, too, have witch potential. Guess what? You do. And with a little training, you can uncover your magickal power and learn to use it to shape your destiny.

WHY IS WITCHCRAFT GAINING POPULARITY TODAY?

Witchcraft resonates with us because it speaks to some key issues of today: respect for the environment, gender equality, and overcoming religious biases and narrow-minded thinking. It also encourages those who follow this path to discover and develop their own, unique powers so they can take charge of their lives and be everything they choose to be.

In general, most witches seek to improve themselves and humankind as a whole, and to live in harmony with the universe. This means working for the greater good—often through the use of magick—and harming none. It also means taking responsibility for your thoughts, words, and deeds because everything you do affects everything else.

Once you learn to harness your natural talents as a witch, you'll discover that a whole new world of possibilities exists. You'll be able to use what's known as the Law of Attraction to improve your financial situation, your relationships, your health, and your overall well-being. You'll also have the power to help others. And, you'll gain a greater sense of your place in the universe.

Magick won't help you finish a project for school or work, or make you taller, or fix a flat tire. However, it can strengthen your concentration and mental receptivity, make you more attractive to other people, or draw someone to you who can repair that flat.

It's a good idea to take it slow in the beginning—just as you would if you were training for a marathon. That way you'll have fun and avoid setbacks.

WHAT YOU'LL LEARN FROM THIS BOOK

We're all born magickal beings. As children we know this, but as we grow up we forget our true nature. We listen to other people whose limited views cause us to doubt our innate powers, and we get caught up in the stresses of everyday life. This book shows you how to reconnect with the magick in you. As you read these pages, you'll learn to pay attention to your intuition and let it guide you. You'll gain a greater appreciation and awareness of the natural world—the cycles of the moon, the energies of the seasons, your links with the animals, birds, and other

The Modern Guide to Witchcraft

creatures who share this planet with you. You'll also discover how to incorporate nature's tools—herbs and flowers, crystals and gemstones, and more—into your magickal workings.

You'll come to realize that witchcraft and magick aren't "hocus pocus." They are your birthright. They already exist deep within you. You already have the power to tap into the energies of the natural world and the cosmos; you just need to recognize that power and learn to direct it. That's what this book is about: reconnecting with your magickal self.

True magick lies in developing your inner potential and spirituality. This book is intended to help you on that journey toward getting in touch with nature, with the Divine, and with your own innate abilities— because ultimately, that's the real source of witchcraft.

PART I

Welcome TO THE WONDERFUL WORLD of WITCHCRAFT

Chapter 1

WHAT IS WITCHCRAFT?

Snow White, Cinderella, The Wizard of Oz, Alice in Wonderland, Beauty and the Beast, Peter Pan, Star Wars. Most of us first discovered wizards and witches, spells and potions, and the never-ending struggle between good and evil through these stories. Fairy tales showed us a world filled with magick—one where inanimate objects like mirrors, stones, and gems can have special powers; animals can talk; plants can think; and with a sprinkling of dust, kids can fly.

Then we grew up and forgot about magick. Our lives became a little less rich and our imaginations started to shrivel as we got mired in the mundane details of our daily lives. But every now and then, we recapture some of that early magick through books and movies like *ET, Lord of the Rings,* and *Harry Potter.* We find ourselves fascinated once again by the supernatural world and eager to reawaken the magick within us.

COMMON MISCONCEPTIONS ABOUT WITCHES

Before we go any further, let's get rid of those ridiculous ideas some people still hold about witches. Misconceptions about witches come from ignorance and fear. For centuries, mainstream religions have encouraged negative images about witches—and during a period known as "The Burning Times" these false ideas led to the deaths of countless innocent people in Europe and the New World. In recent times, the media continue to present a distorted picture of witches and magick, further confusing the issue. For the record:

- Witches do not steal or eat babies—this idea comes from old folklore, and fairies were often blamed for doing the same thing.
- Witches are not Satanists who sell their souls to the devil in return for special powers. Lots of witches don't even believe in Satan—he's a Christian conception.
- Witches don't ride brooms—they get around in cars, trains, and airplanes just like everyone else. (You might see a bumper sticker that says, "I'm driving this car because my broom's in the shop" but that's just a joke.)
- Witches prefer pizza over eye of newt any day.
- Witches don't inherit magickal powers from mysterious ancestors, although if Grandma was a witch and trained you in the Craft from childhood, you'll have a head start on other wannabe witches.
- Not all witches possess remarkable psychic powers, nor do they have the gift of prophecy. Some psychics may be witches, and many witches develop their intuition through practice. But the truth is, everyone has psychic ability, including you.
- Witches don't consort with or battle demons, vampires, zombies, or other monsters—they have better things to do.
- Not all witches worship ancient gods and goddesses—some don't believe in any type of deity.
- Witches aren't immortal; they live ordinary lifespans just like other humans.
- Witches aren't ugly old hags, they can be young and incredibly beautiful, but most of them are just average people like you and me.
- Witches don't engage in rivalries and conflicts with other magickal practitioners. The witches in Salem, Massachusetts, for example, don't have a long-standing rivalry with New Orleans's voodoo priestesses. Trust me on this. I've been a witch for twenty-five years and lived in Salem for eight—and I get along with people from New Orleans just fine.

If you choose to become a witch, you'll have to throw out all the silly and sensational things you've seen, heard, and read about witchcraft. At least for the time being, you'll have to live with being constantly offended

The Modern Guide to Witchcraft

by the ignorance of people who don't (or won't) understand witchcraft. Just put on your magick, protective shield and get on with practicing the real deal.

Wizards, Sorcerers, and Magicians

The words wizard and sorcerer can be used for either a man or a woman. Wizard derives from a term meaning "wise," and sorcerer means "witch" or "diviner." The word magician is also appropriate for both sexes and for witches of all stripes. Depending on the cultural setting, the term magician came to describe people adept in astrology, sorcery, divination, spellcasting, or other magickal arts.

In this book, we'll use some terms repeatedly. Let's clarify a few of them in order to avoid confusion:

- A witch is someone who uses his or her power along with the natural laws of the universe to shape reality in accordance with his/her purposes.
- Witchcraft is the practice of manipulating energy through various means to produce a desired result.
- Magick is the transformation that occurs when a witch/magician bends or shapes energy using paranormal techniques. The "k" at the end of the word distinguishes it from magic tricks and stage illusion (or sleight of hand).

As we go along, you'll see that witches follow any number of paths and use lots of different methods in the practice of their craft. They also perform many types of magick for a variety of reasons. As you explore the art of the witch and learn to use your own magickal ability, you'll discover what suits you best and what direction you wish to take in your own journey.

WITCHCRAFT AND RELIGION

Like people from other walks of life, witches share some concepts and disagree on others—we'll discuss some of these as we go along. Their ideas may be influenced by their cultural traditions and backgrounds, personal life experiences, or individual temperaments. That's okay. You don't have to subscribe to any particular belief system or set of rules to be a witch.

In the past, many witches learned their craft as part of a family tradition in which they were carefully trained, just as other people might learn carpentry or masonry. Villages had "cunning folk" to whom people turned for all kinds of help, from encouraging crops to grow to fixing a broken heart. Healing made up a large part of the witch's work, and many witches were knowledgeable herbalists and midwives. In exchange for such services, the witch might receive a chicken, a measure of grain, or other necessities.

Religious concepts weren't linked with the practice of witchcraft itself, though individual witches often embraced the beliefs of their families or culture. That's still true today. If you belong to a certain religion or are on a specific spiritual path, you needn't give it up to become a witch. In fact, you may choose to incorporate the ideas of your faith into your magickal practice. If you don't hold to any belief system at all, that's fine too. Witches can follow any religion or none. However, the lack of rules, dogma, or religious affiliation does not mean witches lack ethics.

Wicca and Witchcraft

People sometimes confuse the terms *witch* and *Wicca*. Witchcraft is a methodology, a skill, a way of working with energy to produce a result. Wicca is a spiritual philosophy, with its own code of ethics, concepts, rituals, deities, etc. Yes, many witches in the West today consider themselves Wiccan, and Wiccans generally practice witchcraft, but witches are not necessarily Wiccan.

Other Worlds of Existence

Many witches accept that one or more realms beyond our earth exist and that nonphysical beings share the cosmos with us. Some honor certain gods or goddesses, and we'll take a look at these in Chapter 6. Other witches converse with angels, fairies, and nature spirits. Still others believe that everything on earth—animals, plants, stones—possesses a divine essence or soul. But witches do not need to believe in divine beings in order to perform their work, just as computer programmers, electricians, and dental hygienists don't have to be members of a particular faith to do their jobs.

Life after Death and Reincarnation

The cycle of birth–life–death is obvious to all of us, but for many witches the cycle does not stop there. Instead of life ending when the body dies, they believe an individual's soul, spirit, or personal energy travels to a realm beyond the physical one and will eventually be reborn in another body in another time and place. Many of them view earth as a "school" and believe we come here as human beings to learn. This cycle continues until the soul has worked through all the lessons it set out to learn. Having completed the cycle, the soul retires to a place of joy and regeneration.

Of course, this idea isn't unique to witches. Christians, Muslims, and people of many other faiths believe our souls continue on after our bodies die, and Hindus have believed in reincarnation for thousands of years.

Where Do Witches Go When They Die?

Christianity has its heaven. Buddhism has nirvana. Where do witches go when they die? Many Wiccans believe that their souls go to the Summerland, a resting place before reincarnation into new bodies, in an ongoing cycle of birth, life, death, and rebirth.

THE WITCH'S CONNECTION WITH NATURE

Despite their differences and individual ways of practicing their craft, modern witches share some common ground. One of these is a respect for nature. This involves honoring the earth, attuning themselves to her cycles and seasons, and tapping natural forces in magickal workings.

Like shamans, witches see the earth as a living, breathing entity, their home to honor and protect, not a place to conquer and control. Witches regard the earth, its creatures, and everything that exists on our planet as teachers and part of the divine plan. From the witch's perspective, the planet itself and every living thing in this world has a spirit, a unique energy pattern. As a result, witches tend to think globally, mindful of nature and the cosmos.

Living in Harmony with the Earth

Witches celebrate life, and without our beautiful planet life as we know it could not exist. Therefore, witches attempt to establish a dialogue with Mother Nature. Yes, some of them may actually talk to trees, birds, animals, and stones, but more than that they try to observe and listen in order to understand their place in the natural order of things. Witches realize that we are dependent on the earth and therefore it makes sense to engage in practices that enrich both ourselves and the earth. "It's sacred ground we walk upon with every step we take," some witches sing. They seek to live in harmony with all of nature and to balance energies that have gone askew in our technology-driven society.

We often refer to our planet as Mother Earth, and indeed she is mother to us all. In a sense, that makes everyone and everything on earth part of a huge, extended family. When you know that you are a part of a greater whole it becomes more difficult to act against that whole. To do so would be counterproductive and would harm your kin, your friends, and yourself. Witches try to move gently, to respect all life, and to honor the sacredness in all things and in each other. If we can do this, we can heal the earth and the earth will heal us.

Green witches, in particular, devote themselves to this path. (You'll find out more about this in Chapter 7.) Some witches may work to protect endangered lands and wildlife, feeling that the loss of these would be a crime against Gaia (one name for the earth's spirit; in Greek mythology, goddess of the earth). Others donate money or time to ecological causes, and they often send out positive energy through spells and rituals. Later on, you'll learn more about how to do your part to create greater health, peace, and well-being in your own part of the world and beyond.

Signs and Omens in Nature

A rock, a flower, an herb, a tree, or an animal may hold special meaning for a witch, depending on when and where it appears and what's going on in her life at the time. For example, if a wild rose suddenly blossoms in her yard, she might take it as a positive omen of love growing in the home. A clever witch will take this one step further: She'll thank nature for its gift, dry some of those petals, and turn this little treasure into love-inspiring incense. In this manner, a witch may find herself re-inspired by a childlike wonder toward the planet and the small things that we often overlook in our busy lives.

Natural Magick

If you are serious about being a witch and doing magick, you'll need to get in touch with the natural world around you—it has much to teach you and many gifts to offer you. Today, most of us are more familiar with computers and smartphones, offices and shopping malls sealed against the weather, than we are with the sight of crops growing in the fields, the sound of streams rippling over rocks, or the scent of moist leaves on the forest floor.

Go for a walk outdoors. Reconnect with the feeling of the wind blowing through your hair. Listen to the birds that live in a tree in your yard. Watch the sunset. Take time to smell the flowers that bloom in the park during the summer. The natural world is just as natural as it ever was, except there's less of it than there was twenty-five years ago—and most of us don't make a point of enjoying it often enough.

As you begin to rediscover the natural rhythms around you, you'll also start to notice how they affect the flow of your inner life. When you become accustomed to doing this, you'll find that you feel more in sync with everything around you, and with yourself. You may not be able to align your life with the changing seasons the way our ancestors did—nor is it really necessary. However, expanding your awareness of the cycles of the earth and the cosmos will put you in touch with powerful energies beyond your own immediate skills and enable you to do magick more effectively. In later chapters, we'll talk more about tapping into the magick of the natural world around you. You'll learn to make potions, conduct rituals, and cast spells for a happier, healthier, more fulfilling life.

GOOD WITCH, BAD WITCH: WHICH IS WHICH?

Despite the ugly face that religions have tried to put on witches, historically most have been concerned with helping individuals and communities. As we've already said, fear and misunderstanding underlie the foolish ideas many people hold about witches. Once you get to know them, witches are pretty much like everyone else; they just see the world a little differently.

Are there "bad" witches who use their knowledge and power for personal gain and ill will? Yes, of course, just as there are "bad" Christians, "bad" Muslims, and so on. Witches are people. If you shake any figurative tree hard enough, a couple rotten apples are likely to fall off. That's just human nature. The good news is that these rotten apples are the exception, not the rule.

Witchcraft and Ethics

Just like everyone else, witches confront issues that require them to make ethical choices. For instance, should magick be used as a weapon, even if it's only to fight back? Should you use magick to get what you want, even if that means you put someone else at a disadvantage? And where do you draw the line between white and black magick?

Some witches may not concern themselves with the ethical results of a spell or ritual—what counts is that the spell works. With a spell, you're attempting to stack the odds in your favor—or in another person's favor, if the spell is for someone else. You're attempting to influence something in the future. We all do this constantly, of course, in various ways, but when a witch casts a spell she brings her full conscious and creative awareness to the process.

Wiccans and some other witches believe that magick has a boomerang effect: Whatever you do comes back to you. If you do a spell that hurts someone else, you'll hurt yourself in the process or attract someone to you who will cause you harm. For that reason, witches often follow a version of the Golden Rule when doing spells: Be kind to others and be kind to yourself.

Magicians recognize that even though the human mind and spirit have unlimited potential, we can't possibly foresee all the possible outcomes of a spell. Human beings are not omniscient, and sometimes even good intentions lead to terrible results. Just to be on the safe side, you might want to end a spell or ritual with a phrase such as "This is done for the greatest good of all and may it harm none." In essence, this turns over responsibility for the outcome to higher (and wiser) powers who have a better understanding of how to bring about the best possible outcome.

What If Someone Important to You Is Opposed to Witchcraft?

Arguing about it is the worst thing to do. You're not going to change anyone's opinions about spells or anything else. Your best bet is to follow your practice in private. If possible, step back from the situation and try to look at the other person as a teacher. What lesson can you learn from this opposition?

Your Personal Code

Every magickal tradition, from the Druids to Wicca to Santería, has its own code—principles that guide the practitioner, boundaries that she won't cross, a core set of beliefs that permeate everything she does. These core beliefs define an individual's magickal practice. In Wicca, for instance, the primary principle is to harm nothing and no one.

But people also develop their own personal codes. Have you defined yours? As previously noted, cultural differences play a part in sculpting a particular individual's beliefs. In the end, however, each of us must refine our own codes as we evolve from children to adults. What's right for one person might not be okay for another. At the heart of any belief system lies a code by which you live your life, and it may not have any connection to what other people consider good and bad.

Following your own truth will become ever more important as you develop your magickal ability and grow more adept at using your powers. Each witch relies on her inner voice (or conscience, if you will) in determining how she wields magick. There is no cut-and-dried answer to whether anyone is a good or a bad witch.

As a beginner to the wonderful world of witchcraft, you will learn something new every day and experience new sensations and feelings as you explore your newfound path. Some may surprise you, some will challenge you, and lots will fascinate and excite you. One thing you can be sure of now that you've started down this road: You'll never be quite the same again.

Chapter 2

MAGICK AND HOW IT CAN HELP YOU

Have you ever wondered why some days you seem to breeze through life, but on other days nothing goes right? Why it is that when things start sliding downhill, they seem to go from bad to worse? How can you keep the good times rolling and prevent the bad ones from getting a foothold? Is there a way to turn your luck around?

Absolutely! That's what magick spells are for—to give you power over your destiny. Rather than being a victim of circumstances beyond your control, with magick you control the circumstances. Once you start viewing the world from a magickal perspective, you'll be able to see beyond everyday frustrations, disappointments, and aggravations. You'll maneuver around the obstacles that pop up in your path. It's similar to what athletes call being "in the zone."

Considering all the curves life throws us, it only makes sense to use whatever tools are available to give yourself an advantage. Magick spells are just that: tools to help you avoid pitfalls and attract blessings. For thousands of years people have been doing magick. You can, too, and once you start doing spells, you'll never want to stop!

Perhaps you're skeptical. You may be wondering, what's this magick stuff all about anyway? More important, can it really help me? The answer is *yes*. If you didn't believe in magick (at least a little bit), you wouldn't be reading this book.

YOU'RE ALREADY A MAGICIAN

You may not realize it yet, but you're already a magician. You've already done lots of magick spells without even knowing it. Now you're going to learn how to perform magick purposefully, to turn your luck around. Once you discover the secret, you'll be able to chart your own destiny, avoiding the pitfalls and setbacks that seemed inevitable before.

The word "magician" derives from the Latin *magi* meaning wise men or women (singular *magus*). Remember the wise men in the Christmas story? They were also called *magi*, or magicians, and they followed a star they'd seen that foretold of Jesus' birth, which suggests they knew astrology, too.

Every culture, stretching back long before the advent of written history, has had its magicians: medicine men, cunning folk, kahunas, Druids, witches, and shamans. By choosing a magickal path, you are following in the footsteps of ancient seers and healers who knew how to shape the forces of the universe with their intentions.

Simply put, magick is the act of consciously creating circumstances using methods that defy scientific logic. The notorious British magician Aleister Crowley said, "Every intentional act is a Magickal Act." Whenever you form an objective in your mind, then fuel it with willpower, you're doing magick.

TEN GOOD THINGS MAGICK CAN DO FOR YOU

Before we get into *how*, let's consider *why* learning to do magick is worth your time and effort. Here are ten ways magick can help to make your life better. It can:

1. Improve your love life
2. Attract prosperity
3. Keep you and your loved ones safe from harm
4. Enhance your health
5. Protect your home and personal property
6. Open up new career opportunities

7. Give you more control over your life
8. Improve interactions with family, friends, and coworkers
9. Ward off problems and enemies
10. Strengthen your intuition and psychic skills

People who don't understand magick have made it seem weird or evil, and Hollywood sensationalizes it to the point of absurdity. Actually, there's nothing scary, strange, or silly about magick—it's a natural ability you were born with, a talent you can develop just like musical or mathematical talent. All it takes is desire, a little training, and practice.

THE POWER BEHIND MAGICK

Fortunately, you don't really need any special tools to practice witchcraft. Yes, witches frequently do use a variety of tools to enhance their magickal workings—you'll learn about these later. The tools, however, aren't the source of power, the witch is. The truth is, magick is all in the mind—mostly the tools just help you to stay focused.

Thinking Makes It So

In the movie *What Dreams May Come*, the character played by Robin Williams dies and then wakes up in the afterlife. The place looks, smells, tastes, and feels more or less like the so-called real world. But he quickly learns that in this place, whatever he thinks or desires manifests instantly. All of it is a construct of consciousness.

Magick works in the same way. What you think is what you get. The manifestation may not be immediate—although it can be. If your belief and your intent are strong enough, if you bring passion to your spell, and if you can focus your energy clearly toward a specific goal, then you have a good chance of achieving what you want.

Knowing exactly what you want to accomplish and stating your intention with absolute clarity is essential whenever you perform a spell. Otherwise, your spell could backfire.

The fact is, you're doing magick all the time, whether or not you realize it. As noted later, the Law of Attraction states that your thoughts, emotions, and actions affect the energetic patterns around you, and the most significant "tools" in magick are your thoughts and feelings. That's why it's important to use your magickal power with clear intent, so you can produce the results you truly desire.

Underlying all magick is a simple principle of physics: For every action there is an equal and opposite reaction. Remember that old computer axiom, garbage in, garbage out? Magick is like that, too: If you put bad thoughts and feelings in, you'll get bad stuff back and vice versa. So, be careful what you ask for!

What You Believe Is What You'll Get

Belief is the core of magick. Without it, all you have are words and gestures, light and dust, nothing but bluster—rather like the Wizard in *The Wonderful Wizard of Oz* that Dorothy and her companions exposed as just an ordinary man behind a curtain. But what, exactly, is meant by belief? Go back to Oz. The Lion sought courage because he believed he was cowardly. That belief ruled his life until the Wizard pointed out how courageous he actually was. The Lion experienced a radical shift in his beliefs about himself when he realized that he had possessed what he desired most all along. Believing he didn't have courage was what crippled him.

Most of us are just like the Cowardly Lion. We let fear, doubt, and erroneous beliefs limit our power and our ability to create what we desire most in life. Let's say you want abundance. To you, that means financial abundance, money in the bank, freedom from worrying whether the next check you write is going to bounce. However, to those around you, your life appears to be incredibly abundant—you have a loving family, wonderful friends, good health. Sometimes a shift in our deepest beliefs happens because someone whose opinion we respect points out that we really *do* have what we desire. Other times, we reach the same conclusion on our own. One thing you can count on: When your beliefs change, so will your life circumstances.

When you do magick, you must believe in yourself and your ability to produce the result you seek. Doubt pours water on your creative fire. If you doubt you can achieve your goal, you won't. That's true whether you're playing a sport or casting a spell.

The Modern Guide to Witchcraft

The Power of Your Beliefs

A belief is an acceptance of something as true. Thousands of years ago, people believed the world was flat. In the 1600s, men and women were burned at the stake because people in power believed they were evil and consorted with the devil. (You'd be surprised to discover how many people still believe witches are the devil's disciples—more about this later.)

On a more personal level, all of us face the consequences of our personal beliefs in all areas of our lives, every day. Your experiences, the people around you, your personal and professional environments—every facet of your existence, in fact—is a faithful reflection of a belief.

Some common ingrained, self-limiting beliefs that many people hold on to include:

- I'm not worthy (of love, wealth, a great job, whatever).
- My relationships stink.
- I'll never amount to anything.
- People are out to get me.
- Life is a struggle.
- You can't be rich *and* spiritual.
- I live in an unsafe world.

The foundations for many of these notions are laid in childhood, when we adopt the beliefs of our parents, teachers, and other authority figures. Childhood conditioning can be immensely powerful. Inside the man or woman who lacks a sense of self-worth lurks a small child who may believe he or she is a sinner, unworthy, or not good enough.

On a larger scale, our beliefs also come from the cultures and societies in which we live. A woman living in the West, for example, is unlikely to have the same core beliefs about being female as a woman in, say, a Muslim country.

A belief system usually evolves over time. It's something that we grow into, as our needs and goals develop and change. Even when we find a system of beliefs that works for us, we hone and fine-tune it, working our way deeper and deeper into its essential truth. Everything we experience, every thought we have, every desire, need, action, and reaction—everything we perceive with our senses goes into our personal databank and helps to create the belief systems that we hold now. Nothing is lost or forgotten in our lives.

You don't have to remain a victim of your conditioning, however. You can choose for yourself what you believe or don't believe, what you desire and don't desire. You can define your own parameters. Once you do that, you can start consciously creating your destiny according to your own vision—and keying into your magickal nature to make that happen.

THE LAW OF ATTRACTION

Have you heard of something called the Law of Attraction? Actually, it's an ancient concept, but in recent years Esther and Jerry Hicks have popularized and expanded it so that now millions of people around the world are familiar with the idea. At its core, the Law says that you attract whatever you put your mind on. In their best-selling book *Money, and the Law of Attraction* the Hickses wrote, "Each and every component that makes up your life experience is drawn to you by the powerful Law of Attraction's response to the thoughts you think and the story you tell about your life." In *The Secret*, Rhonda Byrne explained that "Your life right now is a reflection of your past thoughts."

What they're saying is, you create your own reality. Your thoughts and feelings generate energy, and they interact with the energy all around you in your environment. Over time, your ideas—especially the ones you feel passionate about—produce "thought forms," which serve as patterns that eventually become physical forms. You could look at it this way: Let's say you're a fashion designer and in your mind you envision a fabulous dress. That creative idea or "thought form" must exist before you can start to develop the physical object. You keep refining your design, doing drawings and maybe even stitching a sample, and eventually produce the dress you'd imagined.

Magick works in essentially the same way. First you create an image in your mind of what you desire and then imbue that image with energy and emotion. In time, what you conjured up mentally will emerge into the material world.

A big part of becoming a powerful witch and performing effective magick is training your mind. This means focusing your thoughts, raising your energy to the highest level you can, and using your will to bring your intentions into fruition. Later in this book, we'll talk more about how to do this—and the more you practice, the better results you'll achieve.

One Thing at a Time

Most of us have grown accustomed to doing several things at once. While eating dinner we also watch TV, send texts to our friends, and make notes of things we need to remember to take care of tomorrow. When you do magick, however, multitasking actually diminishes your returns. As Esther and Jerry Hicks explain in *Money, and the Law of Attraction,* "When you consider many subjects at the same time, you generally do not move forward strongly toward any of them, for your focus and your power is [sic] diffused."

Start paying attention to your thoughts. Are you focusing on what you lack? If so, you'll continue to experience lack. Do you spend time lamenting the problems in your life? If so, you'll keep making more problems for yourself. Whenever you catch yourself thinking something that's *not* what you want, do a mental 180 and start thinking about what you do want instead.

MAGICK ISN'T JUST BLACK AND WHITE

Magick is ethically neutral, just like electricity is neutral. Both magick and electricity can be used to help or to harm. Magick is simply the intentional use of energy. Casting a magick spell is simply a means to an end. A witch uses willpower to direct energy toward a particular goal. Her intention is what colors the magick white, black, or gray.

You've probably heard people describe themselves as white witches, meaning they uphold the "do no harm" rule. The truth, though, is that most magick isn't black or white, it's gray—including the magick most self-proclaimed white witches perform. That doesn't mean it's bad or harmful, however. In fact, the spells of most witches and magicians fall into the gray area.

White, Black, or Gray?

Not every witch will agree with the following definitions of white, black, and gray magick. However, these guidelines can help you sort out the differences:

- White magick's purpose is to further spiritual growth, by strengthening your connection with the divine realm and/or gaining wisdom from a higher source.
- Black magick intends to harm or manipulate another person, or to interfere with his/her free will.
- Every other kind of magick is a shade of gray.

This means that if you do a spell to get a better job or to attract a lover you're operating in the gray zone. Nothing wrong with that. It's easy, though, to stray from the path and inadvertently cast a questionable spell—especially when you're having a bad day or dealing with difficult people. Let's say a coworker is a real pain in the neck and you do a spell to get even with her for a dirty deed. Your revenge may seem justifiable, but it's still black magick.

Here's another little-known fact: Most black magick isn't performed by evil sorcerers or wicked wizards, it's done by ordinary people who don't even realize what they're up to. Have you ever cursed some jerk for stealing your parking space or cutting in front of you in a long supermarket line? That's black magick, too.

Why Doing Black Magick Isn't Such a Good Idea

Maybe you're wondering, why *not* use magick to put someone who's wronged you in his place? It's tempting, for sure. Except remember that in the world of magick, whatever you do returns to you like a boomerang. Indeed, many magicians say it comes back magnified threefold. That's a good reason for keeping your thoughts focused on positive stuff. It's also why usually the best way to get what you want—especially on days when everything seems to be going wrong—is to bless instead of curse.

INTENTION IS EVERYTHING

Admittedly, it can be hard sometimes to determine if you're treading on the dark side of Magick Street. For many people, love spells seem to raise the most questions. What if you want to do a spell to get your yoga instructor to fall for you? Is that okay? It all depends on your intention. If he already has a partner and your goal is to win him away from her, obviously that's *not* a good idea.

Good spells respect other people's free will and right to make their own choices in life. Even if your yoga teacher isn't romantically involved with anybody else, it's manipulative to cast a spell to coerce him into doing something he wouldn't want to do otherwise. How would you feel if someone did that to you? There's another reason, too, to think carefully before casting a spell to win a person's heart. A well-executed love spell creates a strong bond between you and someone else. Later on, if you change your mind, breaking the bond could be tough, to say the least.

Instead, try another angle to accomplish your goal. You could magickally enhance your own attractiveness. You could do magick to remove any obstacles existing between you and the other person. You could do a spell to attract a lover who's right for you, rather than targeting a particular individual. Or you could turn the final decision over to a higher power and let your favorite god/dess, angel, or spirit guide find the perfect partner for you. This kicks your ego out of the driver's seat and lets the universe guide you toward an outcome that's right for you. Maybe you and your yoga teacher would live happily ever after together. On the other hand, maybe you'd be better off with somebody else, perhaps someone you haven't met yet.

Chapter 3

A CONCISE HISTORY OF WITCHCRAFT IN THE WEST

Witches have a rich cultural heritage that they continue celebrating today. Although witchcraft's origins are hidden in antiquity, most likely, people around the world have practiced magick and witchcraft in some form since the beginning of time. Anthropologists speculate that Stonehenge may have been a sacred site where magick rituals were performed thousands of years ago. The famous paintings on the Trois Frères cave walls in Montesquieu-Avantès, France, which date back 15,000 years, may have been put there by Paleolithic peoples as a form of sympathetic magick—by painting these images, cave dwellers sought the aid of spirit animals to help them succeed at hunting.

Today contemporary witches are reviving interest in the Craft. As you join their leagues, you'll become part of the new wave of magicians who are putting a modern spin on an ancient worldview. How exciting is that?

THE OLD RELIGION

Magick and witchcraft go hand in hand. Although not all magick falls under the broad heading of witchcraft, all witches practice magick in one form or another. At the dawn of the human race, when people first came to understand cause and effect, they began trying to explain the mysteries of earth and the heavens. If a wind blew down a tree and hurt someone, the wind might be thought of as "angry" or considered to be a spirit that needed appeasement. In this manner, people began to anthropomorphize aspects of nature. They imagined that gods and goddesses, spirits and demons, and all sorts of fantastic creatures lived in the unseen realms, where they governed everything that happened on earth. Magickal thinking was born.

Magickal Beginnings

As civilizations developed, each brought a new flavor and tone to magickal ideas. One of these ideas was that the universe is a huge web made up of all kinds of invisible interlocking strands. Everything is connected to everything else. If humans could learn to influence one of these connections, they could affect the whole web.

At first, these attempts to influence the world were very simple: one action to produce one result. The action usually corresponded symbolically to the desired result. For example, let's say someone wanted to bind an angry spirit and limit its power. He might tie a knot in a piece of rope and imagine that he'd caught the spirit in that knot. If the action worked, or seemed to work, it was used again. Eventually a tradition developed.

Wise Men and Women

Over time, attempts at guiding "fate" became more elaborate. Our ancestors delegated the tasks of influencing the universe to a few wise individuals, and elevated them to positions of authority in their community. They called these wise men and women shamans, priests and priestesses, magi, or witches. Their job included performing spells and rituals to coerce the ancestors, powerful spirits, or deities into doing their bidding. Although these witches all performed essentially the same basic functions—healing the sick, encouraging crops to grow, predicting the future—how they went about it depended on the culture and era in which they lived.

In early Celtic communities, for example, the Druids served as seers, healers, advisors, astrologers, and spiritual leaders. Their power was second only to the clan's chieftain. An ancient Norse text called the *Poetic Edda*, written in the tenth century, uses the term *völva* to describe a wise woman who did prophecies, cast spells, and performed healing for the community.

Modern witches no longer hand over magickal authority to a select few. Today, everyone is welcome to explore these paths and practices, not just an elite group. Using your personal power is encouraged. Each one of us has a special talent or skill, and ultimately that gift can benefit everyone. Every individual brings something unique to the Craft, which has caused the field of magick to evolve and expand greatly.

WITCHCRAFT IN EUROPE

It's been said that history is written by the victors. History is imperfect and is often clouded by societal, personal, or political agendas; therefore, the study of magickal history is no easy task. To trace the course of events from ancient times to the modern day, let's begin by examining the early practice of witchcraft in Europe.

Not everyone agrees about the evolution of witchcraft in Europe. Some historians believe it developed out of the old fertility cults that worshipped a mother goddess. Others think that the idea of witchcraft was all superstition—when people could not explain an unpleasant event, they blamed it on someone whom they labeled a witch. Still other researchers say witchcraft stemmed from a wide variety of practices and customs including Paganism, Hebrew mysticism, Celtic tradition, and ancient Greek folklore.

As people traveled from one country to another, they influenced the beliefs and practices of the native culture. When the Vikings and the Romans invaded the British Isles, for example, their legends, gods, and goddesses mixed with those of the indigenous people. Traders and travelers, too, brought stories and ideas to the lands they visited. All this cross-pollination had an impact on the way witchcraft evolved.

Additionally, because most people in earlier centuries couldn't read or write, magickal traditions were handed down through generations by oral teaching. The few literate individuals probably recorded information according to their own views. Therefore, it's difficult to figure out what's true and what's fantasy regarding long-ago witchcraft.

Fairy-Tale Witches

Witches show up frequently in our favorite fairy tales, where they're sometimes referred to as fairy godmothers. Certain of these witches can't resist putting enchantments on humans, turning them into hideous beasts ("Beauty and the Beast") or frogs ("The Frog Prince"), or condemning them to unpleasant plights ("Sleeping Beauty"). Others, however, such as the one in "Cinderella," wave their magick wands and make wishes come true. Some of these fairy-tale witches derive from old goddesses in ancient myths, such as the witch in "Hansel and Gretel" who originated in the Baltic fertility goddess Baba Yaga. In old French romance stories, witches and women who practiced magick were called "fairies."

CRIMINALIZING WITCHCRAFT

During the eighth and ninth centuries, the powers-that-be started laying down laws against witchcraft and linking age-old practices with evil doing. As the Christian Church gained power, it attacked the "old religion," which was based in nature and folk traditions. For example, the common people had a custom of leaving offerings for spirits—until 743, when the Synod of Rome declared it a crime. In 829, the Synod of Paris passed a decree against reciting incantations (simple verbal spells for good luck) and idolatry (worshipping the old gods and goddesses). By 900, Christian scholars were promoting the idea that the devil was leading women astray. These events helped prepare the scene for the fury of the Inquisition.

Between the 1100s and 1300s, the Church continued to hammer away at witches. Christian zealots presented a picture of witches as evil creatures who cavorted with the devil, ate children, and held wild orgies to seduce innocents. Witchcraft became a crime against God and the Church. In 1317, Pope John XXII authorized a religious court, known as the Inquisition, to go after anyone who was believed to have made a pact with the devil.

Thousands of trials proceeded. Punishments included burning, hanging, and excommunication. The interrogation process involved torturing people to get them to confess the "truth"—that is, to force them to admit to whatever the inquisitor wished—and to point a finger at other witches.

"In 1484, the Papal Bull of Innocent VIII unleashed the power of the Inquisition against the Old Religion. With the publication of the *Malleus Maleficarum*, 'The Hammer of the Witches,' by Dominicans Kramer and Sprenger in 1486, the groundwork was laid for a reign of terror that was to hold all of Europe in its grip until well into the seventeenth century." —Starhawk, *The Spiral Dance*

Accusing someone of witchcraft also became a bureaucratic convenience. Not only those who actually practiced the Craft were tortured, imprisoned, and killed—anyone whom the authorities disliked or feared was accused of being a witch. Conviction rates soared as many "undesirables" fell prey to the inquisitors.

The atmosphere in England was less radical than on the continent. Because Henry VIII had separated from the Catholic Church, practicing witchcraft in Britain was regarded as a civil violation, and courts handed down fewer death sentences. In part, this may have been due to the influence of John Dee, a well-known wizard who served as an advisor to Queen Elizabeth I.

THE BURNING TIMES

The witch-hunt craze picked up speed in the sixteenth century, during the Reformation period. The public, confused by the religious changes going on, was only too willing to blame anyone whose ideas seemed "different." If someone had a grudge against a neighbor, he could denounce her as a witch. It was the perfect environment for mass persecution.

The legal sanctions against witches became even harsher than before, and the tortures inflicted grew crueler. To force people to confess to witchcraft, inquisitors strapped them to the "rack" and pulled them apart limb by limb, crushed their hands and feet with thumbscrews and "boots," and placed hot coals on their bare skin. If found guilty, the alleged "witches" were burned at the stake.

During the so-called "Burning Times" in Europe, which lasted from the fourteenth until the eighteenth centuries, tens of thousands and possibly millions of people (depending on which source you choose to believe) were executed as witches—most of them women and girls. So thorough were the exterminations that after Germany's witch trials of 1585 two villages in the Bishopric of Trier were left with only one woman surviving in each.

Cats and Rats

During the Burning Times, cats were thought to be witches' familiars and zealots destroyed them by the thousands. It's theorized by some that the Black Plague, which devastated Europe's human population in the fourteenth century, resulted in part because the rat population increased and spread disease once their natural predators were eliminated.

As occurs in all tragedies, some individuals profited from the witch hunts. Payments were given to informants and witch hunters who produced victims. In some instances, male doctors benefited financially when their competitors—female midwives and herbalists—were condemned as witches. Powerful authorities confiscated the property of the victims.

It's hard to know for certain why the witch hysteria finally subsided. Perhaps people grew weary of the violence. In England, the hunts declined after the early 1700s, when the witch statute was finally repealed. The last recorded execution occurred in Germany in 1775.

WITCHCRAFT IN THE NEW WORLD

In the New World, witchcraft evolved as a patchwork quilt of beliefs and practices. Many different concepts, cultures, and customs existed side by side, sometimes overlapping and influencing one another. Each new group of immigrants brought with them their individual views and traditions. Over time, they produced a rich body of magickal thought.

The Modern Guide to Witchcraft

Medicine men and women of the native tribes in North, Central, and South America had engaged in various forms of witchcraft and shamanism for centuries. They tapped the plant kingdom for healing purposes and to see the future. They communed with spirits, ancestors, and other nonphysical beings, seeking supernatural aid in crop growing and hunting. Like witches in other lands, these indigenous people honored Mother Earth and all her creatures. And, like magicians everywhere, they worked with the forces of nature to produce results.

When European settlers migrated to the New World, they brought their customs with them. Not all of these early immigrants were Christians. Some followed the Old Religion and sought freedom to practice their beliefs in a new land. Evidence suggests that some of these people joined Indian tribes whose ideas were compatible with their own.

The slave trade introduced the traditions of African witches to the Americas. Followers of voudon (voodoo), Santería, macumba, and other faiths carried their beliefs and rituals with them to the Caribbean and the southern states of the United States, where they continue to flourish today.

Witchcraft in Salem

When William Griggs, the village doctor in colonial Salem Village (now Salem), Massachusetts, couldn't heal the ailing daughter and niece of Reverend Samuel Parris, he claimed the girls had been bewitched. Thus began the infamous Salem witch hunt, which remains one of America's great tragedies. Soon girls in Salem and surrounding communities were "crying out" the names of "witches" who had supposedly caused their illnesses.

Between June and October 1692, nineteen men and women were hung and another man was crushed to death for the crime of witchcraft. Authorities threw more than 150 other victims into prison, where several died, on charges of being in league with the devil.

Religious and political factors combined to create the witch craze in Salem. A recent smallpox epidemic and attacks by Indian tribes had left the community deeply fearful. Competition between rivals Rev. James Bayley of neighboring Salem Town (now Danvers) and Rev. Parris exacerbated the tension as both ministers capitalized on their Puritan parishioners' fear of Satan to boost their own popularity.

The hysteria also enabled local authorities to rid the community of undesirables and dissidents. Economic interests, too, played a role in the condemnation of Salem's "witches"—those convicted had their assets confiscated and their property was added to the town's coffers. A number of the executed and accused women owned property and were not governed by either husbands or male relatives, which didn't sit well with the male-dominated society of the time. Putting these independent women in their place may have been part of the motive behind the Salem witch trials.

Today, Salem commemorates the victims of the Salem Witch Trials with engraved stones nestled in a small, tree-shaded park off Derby Street, near the city's waterfront and tourist district. Visitors can walk through the memorial and remember Salem's darkest hour.

Hallucinating Witches

One theory suggests that the people supposedly afflicted by witchcraft in Salem were actually "high" on a fungus called ergot that grows on rye bread. The hallucinogen LSD was first derived from ergot. Therefore, the strange behavior exhibited by the "victims" was probably due to eating this psychedelic substance, not demonic possession.

WITCHCRAFT'S REBIRTH

Despite centuries of persecution, witchcraft never died. It just went underground. Witches continued to hand down teachings from mother to daughter, father to son, in secret. Through oral tradition, rituals, codes, and symbols, magickal information passed from generation to generation, at every level of society.

Some parts of the world, of course, never experienced the witch hysteria that infested Europe and Salem, Massachusetts. But even in those places where persecution once raged, witchcraft and magick reawakened during the nineteenth and twentieth centuries.

Magick in the Victorian Era

Interest in magick, mysticism, spiritualism, and the occult in general blossomed toward the end of the nineteenth century, perhaps as a reaction to the Age of Reason's emphasis on logic and science. The magicians of this era had a strong impact on the evolution of contemporary witchcraft and magick.

One noted figure of the time was Charles Godfrey Leland, a Pennsylvania scholar and writer who traveled widely studying the folklore of numerous cultures. His most famous book, *Aradia, or the Gospel of the Witches* became an important text that influenced the development of Neopaganism and modern-day witchcraft. Another was Madame Helena Blavatsky, a Russian-born medium and occultist who moved to New York and founded the Theosophical Society with Henry Steel Olcott. Theosophy, which means "divine wisdom," combines ideas from the Greek mystery schools, the Gnostics, Hindus, and others.

The Hermetic Order of the Golden Dawn, begun by Englishmen William Westcott, S.L. MacGregor Mathers, and William Woodman, was the most important magickal order to arise in the West during the Victorian period. All three men were Freemasons and members of the Rosicrucian Society, which influenced their beliefs and practices. The order's complex teachings drew upon the ideas and traditions of numerous ancient cultures and melded them into an intricate system of ceremonial magick (more about this in Chapter 7).

The Poetry of Ritual

The Golden Dawn's magick rituals were written by the noted British poet and mystic, William Butler Yeats, who was one of the order's most prominent members, in collaboration with founding father S.L. MacGregor Mathers.

The most notorious member of the Golden Dawn was Aleister Crowley, a controversial and charismatic figure who many say was the greatest magician of the twentieth century. After breaking with the Golden Dawn, he formed his own secret society, called Argenteum Astrum, or Silver Star, and later became the head of the Ordo Templi Orientis (Order of the Templars of the Orient or OTO). Much of his magick centered upon the use of sexual energy, which outraged the stuffy, uptight Victorians. The author of numerous books on magick and the occult, Crowley also created one of the most popular tarot decks with Lady Frieda Harris, known as the Thoth Deck.

Neopaganism

Pagan was originally a derogatory term used by the Church to refer to people, often rural folk, who had not converted to Christianity. Generally speaking, today's Neopagans can be described as individuals who uphold an earth-honoring philosophy and attempt to live in harmony with all life on the planet as well as with the cosmos. Pagans tend to be polytheistic, meaning they acknowledge many deities rather than a single god or goddess, although some Pagans may not honor any particular higher being.

The Pagan and Wiccan communities overlap a great deal and share many beliefs, interests, and practices. Not all Pagans are witches or Wiccans, although Wiccans and witches are usually considered Pagans. Because of the similarities between them, they often combine their resources for political, humanitarian, environmental, and educational objectives.

WITCHCRAFT TODAY

In the past few decades, the ranks of witches have swelled rapidly. Although it's impossible to accurately determine how many people practice witchcraft, a study done in 2001 by City University of New York found 134,000 self-described Wiccans in the United States. Certainly, that number has increased since then.

The American Academy of Religions now includes panels on Wicca and witchcraft. The U.S. Defense Department recognizes Wicca as an official religion and allows Wiccan soldiers to state their belief on their dog tags. As of 2006, an estimated 1,800 Wiccans were serving in the U.S. military.

Undoubtedly, the Internet has helped to spread information about the Craft. By enabling witches around the world to connect with one another in a safe and anonymous manner, the Internet has extended witchcraft's influence to all corners of the globe. Today you'll find thousands of websites and blog sites devoted to the subjects of Paganism, Wicca, witchcraft, and magick, along with lots of intelligent, thought-provoking ideas and scholarship.

Witchcraft isn't a static belief system or rigid body of rules and rituals; it's a living entity that's continually evolving and expanding. As education dissolves fear and misconceptions, magickal thinking and practices will gain greater acceptance among the general populace and influence the spiritual growth of all people, regardless of their specific faiths.

Chapter 4

THE MAGICKAL UNIVERSE IN WHICH WE LIVE

We live in a magickal universe. Children often understand this quite clearly, even if adults don't. To a child, the world is alive with possibilities. Most people miss this wondrous fact because they've been trained to look only at the physical world and to focus on the mundane aspects of daily life. Magick, however, teaches that the world most of us see is only the tip of the iceberg. As you develop your magickal abilities, you'll rediscover the awesome power that abides in the universe—and in you.

Maybe, in the deepest recesses of your mind, you have shadowy memories of an ancient time when you lived in constant contact with the earth, the cosmos, and your own instinctual nature. As you strengthen your relationship with nature and the universe, you may reawaken these memories. Perhaps you'll realize that you're a witch in your heart of hearts—and always have been.

There are many ways to tap your magickal power and many ways to harness the creative energy of the universe. This book introduces a number of philosophies, paths, and practices. Some will appeal to you, and some won't. Take what you like and leave the rest. Regardless of which course you choose to follow, when you become a witch and do magick, you enter into an agreement with the universe that if you do your part, the rest will unfold.

THE COSMIC WEB

From the perspective of science, everything is energy. Magicians see the world as surrounded by an energetic matrix that connects everything to everything else. This matrix, or "cosmic web," envelops our earth like a big bubble. It also permeates all things that exist here and extends throughout the solar system and beyond. The web pulses with subtle vibrations that magicians, psychics, and other sensitive individuals can feel. Regardless of whether you are consciously aware of these vibrations, you are affected by them—and your own personal energy vibrations continually affect the matrix.

Energy, Energy Everywhere

Everything in the world emits an energy vibration of some kind. Different things have different energy patterns, resonances, or "signatures." These resonances reach out to touch one another in a series of crisscrossing lines all around the world, rather like a big spider web. They also connect the physical and nonphysical worlds. These energetic connections are what enable witches and wizards to work magick—even over a long distance. You simply send a thought or emotion along one of these energy lines to wherever or whomever you wish to reach—it works faster than sending a text.

Consider this: How many times have you gotten a phone call from someone you were just thinking about? It's not an accident. Your thoughts and the other person's connected in the cosmic web before you spoke to one another in the physical realm. When you do magick, you purposefully tap into this infinite web. You tug a little on one of the lines. As you become skilled at using magick, you'll learn to navigate the cosmic web just as easily as you surf the Internet. The first step is to sensitize yourself to these vibrations and become aware of the energetic field around you.

Sensing Energy Currents

Try these simple exercises to start becoming aware of your own energy and the energy around you. If you like, you can do these exercises with a friend.

1. Close your eyes and hold your palms up in front of you, facing each other, about a foot or so apart. Slowly move your palms closer together but don't actually let them touch. Can you sense the energy flowing between your palms? You may feel warmth or coolness, various degrees of tingling, or something else. You might even sense a color or feel an emotion. Does the feeling grow stronger as your hands get closer together?
2. Choose an object, preferably a natural one such as a stone or plant. Run your hands around the object without touching it physically, trying to feel the energy it possesses. What do you sense? Can you feel warmth, coolness, or any other sensation coming from the object? Do you get any impressions or thoughts? Don't discount them, even if they seem weird.
3. Ask a friend to do this exercise with you. Sit with your eyes closed, while your friend stands behind you. Slowly, your friend moves her hand toward your head, without ever actually touching you. When you sense the energy from her hand, say so. Then switch places and try the exercise again.

Write down what you experienced in what will become your "grimoire" or "book of shadows," a journal of your magick spells and experiences. These notes will help you as you continue working with different energies, and as you grow more aware of how your own energies fluctuate with your mood, your health, and your circumstances.

THE COSMIC INFORMATION REPOSITORY

Like the Worldwide Web, the cosmic web teems with information. All ideas, words, actions, and emotions—going all the way back to the beginning of time—are stored in this energetic matrix. Anyone who knows the password can access this vast storehouse of knowledge.

Maybe you've heard of a psychic named Edgar Cayce, sometimes called the "Sleeping Prophet." Although he had little formal education or medical training, Cayce could go into a trance and discover cures for the thousands of sick people who sought his aid. How did he do it? He psychically "downloaded" wisdom that great minds before him had "blogged" into the cosmic web.

Not only psychics can access information in this way—lots of people do. They just don't realize it. Inventors, artists, musicians, and other creative people often claim to get insights without really knowing where they came from. Mozart didn't plan, structure, or analyze his compositions—he just listened to the music playing in his head and then wrote it down. Van Gogh said, "I dream of painting, and then I paint my dream." Scientific people, too, report having epiphanies that lead to new discoveries in technology, medicine, and other areas. All these people are connecting to the cosmic web and drawing knowledge from it.

Meditate to Quiet Your Mind

You, too, can tap into this awesome repository of information. Being able to key into the wisdom of the ages is a terrific asset to a witch. Wouldn't it be awesome to have the great wizard Merlin guiding you as you cast a spell?

First, you'll need to learn to quiet your mind. Most of us have minds that race like a hamster in a treadmill. In the world of magick, that's counterproductive. You can't "hear" the masters' advice if you're thinking about a zillion other things. One of the best ways to still the inner chatter is to meditate. If you've never meditated, you may think you have to sit in lotus position and chant "Oooommm" for hours. Not true. You can take a walk outside, listen to soothing music (without lyrics), watch the sunset, weed your garden, take a relaxing bath, or fold laundry. The point is to put all your attention on whatever you're doing, without letting distractions interfere. (My book *The Best Meditations on the Planet* includes 100 different meditations—something for everyone.)

Meditation enables you to clear the clutter from your mind and focus your thinking. It also opens the channels of communication between you and the cosmos. Because the mind is the force behind magick, it stands to reason that the more mastery you gain over your thoughts, the more effective your spells will be.

Trust Your Intuition

Whether you call it ESP, a hunch, a gut reaction, an inner knowing, or psychic power, everyone has intuition. It may raise hairs on the back of your neck, cause a twinge in your solar plexus, or make you feel lightheaded. It may speak to you in moments of crisis or utter calm, in the middle of a city traffic jam or while you're taking a shower. Regardless of how your intuition communicates with you, it's important to remember that your so-called sixth sense is just as normal and important as the other five senses.

Think how much you'd miss out on if you lacked the sense of sight, hearing, taste, smell, or touch. The world would be a much duller place. Now try to imagine how much more you could get out of life if you had another sense on top of those five. The good news is that you do!

Because intuition doesn't "make sense" (that is, it doesn't rely on our five physical senses), people tend to discount its validity. Yet many noted scientists have acknowledged that intuition played a significant part in their discoveries. In his later years, Nobel laureate Jonas Salk, who found a vaccine for polio, wrote a book about intuition titled *Anatomy of Reality*. In it he proposed that creativity resulted from the union of intuition and reasoning. Bill Gates said, "Often you have to rely on intuition." Albert Einstein believed "the only real valuable thing is intuition."

What we call intuition is the connection between your conscious mind and the cosmic web. Intuition is a witch's best friend. Sometimes intuition is the most important factor in spell-working. You can memorize the properties of different herbs, gemstones, or colors. You can follow all the prescribed steps in a ritual. But if you don't trust your intuition to guide you, you'll never develop your full potential. To connect with your intuition:

- Listen to the "voice within."
- Pay attention to hunches.
- Pay attention to your dreams and what they're trying to tell you.
- Notice "coincidences."
- Write down impressions and insights that you receive, even if they don't make sense in the moment—they may turn out to mean something more in the future.

As you start paying attention to your intuition, it will grow stronger and begin funneling more useful information your way. Being able to draw on your intuition will enrich your life and enhance your magickal ability in countless ways.

THE MOON AND YOU

One of the most important connections we have in the magickal universe in which we live—and one of the most obvious—is earth's closest neighbor: the moon. We can easily see the impact the moon has on our planet and its inhabitants. For example, the moon's twenty-eight-day cycle influences the oceans' tides; higher tides usually occur during the full moon. It also affects the weather, crop growth, animal and human fertility—as the *Farmers' Almanac* has professed for two centuries—as well as the way we feel and behave. More babies come into this world during the full moon than at other times of the month. Ask police officers or hospital workers about the full moon and they'll tell you they see more crises, more crimes, and more activity in general when the moon is full. No, the full moon won't turn you into a werewolf, but it might bring out your wild side.

Astrologers associate the moon with emotion, intuition, and creativity—the very things that witches rely on when they do magick. So, if you want your spells to be more powerful and effective, pay attention to the moon's cycles and learn to draw upon lunar energy.

Connecting with the Moon

Since ancient times, the moon has fascinated earthlings. Poets, artists, musicians, lovers, astrologers, and magicians all find the moon juicy subject matter for study and inspiration.

"Evidence of Moon worship is found in such widely varied cultures as those of the Anasazi Indians of New Mexico, the Greeks, Romans, Chinese, pre-Columbian Peruvians, Burmese, Phoenicians, and Egyptians. In the Craft, when we refer to the great god by the Hebrew names El or Elohim, we borrow terms that entered Hebrew from Arabic, where the god name 'Ilah' derives from a word that means 'moon.'"

—MORWYN, SECRETS OF A WITCH'S COVEN

Because the moon plays such an important role in magick—and in our lives—you might want to consider getting on closer terms with our planet's satellite. In a practice known as "drawing down the moon," a priestess goes into a trance and invites the goddess (or Divine Feminine energy) to enter her body. While the priestess is in the trance, the goddess speaks through her. Margot Adler wrote in depth about this in her book *Drawing Down the Moon*, but beginners can connect with lunar energy in simpler ways:

- Go outside at night and observe the moon. Let its silvery light wash over you. How do you feel standing in the moonlight, under the dark bowl of the night sky? How is this different from how you feel in the daytime?
- Follow the moon's passage through the heavens, from new to full and back to new again. Pay attention to how you feel during different phases of the moon. Many people feel more energized during the full moon and less vital during the last three days before the new moon.
- The moon moves into a different sign of the zodiac approximately every two and a half days. You might notice that your moods and feelings change every time the moon passes through a different astrological sign—you may feel more impulsive when the moon is in Aries, more sensitive when it's in Cancer, for instance.

Keep notes of what you experience, so you can refer back to them later. What you learn from strengthening your connection with the moon will be useful to you when you start casting spells and doing rituals.

The Moon and Magick

You're more likely to reap the rewards you desire if you do magick during favorable phases of the moon. When casting spells, pay particular attention to the new moon, full moon, the waxing and waning phases. Each has its own unique energy that can add to the power of your spells:

- The new moon, as you might expect, encourages beginnings. Are you looking for a new job? A new romance? A new home? The best time to start anything is during the new moon. As the moon grows in light (and seemingly in size), your undertaking will grow too.

- The waxing moon—the two weeks after the new moon and leading up to the full moon—supports growth and expansion. Do you want to boost your income? Turn up the heat in a relationship? Get a promotion at work? Cast your spell while the moon's light is increasing to generate growth in your worldly affairs.
- The full moon marks a time of culmination. It allows you to start seeing the results of whatever you began on the new moon. Want to bring a project to a successful conclusion? Receive rewards, recognition, or payments that are due to you? Do a spell while the moon is full for best results. The full moon's bright glow can also put you in the spotlight or shed light on murky issues. If your goal is to attract attention—from a lover, boss, or the public—the full moon helps illuminate you favorably. The full moon can also shine light on secrets and deception to let you get to the truth of a shady situation.
- The waning moon—the two weeks after the full moon and before the new moon—encourages decrease. Do you want to lose weight? End a bad relationship? Cut your expenses? Cast your spell while the moon is diminishing in light (and size) to diminish the impact of something in your life.

When two new moons occur in the same month, the second one is called the black moon. It is considerably more powerful than a regular new moon, so any seeding spells you do under a black moon might manifest more quickly. When two full moons occur in the same month, the second is dubbed a blue moon. During the blue moon, you may find you get bigger or better results than on an ordinary full moon, or that you experience a lot more activity or vitality.

THE FOUR DIRECTIONS

You're familiar with the four compass directions: north, south, east, and west. In magick, the four directions are more than mere geographical designations. They have special meanings and associations. Hindu mandalas, Native American medicine wheels, and Celtic stone circles all depict the four directions. Later on, when you learn to cast a circle before performing spells and rituals, you'll work with the four directions in greater depth. For now, let's just look at the directions in a way you've probably never considered them before.

Angelic Connections

Perhaps you've heard of four archangels known as Michael, Raphael, Gabriel, and Uriel. According to some schools of magickal thought, these archangels (an order of divine beings above angels) guard the four directions:

- Raphael guards the east.
- Michael watches over the south.
- Gabriel presides over the west.
- Uriel governs the north.

You can call upon these guardians and ask them to lend their assistance to your rituals and rites. Connecting with them and drawing upon their powers can greatly enhance the effectiveness of your magickal work.

Elemental Connections

When magicians speak of the elements, they're not referring to the periodic table you learned about in school. They mean the four elements: air, fire, water, and earth. These elements are the energetic building blocks that make up our world. We'll go into more detail and depth about the elements later on, but for now let's just note their relationships with the four directions:

- Air relates to the east.
- Fire is associated with the south.
- Water corresponds to the west.
- Earth is linked with the north.

Each has its own connections with the zodiac signs, the suits of the tarot, spirits and angels, the tools a magician uses, and lots of other things. The more you get into magick, the more you'll find yourself working with the elements.

Color Correspondences

Each of the four directions resonates with a certain color. Magickal art, including tarot cards, often depicts these color connections. You might also choose to incorporate them into spells. (Note, however, that Native American medicine wheels do not use these same color correspondences.)

- Yellow relates to the east.
- Red is associated with the south.
- Blue corresponds to the west.
- Green is linked with the north.

Learning to sense the four directions will give you a better understanding of your place in the cosmos. Working with these energies will strengthen your connection to both the earth and to the magickal universe around you.

Three More Directions

In addition to the four compass points, you'll want to consider three other directions when you do magick. The first of these, *Above*, refers to the heavenly realm and all the beings that live there: God, Goddess, angels, spirit guides, ancestors, and so on. The second, *Below*, corresponds to Mother Earth, the foundation of physical existence. *Within* means your own inner self. It's important to align yourself with all seven of these directions and to balance their energies when you're doing magick. They are all sources of power, and they all influence outcomes.

SENSING THE DIRECTIONS

You're going to work with the four directions and their correspondences a lot as your magickal practice expands. Before you actually start using

The Modern Guide to Witchcraft

these energies in spells and rituals, practice sensing what the energies feel like. If possible, try doing these exercises outside as well as inside your home. Many witches prefer to do magick while surrounded by nature whenever they can.

1. Stand facing east and close your eyes. Take a few deep breaths to quiet your thoughts. Keep an open mind as you try to sense the energy at this compass point. This is the energy of dawn, birth, and beginnings. It might take a few minutes, so give yourself time to receive the universe's vibrations. You might feel a slight tingling, warmth or coolness, a subtle emotional shift, or something else.
2. Turn to face south and, again, try to sense the energy flowing toward you. This is the energy of fullness and maturity. Does it seem any different from what you felt when you faced the east?
3. Turn to face west and, again, try to sense the energy flowing toward you. This is the energy of winding down and letting go. How does it seem to you?
4. Turn to face north and, again, try to sense the energy flowing toward you. This is the energy of turning inward, silence, and endings. What do you feel?

If at first you don't succeed in sensing these energies, remember the advice: Try, try again. With practice, you'll learn to pick up on the different resonances and attune yourself to them. Be sure to write down what you experience in your grimoire.

As you continue strengthening your magickal muscles, you'll come to a keen awareness of how intertwined you are with everything else in the cosmos. You'll realize that you can create your own reality by aligning yourself with the dynamic, magickal forces that exist all around you. And you'll notice that possibilities you never imagined before now open up for you.

Chapter 5

THE ELEMENTS OF THE WITCH'S PATH

Wiccans, green witches, shamans, and many other magicians believe that all things in nature—animals, plants, rocks, streams, hills—possess a type of consciousness. The term *animism* refers to this belief. The consciousness within even seemingly inanimate objects enables witches to use them in spellworking. The term *pantheism* is sometimes used to describe Neopagan paths. Often the term is misunderstood as meaning the worship of nature, but it actually means to recognize the Divine in all places, or to identify the Divine with the universe. The root word *pan* means "everywhere," and earth-honoring people believe that their deities are accessible in all places, at all times.

This doesn't mean that witches worship trees, rivers, and stones, any more than astrologers worship the sun, moon, and planets. It means they believe that the entire world, material and nonmaterial, possesses sacred energy, and that each of us holds a spark of divine energy within us.

In the previous chapter, we talked briefly about the four elements. Now let's examine the elements more fully, because earth, air, fire, and water are the four primary substances of creation—not only in nature and the material world, but magickally as well.

EARTH: THE SOLID ELEMENT

Planet Earth is the home of humans and other creatures, as well as a school for learning all kinds of spiritual lessons. When witches speak of the earth element, however, they don't mean simply the physical ground on which we stand. "Earth" in a magickal sense is also an energetic property.

In early agrarian cultures, farmers gave offerings of bread or mead to the soil to ensure a good crop. Soil also served as a component in many old spells. People buried symbolic items in the ground to banish something or to encourage growth. For example, to remove sickness, one healing spell instructs a sick person to spit in the soil and then cover that spot and walk away without looking back. To speed recovery from illness, patients were encouraged to grow health-promoting plants in the soil from their footprints. If you wanted to make sure your lover didn't cheat on you, you'd gather a little soil from beneath your foot and place it in a white cloth bag.

From the Womb of Gaia

Native American stories tell us that the soul waits for rebirth in the earth's womb (under the soil) You'll find dozens of myths, including those of ancient Sumer and Guatemala, that say humankind was shaped from soil. According to the ancient Greeks, the heavens were born into existence from the womb of Gaia, the mother who oversees all the earth's abundance.

Characteristics of the Earth Element

In the material sense, earth serves as our foundation. Thus it corresponds to the characteristics of stability, permanence, groundedness, security, and endurance. Earth energy moves slowly and steadily, so it's good to draw on when a situation or spell requires patience and/or gradual development. Magicians link the earth element with financial matters, material abundance, and fertility. People who have a lot of earth energy in their makeup tend to be practical, reliable, determined, tenacious, sensual, hard-working, cautious, no-nonsense individuals.

Earth Correspondences

Lots and lots of things correspond to the earth element, such as the direction north as you learned in the previous chapter. We'll discuss more as we go along, but here are some that you'll most likely use in your spellworking:

- Zodiac Signs: Taurus, Virgo, Capricorn
- Tarot Suit: Pentacles/Coins/Discs
- Magickal Tools: Pentagram, Salt, Stones
- Colors: Brown, Green, Gray
- Stones: Opaque Stones (such as hematite, onyx, and agate)

AIR: THE ELUSIVE ELEMENT

Air is the most elusive of the elements because it is invisible, intangible, and changeable. The ancients believed that the wind is influenced by the direction from which it originates. This idea translated into magickal methods quite nicely. For example, if a wind blows from the south it can generate passion, warmth, or enthusiasm in spellcraft. If a wind moves from the west it stimulates intuition and imagination.

The Wind Beneath Your Spells

We see a fair amount of directional wind work in spellcraft. For example, always scatter components in a wind moving away from you to carry a message or to take away a problem. Perform magick for new projects with the "wind at your back," for good fortune. When trying to quell anger, opening a window to "air out" the negative energy has great symbolic value.

Think, too, of how the wind scatters pollen to fertilize plants. In a similar way, the air element describes how words are spread far and wide, fertilizing our minds and cross-pollinating our societies with new ideas. Air can be gentle or fierce, damp or dry, hot or cold, and each of these "moods" has slightly different magickal connotations. For example, a damp wind combines the power of water and air to raise energy that is dreamy and nourishing.

Characteristics of the Air Element

The air element relates to flexibility, instability, intellect, and detachment. Air energy moves quickly, so it's good to draw on when a situation or spell involves change, movement, or you want things to happen fast. You can also use air energy to contact spirits or other nonphysical beings. Magicians link the air element with mental activity, communication, the world of ideas, and social interaction—use it for spells that involve these things. People who have a lot of air energy in their makeup tend to be friendly, curious, fickle, adaptable, idealistic, talkative, and interested in all sorts of ideas.

Air Correspondences

As you continue your magickal studies, you'll find many things correspond to the air element, such as the direction east as you learned in the previous chapter. We'll discuss more as we go along, but here are some that you'll most likely use in your spellworking:

- Zodiac Signs: Gemini, Libra, Aquarius
- Tarot Suit: Swords/Daggers
- Magickal Tools: Athame, Incense
- Colors: Yellow, Pale Blue, White
- Stones: Transparent Stones (such as aquamarine, diamond, and clear quartz)

FIRE: THE ELEMENT OF CLARITY

For millennia, our ancestors gathered around fires to cook, tell stories, and celebrate life. Because of its warmth, fire represents our passions, enthusiasm, and kinship. Fire also allowed early people to see in the darkness, therefore, magicians connect it with clarity, vision, and enlightenment. When humans discovered fire and learned how to use it, their lives were transformed; thus the fire element is associated with transformation. Think of the mythical phoenix rising from the flames— a symbol of fiery transformation.

Characteristics of the Fire Element

The fire element conveys inspiration, enthusiasm, vitality, and daring. Fire energy moves rapidly; it's volatile and unpredictable—think of how a wildfire can rage out of control or how lightning bursts in the sky. You can draw on the element of fire when you want to kick your spell's power up a notch or you want to see rapid results. Of course, if you seek to transform something in your life—a relationship, career path, or health condition—you can tap into fire's dynamic power. Magicians link the fire element with creativity, action, and the will to make things happen. You can also employ fire energy to banish fear, see the future, or in purification spells and rituals. People who have a lot of fire energy in their makeup tend to be self-confident, passionate, impulsive, outgoing, vigorous, and courageous individuals.

Your Power Element

Each witch has one element to which she most strongly responds, called a power element. By working with and tapping into that element, a witch can energize herself and her magickal processes. Determine your power element by going to places where you can experience each element intimately. For example, sit beside a stream, lake, or ocean to connect with the water element; stand high on a windswept hill to feel the air element. Pay attention to your reactions. Once you determine which element energizes you, find ways to expose yourself to it regularly, to refill your inner well.

Fire Correspondences

You'll discover many more things that correspond to the fire element as you progress in your magickal studies. We'll discuss more as we go along, but here are some that you'll use often in your spellworking:

- Zodiac Signs: Aries, Leo, Sagittarius
- Tarot Suit: Wands/Rods/Staves
- Magickal Tools: Wand, Candles
- Colors: Red, Orange

- Stones: Stones that contain sparks of light or rutiles, such as fire opals, star sapphires, and red phantom quartz

WATER: THE ELEMENT OF MOVEMENT

Water comprises more than 70 percent of our earth's surface and about 60 percent of our bodies. Of course, water is essential for life. Consequently, we associate the water element with nourishment. Water moves constantly—the oceans' shifting tides, the rolling rivers and rippling streams, the rains that fall to earth—and so we sense change and movement in this element. Because we wash in water, we think of this element as cleansing, clearing, and healing. Even today, people go to hot springs and spas to "take the waters." Since ancient times, people have gathered at sacred wells and reported seeing holy visions in streams and other bodies of water. Thus, water relates to spirituality and mysticism.

Ancient Water Healing Practices

According to an old European custom, dew gathered at dawn banishes illness, making it a good base for curative potions. Bathing in the water from a sacred well, dipping your hands into the ocean's water three times and then pouring it behind you so the sickness is likewise "behind" you, or releasing a token that represents your sickness into the waves are old spells that you can still use today.

Characteristics of the Water Element

The water element embodies the characteristics of nourishment, healing, purification (physically and spiritually), intuition, emotion, and creativity. Tap this element to "water" spells for growth and abundance, or to nurture your creativity. Water energy is changeable and unpredictable—it can manifest as a gentle rain or a typhoon. Thus, it's a good energy to draw upon when you're doing spells for change or to stimulate movement—the trick is to control the energy so you get just the right amount. Because the moon affects the tides, it has connections with the water element. Purification spells and rituals also draw upon the water element. Magicians often take ritual baths before doing spells and wash magick tools with water to purify them. People who have a lot of water energy in their makeup tend to be emotional, sensitive, intuitive, imaginative, and compassionate individuals.

Water Correspondences

We've already talked a bit about the use of lunar energy and intuition in spellwork, and you'll learn more as you go along. We'll discuss the water element in later chapters, but for now make note of these correspondences that you'll most likely use in your spellworking:

- Zodiac Signs: Cancer, Scorpio, Pisces
- Tarot Suit: Cups/Chalices
- Magickal Tools: Chalice, Cauldron
- Colors: Blue, Aqua, Indigo, Purple
- Stones: Translucent stones and gems such as pearls, opals, moonstones, and rose quartz

SPIRIT: THE FIFTH ELEMENT?

Spirit (also known as ether) isn't an element *per se*, but you'll often see it included in a list of magickal elements as the fifth point of the pentagram. It's even harder to define than air. Spirit links the four quarters of creation and thus is the source of magick. Spirit resides within and without, around, above, and below all things. Although we can experience earth, air, fire, and water directly with our physical senses, spirit is elusive. You can only engage it with your spiritual senses.

In spells and rituals, spirit usually comes into play if a witch chooses to call upon a divine figure to bless and energize her magick. Or, it may become part of the equation if you invite devic entities (nature fairies) to work in harmony with you.

NATURE SPIRITS: THE WITCH'S ALLIES

No matter how much access a witch has to nature, she's likely to work closely with the earth. You can live on the forty-seventh floor of a high-rise apartment building in the middle of a metropolis and still have a meaningful relationship with the earth.

Among the witch's allies in the magickal world are the nature spirits. Sometimes called devas, elementals, or fairies, these spirits can be valuable partners and aides in your practice. Although most people don't see them, you can think of these spirits as the intelligence or awareness attached to a particular place, a plant or tree, a natural object such as a rock or stream, or a specific type of weather. They are not deities.

Do all witches work with nature spirits? No. Most do recognize that nature has an intelligence, or a sense of spirit, that varies according to the location. How each witch relates to these spirits or forces depends on how she perceives them.

How you visualize these spirits is completely up to you. You may see them as tiny people or orbs of light. You may not see them at all but experience emotions or sensations when you are near the tree, flower, standing stone, or phenomenon with which the spirit is associated. Whether your visualization matches the visualizations of other witches is unimportant. What *is* important is that if you choose to work with them, you must honor the spirits as allies and work with them to heal and harmonize the earth and its inhabitants.

You can encounter nature spirits in many places and through a variety of methods. The simplest method is to reach out and connect with the spirit of a single plant, then ask the plant spirit for information on the plant's uses and properties. In his book *Plant Spirit Medicine*, Eliot Cowan stresses that the energy possessed by each individual plant is entirely personal. The information and/or gift the spirit of that plant offers to you is exactly what you need at that moment. This gift is not necessarily an energy traditionally associated with the plant. For example, the energy you receive from a rose bush will not necessarily be love, even though we usually connect roses with love and romance. The spirit of the rose bush may perceive that you require something different and offer it to you. The key to working with nature spirits like this is to remain open to what they bring to you, without expectations or preconceived ideas.

ELEMENTALS

Since ancient times, myths and legends have spoken about supernatural beings who fly through the air, burrow beneath the earth, or swim in the ocean's depths. But these magickal creatures don't simply reside in these regions; they serve as guardians and ambassadors of their respective realms. Some people might describe them as energetic forces, rather than specific entities, and they go by different names in different mystical traditions. Witches often choose to work with four elementals known as gnomes, sylphs, salamanders, and undines. These elementals correspond to the four elements: Gnomes are earth elementals, sylphs are air spirits, salamanders abide in the fire element, and undines are found in water.

The Earth Spirits at Findhorn

In the early 1960s, Eileen and Peter Caddy and their associate Dorothy Maclean founded a spiritual community in a wild and windswept area of northern Scotland known as Findhorn. Even though the soil there was mostly sand and the climate inhospitable, Findhorn became famous for its amazing gardens, which produced tropical flowers and forty-two-pound cabbages. How could this happen? According to Dorothy, the elementals who govern plant growth—she described them as "living forces of creative intelligence that work behind the scene"— guided Findhorn's founders in planting and maintaining the incredible gardens. In his book *Faces of Findhorn*, Professor R. Lindsay Robb of the Soil Association writes, "The vigor, health and bloom of the plants in this garden in midwinter, on land which is almost barren, powdery sand, cannot be explained ..." Well, not by ordinary thinking anyway!

Gnomes: Earth Elementals

Those little green guys you see in the garden might be gnomes, though not all gnomes are green or little. Some of them look like leprechauns or trolls. Known as sprites or dryads in some cultures, these nature spirits aid the growth of flowers, trees, and other plants—if you look closely, you might spot them sitting in a tree or resting beneath a blackberry bush. When autumn comes, they change the leaves from green to red, orange, and gold. Earth elementals also play an important role in helping the earth heal from the effects of pollution, deforestation, mining, and other forms of destruction.

Practical, no-nonsense beings, they can seem a little gruff at times. However, they have a wonderful appreciation for material things and wealth—remember the leprechaun's pot of gold? Ask the earth elementals to lend a hand with prosperity spells.

Sylphs: Air Elementals

Most people think of fairies as small, flying creatures like Tinker Bell, but these are probably air elementals. Sylphs aren't just cute and delicate winged beings, as contemporary films and children's books portray them—they handle lots of things related to the air and sky. They have the power to manipulate the winds, influence air quality, and help earthlings breathe. They also assist birds and flying insects.

In magickal work, sylphs can help you with verbal spells such as incantations. If you want to ace a test, learn a new subject or skill, or communicate clearly with someone, ask a sylph for assistance. Air spirits also like to get involved with legal matters and contracts.

Salamanders: Fire Elementals

No, we're not talking about a type of lizard. Salamanders, in the magickal sense, are the fire elementals. You may see these shining beings in a candle flame or the sun's rays, and they abide in all types of fire. They stimulate inspiration—when you have an Aha! moment and suddenly "see the light" you may have connected with a fire elemental.

Salamanders like to work with people who have a spiritual bent and with those who exhibit initiative or daring. Invite them to join you when you do spells that involve passion, vitality, courage, or action.

Undines: Water Elementals

These spirits splash about in the waters of the world. The Greeks' water nymphs and mermaids fall into this category, too. Usually depicted as beautiful young females, undines perform a variety of tasks, from nourishing life on earth to regulating the tides to inspiring artists and poets. They also protect fish and aquatic creatures, and—if they choose—guide humans on sea voyages. In recent times, these elementals have been working hard to offset the effects of water pollution and the destruction of marine habitat.

Capricious creatures, they gravitate toward sensitive, artistic people and you can call upon them if you need help with a creative project. Want to get in touch with your psychic ability? Ask an undine for assistance. These elementals will also come to your aid when you're doing love spells.

Always remember to thank the elementals that assist you in your spellworking. These beings enjoy receiving small gifts that express your appreciation:

- Gnomes adore jewelry and crystals. Bury a token in the ground as a way of saying "Thanks."
- Sylphs enjoy flowers. Place fresh blossoms on your altar or lay them in a sacred spot outdoors as an offering.
- Salamanders like candles and incense. Burn these to honor your fiery helpers.
- Undines are fond of perfume. Pour some in a stream, lake, or other body of water.

If you behave disrespectfully toward the elementals, they may retaliate by playing nasty tricks on you. Be generous, however, and your elemental friends will continue to serve you faithfully.

Chapter 6

GODS AND GODDESSES

How do you envision the Divine? How do you integrate sacred energy into your own life? Do you believe in many gods and goddesses, one deity with many faces, or a single Supreme Being?

Throughout history, virtually every culture has entertained visions of a divine realm populated by one or more beings with supernatural powers. Early people who lived close to nature often revered female creator/fertility figures. A great Mother Goddess shows up in many different civilizations as Mary, Demeter, Ceres, Isis, and various other deities. The ancient Greeks, Romans, and Norse worshipped numerous gods and goddesses. The Hindu pantheon includes many diverse spiritual beings, too.

Witches, Wiccans, and Neopagans—just like followers of other belief systems—often disagree about the nature of the Divine. Some follow a specific faith and worship one or more gods or goddesses; some aren't religious at all. Wiccans honor a Goddess and a God as her consort; Neopagans often recognize a number of deities. Many witches consider all spiritual paths equally valid and that all lead to the same place. Who or what you believe in—if anything—is totally up to you.

FACETS OF THE DIVINE

Early people connected spirits with the wind, nature, the stars, and the forces behind phenomena they couldn't explain in other ways. These divine beings were said to watch over creation and guide human destiny. As the earth's population grew and cultures interacted with one another—through war, trade, and migration—our conceptions of the heavenly realm evolved.

Some spirits fell out of favor as our ancestors learned more about the actual workings of the physical world and the universe. In some instances, minor tribal gods and goddesses merged with or gave way to deities with greater powers. Some deities went by different names and faces in different countries—Venus in Rome, Aphrodite in Greece, Amaterasu in Japan—although their attributes were essentially the same.

A popular metaphor describes divine energy as a gemstone, and every facet on that gemstone as a different manifestation of the core energy. These manifestations present themselves differently, but they are all, in the end, from the same divine source.

Some witches naturally relate to the gods and goddesses that are part of their personal heritage. Scandinavians might gravitate to Freya, Greeks to Sophia, Irish to Brigid. Santeríans combine Catholicism with African Paganism, and honor deities from both traditions.

One Deity or Many?

- Monotheism means a belief in a single supreme being.
- A dualist believes in two deities; in a Wiccan context, this would be God and Goddess.
- Polytheism is the belief in many separate gods.
- Henotheists believe in one god without denying the existence of others.

DUAL FORCES IN THE UNIVERSE

Wiccans believe that instead of one divine source or entity, there are two distinct deities—Goddess and God—and they in turn manifest as the gender-related god-forms. But the concept of dual forces operating in the universe isn't limited to Wiccans. Many cultures speak of a feminine and a masculine principle that exist in and around us. The Chinese refer to these two energies as yin (feminine) and yang (masculine). Native Americans respect Mother Earth and Father Sky.

These two polarities function in tandem to balance one another and create wholeness.

The Divine Feminine

When we talk about feminine and masculine, we don't mean woman and man. Think energies instead. Receptivity, emotion, passivity, and intuition are all expressions of feminine energy. You can see it operating in water, earth, the moon, darkness, night, silence, cool colors, and lots of other things. When you do magick, you use these ingredients in order to bring a specific energy into your spells and rituals. (In later chapters you'll learn ways to combine certain ingredients to produce the outcome you seek.) The Goddess is merely a depiction of the feminine force—the face we put on the energy to personify it.

The Earth Mother

Perhaps the most omnipresent symbol of the Divine Feminine is Mother Earth herself. Concern for the environment and "green" practices show respect for the Goddess, who appears in all of nature. It's no accident that movements honoring the earth and the Goddess evolved simultaneously. Indeed, many witches believe that unless Goddess energy reawakens within each of us and in the world as a whole, the planet may be destroyed.

The Divine Masculine

The feminine is not complete without the masculine; together, these energetic polarities form a whole. Go online and look at the yin-yang symbol. The white part represents the masculine force, the black side the feminine. Notice how, when joined, they form a circle, the symbol of wholeness. Masculine energy expresses itself outwardly as action and assertiveness. You can see this principle operating in fire, wind, the sun, light, daytime, noise, warm colors, and many other things—and you'll use these in specific ways when you do magick. Gods such as Thor, god of thunder and lightning, and the war god Mars symbolize the qualities of the masculine force.

Tripartite Deities

Sometimes the God and Goddess are shown as tripartite beings. This means that they are represented by three different images that signify the three stages of human life. The Goddess is frequently depicted in three aspects—maiden, mother, and crone—that signify the three phases of womanhood. Likewise, witches often see the God as having three faces, which represent the stages of a human's life: youth, maturity, and old age.

Depending on the type of magick you're doing, you might choose to call upon a certain aspect of the God or Goddess. For instance, if you need extra vitality to win a big ballgame, invite the youthful side of the Divine Masculine to assist you. If you're trying to get pregnant, ask the mother aspect of the Divine Feminine to lend you her fertility.

SEEING THE DIVINE IN NATURE

Honoring the earth and being aware of the natural world are part of many modern alternative spiritualities. A person who honors the earth and considers the natural world her primary teacher is sometimes labeled a nature-worshipper or called a Pagan (see Chapter 3). In modern use, however, the terms are not generally pejorative. In New Age spiritual practice, the word "Pagan" is being reclaimed by people who resonate to the heartbeat of the earth itself. Green witches, for instance, see the Divine in all of nature. If you ask a green witch, "Is there a God or Goddess?" she'll probably reply, "Of course." If you inquire further, "Who is he or she?" the green witch might say, "God is everywhere in nature."

GODDESSES FROM AROUND THE WORLD

Whatever she's called, however her story is told, the characteristics of the Divine Feminine—fertility, creativity, compassion, wisdom, beauty, love, healing—can be seen in the goddesses of all cultures. Here are some of the world's many goddesses and the attributes usually associated with them.

Name	Culture	Attributes
Amaterasu	Japanese	beauty, leadership, brightness
Aphrodite	Greek	love, beauty, sensuality
Artemis	Greek	courage, independence, protection
Axo Mama	Peruvian	fertility
Bast	Egyptian	playfulness, joy
Brigid	Celtic	creativity, smithcraft, inspiration, healing
Ceres	Roman	nourishment, health
Ceridwin	Celtic	inspiration, wisdom
Cybele	Asia Minor	fertility
Diana	Roman	hunting, purity, independence
Freya	Norse	love, healing, sensuality
Hathor	Egyptian	love
Hecate	Greek	magick, death, wisdom
Inanna	Sumerian	journeys, facing fears, courage, grief
Isis	Egyptian	art, nourishment, wholeness, awakening
Kali	Indian	transformation, death, destruction, change
Kuan Yin	Asian	compassion, humanitarianism, mercy
Lakshmi	Indian	wealth, abundance
Pele	Hawaiian	fiery spirit, destruction and rebirth, vitality
Sekhmet	Egyptian	grace, dignity, strength
Siva	Slavic	fertility
Sophia	Greek	wisdom, power
Tara	Indian	nourishment, protection, compassion
Tiamat	Babylonian	power, magick, protection
Yemaja	Nigerian	secrets, dreams, childbirth, purification

On days when a witch wishes to connect with certain qualities in herself or wants to strengthen abilities she feels are weak, she can ask for help from a goddess who embodies the qualities she seeks. Say you have an important business meeting coming up and you want to make a good impression. The Egyptian sun goddess Sekhmet, depicted as a lioness, symbolizes the attributes you need. Ask her to help you accomplish your aims.

Goddess-Named Products

Goddesses have loaned their names to various products in popular culture. The sportswear company Nike, for instance, took its name from the Greek goddess of victory. But some associations seem a bit curious, such as Gillette's razor for women, called Venus—does this imply that shaving off all your body hair makes you more loving? Or how about Kali Mints, named after the Indian goddess of death—they don't sound very appetizing do they?

GODS FROM AROUND THE WORLD

Since the beginning of time, cultures around the world have honored a masculine force. The many faces of the God express qualities associated with the male archetype: strength, virility, daring, leadership skills, logic, protection, knowledge, and courage. Here are some of the gods found in various cultures around the world and the attributes connected with them.

Name	Culture	Attributes
Aengus	Irish	youth, love
Apollo	Greek	beauty, poetry, music, healing
Damballah	Haitian	wisdom, reassurance
Ea	Chaldean	magick, wisdom
Ganesh	Indian	strength, perseverance, overcoming obstacles
Green Man	Celtic	fertility, nature, abundance, sexuality
Horus	Egyptian	knowledge, eternal life, protection
Lugh	Celtic	craftsmanship, healing, magick
Mars	Roman	aggression, war, vitality, courage

Name	Culture	Attributes
Mercury	Roman	intelligence, communication, trade, travel
Mithras	Persian	strength, virility, courage, wisdom
Odin	Scandinavian	knowledge, poetry, prophesy
Osiris	Egyptian	civilization, learning
Pan	Greek	nature, fertility
Shiva	Indian	destruction, transformation
Thoth	Egyptian	knowledge, science, the arts
Tyr	Teutonic	law, athletics
Vishnu	Indian	preservation, stability
Zeus	Greek	authority, justice, abundance, magnanimity

Want to take a trip? Invite Mercury to help you plan your itinerary. Need some extra power on the gridiron? Consider adding Mars or Mithras to your team. You can develop a personal relationship with the gods and goddesses, no matter what their origin, and learn more about yourself through working with them.

GETTING HELP FROM GODS AND GODDESSES

Once you've familiarized yourself with a number of gods and goddesses, you may opt to petition one or more for help with a specific task. If you are facing a big challenge or obstacle, you could call on the Hindu god Ganesh to assist you. Perhaps you admire a certain deity's attributes and want to add them to your own character. If you'd like to be more compassionate, say, you could align yourself with Kuan Yin, the Asian goddess of mercy. Many witches believe that gods and goddesses are willing to help us if we ask and show them due respect.

Guides, Guardians, and Other Spirit Helpers

Most witches believe we share this universe with all sorts of non-physical beings—not just gods and goddesses—including lots of good guys who are willing to help us. They guide, protect, and aid us in our daily lives. When things go wrong, we can call on them for assistance.

Some people envision these divine helpers as angels. Others prefer to think of them as sages, guardians, or parts of their own higher consciousness. Native Americans often look to revered ancestors and spirit animals for guidance. We've already talked about teaming up with fairies, nature spirits, and elementals. These supernatural beings can be tremendous assets in magickal work—indeed, they could be essential to a spell's success.

Tips for Working with Deities

When working with spirit helpers, certain rules of etiquette apply, as is the case in any personal or business relationship:

- Ask for assistance—guides, guardians, and deities recognize your free will and might not intervene unless you invite them to do so.
- Show respect—treat spirit helpers as honored teachers and allies, not servants.
- Don't try to micromanage deities—if you seek aid from spirit beings, turn over the reins and allow them to carry out your request as they see fit.
- Don't seek help to do harm—although some evil entities lurk out there, you don't want to join forces with them, and the good spirits won't get behind a bad cause.
- Express gratitude—remember to thank the beings who assist you, and perhaps give them an offering.

Ways to Attract Divine Assistance

How can you go about connecting with deities? They might come to you in a dream, meditation, or vision. Countless people throughout history have experienced visitations from divine beings. Myths and legends from many cultures speak of gods and goddesses interacting with humans in this way. Such appearances aren't just a thing of the past—they can happen to anyone, any time.

The Modern Guide to Witchcraft

But if that doesn't happen to you, don't despair. You have other ways to catch a favorite deity's eye. Consider these suggestions:

- Learn as much as you can about the god/dess you wish to attract. Read myths, spiritual literature, and folklore. Many websites and blog sites provide in-depth information about deities, from the best known to the most obscure.
- Set up an altar and dedicate it to the deity of your choice. In Chapter 9, we'll talk more about creating altars and shrines.
- Collect artwork depicting the deities you want to petition. Again, you'll find lots of images online, but New Age stores and some religious shops also sell spiritual artwork. Display these images in a prominent place where you'll see them often, such as on your altar.
- Find out what things certain deities like. Many of them have preferences for particular plants, foods, stones, etc. Place these on your altar or in a special place outdoors as offerings to the god, goddess, or other spirit.

Keep an open mind and an open heart when you're working with deities. Trust your intuition—when you're dealing with forces beyond the mundane world, you need to rely on a type of knowing beyond your everyday awareness, one that will let you tune in to higher frequencies. Finally, believe that the spirits will speak to you, in one way or another. Doubt slams the door between you and magickal beings. When you're dealing with other realities and supernatural forces, remember this: You'll see it when you believe it.

Chapter 7

DIFFERENT TYPES OF WITCHCRAFT AND MAGICK

Now that you have a better understanding of the magickal universe in which you live and perhaps have met some of your spirit helpers, it's time to start thinking about how you might like to proceed along your journey as a witch. Just as musicians approach their craft in very personal ways, so do witches. Some musicians are classically trained and perform complicated pieces in concert halls or with orchestras. Others can't even read music and prefer to jam in a more casual manner. Witches, too, may choose to tread a simple path or an incredibly complex one. Kitchen and hedge witches, for example, generally practice uncomplicated, natural magick. They usually don't belong to a coven—though they may join forces with other witches for special purposes. Solitary practitioners, they depend on self-study, insight, creativity, and intuition as their guideposts. Their practice usually includes plant and herbal magick, often for the purpose of healing.

Other witches perform magick with more ritualistic overtones, drawing inspiration from various mystical and spiritual movements, such as the Qabalah (a body of Jewish mysticism and magick). They look at every aspect of a spell or a ritual as part of a huge picture. Each piece must be in the right place for everything to turn out as it should. For instance, the astrological phase of the moon during which the spell is performed should be suited to the task. The witch might wear special clothing and move in carefully choreographed patterns. Every part of the working should be designed to build energy toward a desired outcome.

Which path you choose depends on your personality, preferences, and talents. Do you enjoy group activities and working with other people toward a common goal? Perhaps you'd like to join a Wiccan coven. Or are you a loner and a homebody? You may be a natural hedge witch. Do you feel a strong connection with the earth and love the outdoors? If so, green witchcraft might be your thing. If you have a flair for the dramatic, ceremonial magick might appeal to you. Where you live could be a factor too. In the Southwestern states, shamanism influenced by Native American traditions is popular; in Salem, Massachusetts, you'll find plenty of Wiccans. Let's look at a few of these different practices now—you may find one that intrigues you enough to investigate it further.

Origins of the Freemasons

During the Middle Ages, some Medieval tradesmen became members of secret, mystical guilds. Because they possessed special knowledge of magick and symbolism as well as skills in carpentry, masonry, or glasswork these artisans were hired to work on Europe's great cathedrals. The famous rose windows they created had unique healing properties, due to a type of magick that we still don't fully understand today. These early guilds spawned the Freemasons.

GREEN WITCHES

Green witches are the original "tree huggers." The green witch walks the path of the naturalist, the herbalist, the wise woman, and the healer. Earth is her primer, the natural world her classroom. The natural world offers many gifts, but comparatively few people in today's technology-driven society embrace them. With the resurgence of nature-based practices and environmental awareness, however, green witches are once again emerging as guardians of nature and of humanity's relationship with our planet.

The green witch uses nature's gifts to improve the well-being of the physical body, the spirit and soul, and the environment. In earlier times,

The Modern Guide to Witchcraft

many people practiced green witchcraft, whether or not they called it that. Midwives, herbalists, shamans, and other healers knew the powers of plants—both medicinal and magickal—and tapped botanicals for all sorts of purposes. They also felt a strong connection to the earth, the seasons, and the cycles of life. In fact, their very lives depended on existing in harmony with nature.

The Modern Green Witch's Work

Today's green witches follow in the footsteps of their ancestors. They honor the earth and all its inhabitants—rocks, plants, and animals. They utilize ingredients from nature to concoct remedies and in spellcasting, particularly herbs and crystals. (You'll learn more about this in Chapters 11 and 12.) They work to protect the environment and try to live in harmony with all of creation. They may interact with the devas, elementals, or spirits who guard nature. Using their intuition, they create a channel of communication between the natural world and the human one.

A green witch usually works alone with nature as her partner. Historically, green witches lived apart from the community. Those who needed the services of such a witch traveled to see her, perhaps high into the hills or at the edge of the forest. She used the properties of the plants and trees around her to heal others. These days, you're more likely to find a green witch living in the middle of a city or in the suburbs, and her garden is likely to be small—maybe just some containers on a porch or a kitchen window "greenhouse."

She might work in an office or in sales or in the service industry. Perhaps she's in the medical field. Or she's a teacher or a full-time parent. Today's green witch understands that she can't restore nature's balance by isolating herself in the wild, she must bring her knowledge and gifts into the rest of the world. Cities, superhighways, and deforested areas— places where humankind has damaged nature—need the green witch's healing powers.

Living the Green Path

A green witch isn't defined by where she lives or what she does to bring home a paycheck. Nor is she limited to working with flowers, trees, and herbs. What makes a green witch is her relationship to the world around her, her ethics, and her affinity with nature. She doesn't merely practice green witchcraft, making potions and lotions, healing salves and teas—she *lives* the green path.

The path of the green witch combines aspects of both witchcraft and shamanism, but is wholly neither. It is an intensely personal path that integrates ability, likes and dislikes, the climate of a particular geographic location, and interaction with the energy of the environment. Healing, harmony, and balance are all key to the green witch's practice and outlook on life. These concepts embody three distinct focuses:

1. The earth (your local environment, as well as the planet)
2. Humanity (in general, as well as your local community, friends, and acquaintances)
3. You

Whether you choose to grow your own garden, install solar panels on your home, pick up trash by the side of the road, or get involved in a movement to protect wildlife is totally up to you. Although rooted in the ancient past, green witchcraft isn't a tradition so much as a personal adaptation of an ideal. No body of formal knowledge is passed on through careful training, no established group mind to which you are connected by sacred ceremonies performed by elders.

The green witch's power comes from participating in the miracle that is life, from attuning yourself to the energies of the environment around you. Instead of striving to amass power, you tap into the flows of energy that already exist in and around the earth. The challenge is how to walk a green path today, in a time of environmental stress, mass industrialization, and urbanization.

HEDGE WITCHES AND KITCHEN WITCHES

The terms *hedge witch* and *kitchen witch* can refer to someone who follows a home-based, freeform spiritual path that can't be clearly defined or identified as an existing Neopagan path. In some circles they connote a person who engages in a shamanic practice involving spirit journeys or trancing (more about this later), often with the aid and support of herbal knowledge. A kitchen or hedge witch can also be someone who pursues a solitary nature-based spiritual path. In earlier times, wise women, cunning men, and other such practitioners were sometimes called green witches or hedge witches; they worked to heal individuals, communities, and any malaise in the natural world.

Home as a Sanctuary

Similar to green witchcraft, hedge witchcraft is nature based. Hedge witches are often solitary practitioners, meaning they work alone rather than with a coven or group of other people. They may be self-dedicated, but they are rarely publicly initiated into the field—they're more likely to have learned the Craft at Grandma's side or eased into it as an extension of growing herbs in a backyard garden.

Hearth and home occupy a central place in their spiritual and magickal work—often kitchen witches work out of their own homes, making those homes places of healing energy and knowledge. Their homes provide shelter and nourishment, for both the body and the spirit. The hedge witch's home is her temple and her sanctuary, which she tends in order to keep energy flowing smoothly and freely. She seeks to support, nurture, and nourish her family (and extended community), both spiritually and physically. That neighbor who always makes you feel comfortable and peaceful in her home, who serves you soothing herbal teas and healthy, homemade meals might be practicing kitchen witchery, even if she doesn't call it that.

Home-Based Spirituality

We find the concept of the home as a spiritual center in many cultures and throughout many eras. The home, and in particular the hearth, has often served as a point of connection for god/desses and humankind. In China, the Kitchen God is viewed as an important domestic deity, and families hang paper images of the god near their stoves. In the West, kitchen witches use two symbols as joint keystones: the cauldron and the flame. (We'll talk more about these symbols in later chapters.)

Traditionally, the cauldron represents abundance and hospitality. In magick, it also symbolizes rebirth, mystery, creation, fertility, transformation, and feminine power. The flame is a symbol of life, activity, the Divine, purification, inspiration, and masculine power, making it an excellent partner for the cauldron.

A Clean Sweep

The kitchen witch bases her magickal practice in her everyday household activities—cooking, cleaning, baking, and so forth, all form the basis for her magick. For example, sweeping the floor free of dust and dirt may simultaneously cleanse the space of negative energy. That's the real reason witches use brooms, by the way—not to fly across the sky.

Although we usually think of hedges as surrounding property, for witches the hedge is more than a physical barrier. It symbolizes spiritual protection from the stresses of the outside world. It can also be seen as a barrier between the world of humans and the spirit realm.

WICCA

The words *Wicca* and *witch* come from the Anglo-Saxon term *wicce* meaning "to bend or shape." Wicca's tenets reach back to the "Old Religion" of pre-Christian Europe, especially that of the early Celts. Its roots also dig deeply into prehistoric times and the ancient fertility goddesses worshipped by Paleolithic peoples.

Writer Gerald Gardner is commonly given credit for coining the term *Wiccan* and jump-starting the modern movement in the 1950s. During the 1960s and '70s as feminism emerged Wicca gained popularity because it offers greater balance and equality than patriarchal religions. It is one of the few faiths that honors a primary feminine deity; however, you needn't be female or a feminist to pursue a Wiccan path. Today, Wicca is among the fastest-growing religious systems in the United States; it is even recognized by the U.S. military.

As mentioned earlier, people sometimes mistakenly think Wicca and witchcraft are interchangeable terms. Wiccans generally practice witchcraft, but witches may not necessarily share Wiccan beliefs and therefore would not consider themselves Wiccan. Simply put, Wicca is a religion, like Christianity or Judaism. It has defined practices, beliefs, and ethical codes. Within this religion, however, you'll find plenty of room for personal expression.

How Many Wiccans Are There?

According to ReligionFacts (*www.religionfacts.com*) between 1 and 3 million men and women worldwide consider themselves adherents of Wicca. Other estimates put that number closer to 800,000. Indiana University of Pennsylvania places Wicca among the eight largest faith groups in the United States.

Although Wiccans observe certain customs, rituals, and practices, the religion is flexible with no dogma, no sacred texts, and no laws save one: Do no harm. Wiccans follow what's known as the threefold law. The law basically states that whatever you do, whatever energies you "put out," will return to you threefold (three times over) in this lifetime or in the next. Therefore, Wiccans attempt to abide by what's known as the Wiccan Rede.

The Wiccan Rede

Bide the Wiccan law ye must,

In perfect love and perfect trust,

Eight words the Wiccan Rede fulfill:

An' ye harm none, do what ye will.

What ye send forth comes back to thee,

So ever mind the Rule of Three.

Follow this with mind and heart,

And merry ye meet, and merry ye part.

Various branches of Wicca, each with somewhat different views, already exist. Dianic Wicca, for example, has a strong feminist component. Gardnerian Wicca is more formal and hierarchal than some other branches, and its practitioners perform rituals "skyclad" (nude). Visit *www.wicca.com* for more information about these and other types of Wicca. Like all belief systems, Wicca continues to evolve, and young enthusiasts coming to it today will surely expand its ideas, practices, and forms of expression in the future.

SHAMANISM

One of the earliest depictions of a shaman was found in France, in the cave of Les Trois Frères. Estimated to be at least 15,000 years old, the painting shows a man disguised as a bison and armed with a bow. Originally, the term *shaman* referred to a Siberian medicine man, but it can apply to anyone who engages in shamanistic practices, regardless of the era and society in which the person lives. In simple terms, a shaman is someone who understands both the spirit world and the natural world, and who uses that knowledge to provide healing, guidance, and protection to his people.

The Lessons of Don Juan

In the 1970s, the best-selling books of Carlos Castaneda introduced readers to the concepts of shamanism. Castaneda wrote about his five-year apprenticeship with a teacher whom he called Don Juan, and described his experiences in what he termed "nonordinary states of reality." He also discussed shape-shifting, a shamanic practice that involved projecting his own consciousness into animals and plants.

Among the indigenous people of North, Central, and South America, shamans have long served as medicine men, midwives, visionaries, wisdom keepers, and healers. These shamans worked with the forces of nature, the deities and ancestors in the spirit realms, and totem animals to ensure the well-being of their tribes.

Walking Between the Worlds

From the shamanic perspective, the physical world is only one facet of reality. Many other realms exist, and it's possible to travel to these other realities at will. Shamans have learned to erase the barriers that ordinarily separate the physical and nonphysical realms in order to "walk between the worlds."

The Modern Guide to Witchcraft

As seers and diviners, Native American shamans use drumming, dancing, herbs and botanical substances, fasting, and other practices to induce altered states of consciousness. While in these trance states, the shamans journey beyond the limitations of matter and space to gain knowledge, communicate with entities in the spirit world, effect healing, and observe the future. Dreams, too, provide access into other levels of reality. Although we tend to associate shamanism with Native Americans, you'll find shamans in many other cultures too. Celtic magicians might not use the term shamanism, but they engage in shamanic practices. They explore what's known as the Otherworld, a nonphysical place of wisdom, creativity, and imagination, as well as the fairie realm.

Often a shaman uses a technique called "astral projection" to visit other worlds beyond our earthly one. This allows the person's spirit to journey freely while the physical body remains in a trancelike state. The spirit is also able to temporarily leave the body during sleep and explore the nonphysical realms. In these other levels of reality, the shaman might meet spirits that once occupied human bodies as well as gods, goddesses, and other beings that have never incarnated.

Spirit Animals

When journeying in this way, shamans sometimes seek the assistance of spirit animals or other guides to provide protection and direction. In ancient times, people in many parts of the world believed spirit animals lived in an invisible realm that intersects with our own physical one. These spirit beings helped our ancestors in countless ways, from providing protection to offering healing wisdom to predicting the future. Early humans considered these animal guides and guardians as types of deities—somewhat like angels—and paid homage to them.

Native American tribes traditionally established special affinities with certain animals, which became the tribe's totems or sacred animals. They assisted the shamans' personal spirit guides in magickal work. Tribes carved totem poles with the images of various spirit and animal guides as a way of showing gratitude and to request continued aid in the future.

SORCERERS

Like shamans, sorcerers understand that our planet is not the only realm of existence, nor are we earthlings the only forms of intelligent life in the cosmos. Sorcerers believe the universe contains an infinite number of worlds just waiting to be explored. Furthermore, they're adept at traveling to these other worlds and interacting with the beings who reside there—and they don't need a passport to get in.

In her book *The Sorcerer's Crossing*, Taisha Abelar describes sorcerers as people whose goal is "breaking the perceptual dispositions and biases that imprison us within the boundaries of the normal everyday world and prevent us from entering other perceivable worlds." What she means is, we limit ourselves with narrow, conditioned thinking and miss out on a lot.

Through training and practice, sorcerers develop the ability to expand their sight beyond ordinary vision and see things the rest of us can't. They can perceive the life in rocks and trees, as well as see the spirits who live all around us. With practice, the sorcerer attunes herself with her nonphysical, energetic body—known as the "double"—controlling and expanding it in order to accomplish feats far beyond what most of us consider normal. For example, a sorcerer might project her double someplace other than where her physical body happens to be at any given time, so that she can be in two places at once. While she's sitting at her desk, performing her everyday job, she may simultaneously be chanting in a temple in India or visiting Machu Picchu in Peru.

DRUID MAGICK

The word *Druid* derives from the Indo-European root *drui*, meaning "oak," as well as "solid and true." Originally, Druids served as the bards, teachers, healers, judges, scribes, seers, astrologers, and spiritual leaders of the ancient Celts. They conducted rites and rituals, gazed into the future, healed the sick, kept the history of their people, and addressed legal matters within their communities. These wise men and women were highly revered and wielded authority second only to the king's.

The Modern Guide to Witchcraft

Much of what we know today about the early Druids has been handed down through oral tradition, folklore, legends, songs, and poetry. As the Romans and Christianity moved into Ireland and Britain, the conquerors destroyed the Druids and their tradition. Thus, most of Druidic history remains shrouded in mystery.

Druids and Magick

Maya Magee Sutton, PhD, and Nicholas R. Mann, authors of *Druid Magic*, explain that in contemporary Irish dictionaries, the word *draiocht* means "magick" as well as "spells." Its root, *draoi*, translates as "magician," "sorcerer," or "Druid." This suggests a strong connection between the Druids and the practice of magick.

Modern-day Druids follow beliefs and practices associated with their early ancestors. With little actual information available about the old ways, however, neo-Druids interpret the spiritual tradition by blending ancient with contemporary wisdom. A reverence for nature, knowledge of astrology and divination, healing, and shamanic journeying continue to be part of today's Druidic practice.

The Druids consider trees to be sacred. Oaks, in particular, have long been linked with Druid spirituality. Sacred rituals were—and still are—performed in oak groves. Druids believe trees embody wisdom that can be passed along to human beings. Each tree possesses certain characteristics and unique properties that Druids use in their magickal work. Rowan trees, for instance, offer protection. Oaks give strength and endurance. Willows are associated with intuition and divination—they're a favorite wood for making magick wands.

CEREMONIAL MAGICK

Also called high or ritual magick, ceremonial magick evolved out of the teachings of early mystery schools in various parts of the world. Its practitioners are more likely to describe themselves as magicians than as witches. The Hermetic Order of the Golden Dawn, an organization that formed in the latter part of the nineteenth century as a secret society (see Chapter 3), has greatly influenced this type of magick and its practice today. The group's philosophy is founded on the Hebrew Qabalah and the doctrines of Hermes Trismegistus, and draws upon the belief systems of the Freemasons, Rosicrucians, Gnostics, and others.

More formalized and intellectualized than Wicca and other Pagan spiritual paths, ceremonial magick involves study of the Qabalah, astrology, alchemy, tarot, and many other subjects. It emphasizes the use of ritual and ceremony, along with mental training, to facilitate spiritual enlightenment, healing, extrasensory powers, and understanding of the cosmic order. Carl Weschcke, president of the publishing company Llewellyn Worldwide, has called this field of magick "spiritual technology." Indeed, if you have a fondness for highly developed systems, this path might be for you.

Why engage in complicated and sometimes lengthy rituals? Rituals focus the mind and transport you from the everyday world into a magickal one—that's a key reason for enacting them. Rituals rely on symbolic associations that the magician's senses and subconscious mind intuitively understand. Gestures, diagrams, postures, words, images, sounds, scents, and colors all play symbolic roles in magick rituals and ceremonies.

Ritual magick often involves elaborate and carefully orchestrated practices that are designed for various purposes. Purification rituals, for instance, cleanse the mind, body, and energy field. Protection rituals define sacred space and prevent unwanted influences from interfering. The rituals themselves are magickal acts.

The Magickal Qabalah

The Qabalah (sometimes spelled Kabbala, Cabala, and other ways) is a body of collected teachings that underlie Hebrew mysticism. It includes four sections that cover doctrines, magickal practices, orally conveyed wisdom, and techniques for working with words, letters, and numbers. It also describes the Tree of Life, which plays an important part in ritual magick and shows the stages of development and pathways to spiritual enlightenment.

The Modern Guide to Witchcraft

SEX MAGICK

Mystical rites, rituals, and ceremonies involving sex have been practiced in numerous cultures, East and West, for longer than anyone can document. The early Celts engaged in sexual activity, particularly during the spring planting season and on Beltane, as a form of sympathetic magick to encourage the land's fertility. Temple priestesses in ancient Greece combined sex and mysticism. Tantric yoga channels sexual energy toward spiritual goals and also promotes health and longevity. In Wicca's Great Rite, a couple invites the God and Goddess to enter their bodies during sex, and the act is considered sacred.

The Origins of Sex Magick

Western sex magick is rooted in the teachings of Sufis, adherents of a mystical branch of Islam, who supposedly shared their knowledge with the Knights Templar during the Crusades in the Middle East. The Templars brought these practices back to Europe, where they were incorporated into other mystical and occult philosophies. Magick's notorious bad boy, Aleister Crowley, did much to promote and influence the course sex magick has taken in the West. Crowley learned sex magick while traveling in India and Africa, and he emphasized its practice through the organization he headed, the Ordo Templi Orientis (OTO).

Sex magick can be great fun, but that's not its purpose. In simple terms, it's a way to supercharge your magickal work and generate results faster. According to sex magick's tenets, this creative force, which is responsible for all human and animal life, can be directed to create abundance, success, healing, spiritual growth, and so on—like other types of magick. It taps the powerful creative energy inherent in sexual activity for specific purposes other than human reproduction. Some witches engage in sex magick, others don't. It can be added to any other form of witchcraft, magick, or spiritual practice, and can be done by anyone. (For more information, see my book *Sex Magic for Beginners*.)

VOUDON OR VOODOO

When people hear the word *voodoo*, they often envision dolls stuck with pins, zombies, and hideous rituals carried out secretly in darkness. But voudon (or voodoo) is simply a belief system. First brought to Haiti by African slaves sometime during the sixteenth century, it emerged in Louisiana 200 years later.

Voudon involves the interaction of humans with spirits. Numerous deities and spirits play parts in voudon's elaborate rituals and spells. In a traditional voudon ceremony, worshippers work themselves into a frenzy through music, chanting, and dancing, sometimes accompanied by various forms of drugs and alcohol. During an altered state of consciousness, they become possessed by one of the spirits and collapse to the ground, writhing and speaking unintelligibly. Once possessed, a worshipper is believed to be able to bring about a cure, good fortune, or some other desire. In some instances, animal sacrifices might be offered to the spirits to win their favor.

The dark side of voudon, however, has captured the public's imagination. Some practitioners, it's said, turn the dead into zombies— reanimated corpses who are slaves without wills of their own. The extremes of voudon's black magick can include all the stuff of horror movies, including control over others, ritual murders, and cannibalism.

SANTERÍA

Often referred to as a Cuban mystery religion, the word *santería* literally means "the worship of saints." A blend of Catholicism and Nigerian Paganism that evolved centuries ago, when Yoruba slaves were taken from Nigeria to Cuba, santería consists of a pantheon of *orishas* who are a combination of Catholic saints and Yoruba gods and goddesses. If you were raised Catholic you might find this colorful tradition intriguing, a way to incorporate witchcraft into the religious training and experience you already have.

When a man joins the religion and becomes a *santero* (or *santera*, if she's female), he agrees to "worship the saints, to observe their feasts, obey their commands, and conduct their rituals," writes Migene

The Modern Guide to Witchcraft

Gonzalez-Wippler, author of *The Santería Experience*. "In exchange for this absolute submission, he gains supernatural powers, protection against evil, and the ability to foresee the future and even to shape the future according to his will."

Casting spells and practicing witchcraft are part of a *santero*'s work. A *santero* often keeps icons or statues of the *orishas* and other saints on his altar, along with flowers, a bowl of water, and a bottle of Florida water (a type of cheap cologne used in many of the spells). The darker side of santería, known as mayomberia, is a type of black magick.

Of course, many other types of witchcraft and magickal practices exist around the world. The Polynesian spiritual path known as Huna teaches you to unite three aspects of yourself and channel your primal energy to bring about the results you desire. Practitioners of the ancient Chinese art of feng shui (pronounced *fung shway*) use a form of magick when they make changes in your home and workplace in order to attract money, love, health, etc. Wherever you go, you'll find people performing magick and doing witchcraft—even if they don't always call it that.

Chapter 8

SACRED SPACE

The Buddha once said, "Wherever you live is your temple if you treat it like one." Sacredness is more a matter of attitude and behavior than of trappings, and it doesn't require a building or props. Nonetheless, creating a sacred space is an important part of practicing magick, and witches often use tools and processes to establish safe havens in which to work.

WHAT IS SACRED SPACE?

Sacred space is an area you've cleansed of distractions and energy that you don't want to interfere with your magickal work. Within this purified zone you may choose to meditate, make offerings, and conduct spells or rituals. If you are lucky enough to have a temple or dedicated worship space in your home, then that is your permanent sacred space.

You've probably heard of magick circles. What makes sacred space different from a circle? A circle is a consciously constructed area that partially overlaps both our material world and the divine world. The resulting region is said to be "between the worlds," not wholly in one or the other. Sacred space is a place of peace and calm, but it is not necessarily "between the worlds." Sacred space is what goes into the circle, or it can simply exist on its own.

When you're in your sacred space you can still interact with the world beyond it—it doesn't set up a barrier the way a circle does. When you use sacred space, you make the existing environment holy, as opposed to creating a whole new surrounding. You remain open to the good energies in the area instead of sealing yourself away from them.

Sacred space is a wonderful alternative to a circle if you seek to create a harmonious atmosphere for a family gathering, particularly if the attendees are of mixed spiritualities or if the space you are using is unfamiliar to you. You can create it without anyone else's knowledge by purifying and harmonizing the energy of the area. You remove distracting, harmful, or stale energy and leave a positive, comfortable feeling instead.

Creating sacred space for other people who may not share your beliefs does not manipulate them in any way, nor does it disrespect their own religion. You are offering them a peaceful and balanced environment in which to study, discuss, eat, or mingle. Try creating sacred space before a dinner gathering during the week, when everyone is tired and stressed out. Watch how everyone relaxes in the serene energy.

CREATING SACRED SPACE

Creating sacred space includes four basic steps. The process takes place both inside you and outside, both in your mind and in a physical space.

- *Create*: This means eliminating thoughts, feelings, and energies that would distract you, so that your psyche is calm and all those everyday annoyances have been left behind.
- *Cleanse*: Clean up the area you will be using so that you have a tidy, pleasant place in which to work.
- *Purify*: This is the magickal counterpart to cleansing. Purification removes negative energy.
- *Consecrate*: This step involves blessing the space in some fashion.

From here you can go on to cast a circle if you so desire, or if your ritual requires it. (You'll learn how later in this chapter.) Otherwise, you're ready to begin doing whatever you choose to do within the sacred space you've created with these four steps.

The Modern Guide to Witchcraft

Creating Internal Sacred Space

Before you perform any magick spells or rituals, you need to calm your spirit and your mind. Begin by putting aside your daily concerns and taking a few minutes to relax your body. Your goal is to shift your thinking and feeling from ordinary consciousness to a more serene and elevated consciousness. Giving yourself just five minutes to meditate will help you get in the right frame of mind to create sacred space.

Cleansing

Cleansing the physical space where you will work removes the distraction caused by dirt and clutter. Physical clutter and dust create chaotic energy, as any feng shui expert will attest. Cleansing also signifies your intention to honor this space and make it special. Sweep the floor with a regular broom and dustpan, clear off your altar or workspace, and tidy the general area. Put away loose papers, piles of books, clothes, toys, and other clutter from the area. Once you've removed the physical clutter, clean and polish the surfaces.

Cleanse yourself, too. Some witches like to take a relaxing bath or shower before a ritual. Although this step technically focuses on physical cleansing, it also helps you to mentally and emotionally prepare yourself to do magick.

Purifying Ritual Bath

Try this fragrant purifying scrub before doing a ritual or other magick work. Use warm—not hot—water. Do not use this scrub on your face. If you have sensitive skin, blend the herbs and essential oils into the almond or jojoba oil and omit the salt. Rub the oil gently into your skin prior to your bath or shower, and then rinse off.

CLEANSING BATH SCRUB

½ cup sea salt

1 teaspoon lemon zest (fresh)

1 cup fine Epsom salts

½ cup sweet almond or jojoba oil

3 drops lavender oil

3 drops frankincense oil

2 teaspoons lavender flowers (fresh or dry)

A lidded jar large enough to hold at least two cups of scrub

A small glass bowl

A damp washcloth

1. Purify the ingredients first. You can do this by visualizing white light around them. Grind the dried flowers finely while you state aloud that they will cleanse and purify your body, mind, and spirit.

2. In the covered jar, shake the two salts together. In the bowl, mix the oils. Open the jar and add the oil blend to the salt. Close the jar and shake to combine thoroughly. Open the jar and sprinkle the herbs over the oil and salt blend. Close the jar and shake to blend one final time.

3. To use the salt scrub once you are in the bath or shower, place about a tablespoon in the center of a clean, damp washcloth or in the palm of your hand. Gently rub the salts against your skin. Imagine them loosening any negative energy that may cling to you. Feel the purifying salt, lavender, frankincense, and lemon soaking into your body, cleansing your aura and calming your mind.

4. When you feel cleansed, rinse the salt scrub and the negative energy away with water.

5. Step out of the bath and dry yourself gently with a clean towel.

Purification

In this step, you purify yourself and the area where you'll be working. Cleansing deals with physical dirt; purification gets rid of the negative energy that clutters up an area. You can do this by sweeping in a counterclockwise motion with a besom (a witch's broom). If you enjoy aromatherapy, spritz some lavender scent into the air or burn your favorite calming incense. Some witches prefer to burn a smudge stick and waft the smoke around the area. Others sprinkle small amounts of salt in the space. Or, you can simply visualize a ball of white light materializing in the center, then growing outward and driving away negativity.

Purifying with a Stone

You can also purify your sacred space with a crystal or gemstone. Citrine, a yellowish-colored quartz crystal, is a good choice, although clear quartz will work as well. Before you use your chosen stone to purify a space, wash it in warm water and pat it dry. (Remember to cleanse your stone(s) often to get rid of any negative energy that may cling to them.) Then program or "charge" it with the purpose of purification. You can do this by speaking your intention to the stone. Rather than visualizing the negative energy being absorbed into the stone, imagine the stone pushing away unwanted vibrations.

1.   Beginning at the perimeter of your area, slowly walk counterclockwise in circles that grow decreasingly smaller, spiraling in toward the center. As you do this, hold the crystal out and visualize it repelling the unwanted energy away from your space. If you notice a place that feels as if it has collected lots of negative energy, pause there and move the crystal around and up and down slowly, until you feel that the energy has been dispersed.

2.   Finish in the center of the space. As an added precaution, you can leave the crystal lying on the floor to allow it to continue chasing away unwanted energy.

Consecration

Once both you and your ritual space have been physically cleansed and spiritually purified, you're ready to consecrate the space. To consecrate means to sanctify, and this is the definitive step that makes the space sacred.

One way to do this is to bring into your space the energies of the four elements we discussed in Chapter 5. Choose an object that represents each element; for example, a candle could symbolize the fire element, a stone could signify earth, a bowl of water could stand for the element of water, and a smoking stick of incense could bring in the air element.

Here's another method: Stand in the center of the area and feel yourself drawing up energy from the earth beneath your feet into the center of your body. Next, connect with the energy of the sky and sense it flowing down into the center of your body. Allow these two energies to mingle within you—feel them swirling around and blending in your core—then envision yourself radiating this dual energy outward until it fills the space. Stop the flow of energy from both sky and earth when you sense that your sacred space is filled.

After Your Ritual

Sacred space does not need to be dismantled, as a circle does, when you've finished your magickal working. You can leave it and come back whenever you choose, knowing that your sanctuary awaits you. To signal that your work here is finished, simply say something like, "This [ritual/spell/meditation] is ended. I go in peace." How long does sacred space last? It depends on where you created it. If your sacred space is in a room of your home, its sanctity will linger longer than if you set up a temporary space in a public mall. The more often you use this space, the more you reinforce its sanctity.

PREPARATION FOR CASTING A CIRCLE

Since ancient times, circles have symbolized both power and protection. When you cast a circle, you're working on several levels simultaneously. At a physical level you're defining the boundaries for your work, and on a spiritual level you're filling the space with your personal power. Modern witches still perform spells and rituals within a circle. Group work, especially gatherings and public rituals, frequently takes place in a circular sacred space. The circle represents unity, accord, and wholeness. It provides a protective psychic "fence" that keeps unwanted energies out and desired energies in, until you're ready to release them. A circle also shows that each person present is important to the success of the magickal working.

Creating the Proper Ambiance

The time spent creating sacred space is important psychologically for the participants. This allows everyone to adjust to spirit-thinking rather than mundane thinking. That attitude is important to the success of even the simplest magickal process. Everyone involved must be focused on your agreed-upon intention, in order to harness the energy needed for your spell or ritual. Once you're inside the circle, no one should leave unless absolutely necessary. The following guidelines will help you create the right ambiance for your sacred space:

1. Ensure that you (or the group) won't be interrupted. Turn off cell phones, TVs, etc.
2. Choose the right space for your task, taking into account weather, personal time, physical constraints, and what's going to take place in the sacred space.
3. Make sure the area is safe and tidy; get rid of anything that might distract you from the task at hand.
4. Set up your purified tools so they're readily accessible.
5. If you light candles, make sure you do it in a safe place to avoid the danger of fire. Keep them away from flammable materials (such as curtains).

Don't use potentially harmful chemicals in your sacred space. Whatever you put into sacred space—physical, emotional, and mental—gets amplified. Outdoors, use natural insect repellents, and salt or mulch to inhibit weed growth. Indoors, use only "green" cleaning materials.

Your Magickal Workspace

Your circle should be large enough to accommodate the number of people who will be working inside of it, as well as any objects that you'll bring into the circle. It's also your workspace, so if you'll be dancing, drumming, or otherwise moving about inside the circle, allow plenty of room for your activities.

Do You Need to Cleanse, Purify, and Consecrate Your Space Before Casting a Circle?

Some witches believe that you must always cleanse, purify, and consecrate the space where you will construct your circle. Others believe that cleansing and purifying are necessary, but that the act of creating the circle consecrates the space. Still others believe that you don't need to prepare the space in any way before you raise your circle. Do what feels right to you.

A circle isn't a flat ring, nor is it a dome over you. Your circle is actually a sphere surrounding you above and below your workspace, as if you were standing in a bubble. You draw a circle, but envision a sphere growing out of the line you draw—it's a circle in three dimensions, a shell that allows the sacred space within the circle to exist between the worlds.

CASTING A MAGICK CIRCLE

Casting a circle begins as an act of faith; you *believe* the circle is there. Although many methods exist for circle casting, some of them quite elaborate, you can begin by following these simple steps:

1. Stand in the center of the space you will define as your circle.
2. Facing east, extend your "projective" hand outward, pointing to where you're going to draw the circle's wall. (Your projective hand is the hand with which you send out energy.)
3. Center your personal energy within your body. Then ground your energy by envisioning it flowing down through your feet and into the earth, where it connects with the energy of the earth.
4. With your projective hand still extended, draw energy up from the earth, through your body and out to your hand.
5. Allow this energy to flow out to the point where you intend to begin forming your circle. Slowly turn in a clockwise direction until you are again facing the original starting point and the flow of energy joins up with where it started, forming a seamless ring.
6. Visualize the ring thickening and curving inward until it meets above your head and below your feet, forming a perfect sphere of energy.
7. Drop your hand to shut off the energy flow.

You are now ready to begin your magick spell or ritual.

Some witches prefer to use a tool to draw the circle, usually either an athame (ritual dagger) or a magick wand. We'll talk more about these and other tools later. Some witches like to actually walk the perimeter of the circle. If you want to do this, start in the east (make sure you know where the four compass directions are before you begin) and walk clockwise (or deosil), so that when the circle is completed you'll be inside of it. On a physical level, you create your circle by walking around its outer border, but for the circle to exist both in the physical realm and in the mental and spiritual realms, you must also visualize it with clear intent, channeling your energy and that of the earth into your visualization.

The Four Elements Technique

This technique combines the four elements—earth, air, fire, and water—to cast a circle. First, fill a bowl with salt water, which symbolizes the elements of earth and water. Beginning in the east, walk in a clockwise direction, sprinkling the salt water on the ground to define a circle as you say, "With earth and water I cast this magick circle." Next, light a stick of incense, which represents fire and air (smoke). Again, start in the east and walk clockwise around the circle, trailing the fragrant smoke behind you while you say, "With fire and air I cast this magick circle."

If you prefer, two people can perform this circle-casting ritual together. In this case, one person holds the bowl of salt water, and the other carries the stick of burning incense.

What If You Have to Leave a Circle?

Sometimes you just have to leave the circle, to retrieve something you forgot, go to the bathroom, or deal with some emergency. In this case, you'll need to open a door in the circle's "wall" to keep from breaking it—like popping a balloon—and letting all the power you've raised escape. You can cut a door with an athame, but the simplest method is to use your hands:

1. Hold your hands out in front of you, palms together. Slowly insert them into the energy of your circle wall.
2. Carefully pull your hands apart and visualize the wall of energy parting like a pair of curtains.
3. Step through and close the "curtains" behind you. Do what you need to do quickly and calmly, then return to the circle and open the curtains again, from the outside.

4. After stepping through the energy curtains and back into the circle, close the curtains.

DISMANTLING A BASIC CIRCLE

Dismantling the circle is just as important as raising it. Unlike sacred space, which slowly loses its energy over time, a circle must be taken down with as much care as you used to cast it. Perform the steps with reverence, closing the ritual with the same degree of respect as you entered into it. Basically, you dismantle a circle by repeating the motions you used to cast it, but in reverse:

1. Stand in the center of your circle and extend your "receptive" hand (the opposite of your projective hand) toward the wall of the circle. Center your personal energy, then ground it into the earth below.
2. Facing east, begin drawing the energy of the circle into your hand and let it flow through your body, then down into the earth. Turning counterclockwise, continue removing the energy in this manner until you face your original starting point again and the energy of the circle is all gone.
3. Drop your hand, shutting off the energy flow. Your hand may feel tingly or odd after collecting the energy—shake it a few times to get rid of any traces of the circle energy that may still be clinging to it. Disconnect your personal energy from the earth, bringing it back into your body.

You may wish to experiment with various circle-casting methods to see which ones you like best. Your circle may or may not be visible—it depends on you and your objective. Some magicians actually draw on the floor or ground with chalk. Some sprinkle flour or cornmeal to define the circle. Some witches light candles around the perimeter, or position stones in a circle. You might even choose to use a material that relates to the purpose of your spell; for example, if you're doing a love spell you could scatter rose petals in a circle. However, your intention and the love, passion, and joy that you project into the process are more important than the material you use.

The Modern Guide to Witchcraft

Chapter 9

ALTARS AND SHRINES

If you plan to do magick frequently—and why wouldn't you?—you may decide to erect an altar in your home. An altar can be a TV table draped with a beautiful cloth, an ornate antique cabinet, or anything in between. Your altar is your basic "workbench" for doing magick. It establishes a sanctuary in your home and provides a focal point for casting spells, performing rites and rituals, and meditating. You go there to temporarily leave the ordinary, everyday world behind and enter sacred space.

SETTING UP YOUR ALTAR

Many witches include at least one central altar in a sacred space. Some believe it's important to place their altars in the east, others prefer the north, but wherever you choose to put yours is fine—go with what feels right. For practical purposes, setting the altar in the middle of your circle makes sense, especially if a number of people will join you there for rituals. Everyone can gather around it easily, and a central candle placed on the altar can symbolize Spirit as the guiding force for the ritual.

You can set up a permanent altar if your living circumstances permit. If you don't have enough space or share your home with other people who may not respect your altar, you can create a temporary one and dismantle it when you're finished doing your magick. If you're lucky enough to have a nice area outside to work in, you might position an altar there. Perhaps you could dedicate a special, large stone to that purpose.

What Goes on Your Altar?

Witches usually set up something depicting the four elements some-where on their altars. These can be physical representations such as salt for earth, water for water, a candle for fire, and incense for air. Some magicians display their wands, pentagrams, athames, and chalices openly on their altars. If you decide to lay out your tools on your altar, be sure to include all four. (We'll discuss these tools in depth in the next chapter.) You might also like to place candles in handsome candleholders, some crystals, statues of favorite deities, flowers, and other meaningful objects there. Many people store their magickal gear in their altars. A cabinet with drawers is the perfect place to stash additional candles, incense, herbs, oracles, ritual clothing, and various other ingredients that you will use in your spells.

Your altar should bring you a sense of peace, joy, harmony, and per-sonal power. Choose only things that hold positive associations for you to display on your altar.

Attuning Your Altar to Your Purpose

The items and symbols you bring to your altar largely depend on the purpose of your magick. Therefore, they may change regularly, depend-ing on the type of spell or ritual you're doing. For example, for a ritual to honor your ancestors, you might want to include their photographs or personal effects. If you're doing a spell for love, you might set a vase of roses there.

Some witches enjoy decorating their altars according to the seasons or holidays. Spring flowers and some painted eggs add a pretty touch at Ostara. A cornucopia of fruits and vegetables could bring the flavor of the harvest festival Lughnasadh to your sacred space. At Yule, use ever-green sprigs and pinecones to set the scene. (We'll talk more about these holidays and how to celebrate them in Chapter 21.)

It's a good idea to cleanse and purify all the things you plan to use for magickal workings or to place on your altar beforehand. An easy way to do this is to light a stick of incense, such as cedar or sandalwood, and then pass the objects through the smoke.

Mobile Magick

You can even make a mobile altar to take along with you when you travel. You can transform a small box into a portable altar. Decorate it with images that imply "magick" to you, or pack a pretty scarf to drape over it. Fill the box with a few of the basics—tea light candles, incense cones, small crystals, etc. Or, consider putting an "altar" on your smartphone or iPad. Photograph your home altar or choose images that speak to you, and look at them whenever you want, wherever you go. Add some peaceful music to set the mood and you're good to go.

ADDING ALTARS IN YOUR CIRCLE

To connect with the four elements and the four corners of creation, some witches erect four small altars within their sacred spaces. If you decide to do this, position one altar at each of the four main compass points of your working space; these are known as the "quarters." You can either create permanent or temporary altars for a specific purpose. Consider placing items that represent the element on its respective altar—this can help to strengthen your connection with that element and enrich your experience during your magickal working. Here are some suggestions:

Direction	Element	Suggested Objects
East	Air	yellow candle, feathers, incense, wind chimes
South	Fire	red candle, red-colored stones (bloodstone, carnelian, ruby), figurine of a dragon
West	Water	blue candle, shells, bowl of water
North	Earth	green candle, stones or crystals, potted plants, marble or ceramic statue

An easy way to assign each altar to an element is to cover it with a cloth of the element's color: air/yellow, fire/red, water/blue, north/green. You might also consider putting a picture of the archangel who presides over each direction on the appropriate altar: east/Raphael, south/Michael, west/Gabriel, north/Uriel. Later in this chapter, you'll learn to call upon these deities to assist you in your magickal workings.

Elemental Shrines

A shrine is a place to honor something or someone, and to leave offerings. It serves as a physical point of contact where you can connect to a god or goddess, your guardian angel, a spirit animal, or an ancestor. Your altar can be used for these things as well, but a shrine is not a workspace for doing magick, like an altar. Shrines are easier to set up and maintain because they aren't as complex. A shrine can consist of a postcard, a specially charged crystal, a plant, or a small statue. If you don't want your family or roommate to know what you're doing, keep it simple. You know why those particular things are together; anyone else looking at them will think that it's just a decorative arrangement. Using a shrine as a focus for specific activities can also help unclutter your main altar area.

Famous Shrines

Since ancient times, all cultures have created shrines to honor deities and to mark sacred space. Stonehenge, a giant, megalithic circle in Wiltshire, England, remains a mystery today, but anthropologists think it might have been a sacred site for rituals or perhaps a shrine to deities. The Sekhmet Sanctuary at Luxor, Egypt, is a stunning shrine to the lion-headed goddess. Other amazing shrines include the Hanging Gardens of Haifa in Israel, Machu Picchu in Peru, and the Grand Mosque in Mecca. (See Judy Hall's book, *Crystals and Sacred Sites* to learn more.)

An element shrine is a place where you can connect with one element or all four. For example, if you build a water shrine, you can include a goblet of water, a small fountain, shells, river stones, or even just pictures of a waterfall or a calm lake. A fire shrine may be a collection of candles in reds and golds set on a crimson cloth, perhaps with a small brass figurine of a lion. The important thing is to think about what each element means to you and to gather a few items that represent your feelings and intentions regarding it.

Shrines for Harmony in the Home

Experiment with creating four separate shrines in four different places in your home. You can try building the earth shrine in the northern part of your house, the air shrine in the east, the fire shrine in the south, and the water shrine in the west. Make sure to have one shrine for each element so that your home remains balanced.

Does your home have a room where people tend to lose their tempers or energy runs too high? It may have an excess of fire energy that arises from its décor or as a result of how the energy flows through it. Try setting up an earth shrine or a water shrine in that room to ease tension and bring harmony. Choose a peaceful picture, a pretty blue or green stone, a shell, or a plant.

If an area of your home or workplace seems sluggish or heavy, consider building a fire shrine there. A photo of a sunny beach, a red stone, a vase of red or orange flowers—whatever feels right to you. You can do this in your office or workplace, too. Nobody has to know!

Memorial Shrines

Around the world, people create shrines to honor people who have died in battles or other catastrophes. These memorials, such as Footprints Fountain at Ground Zero in New York, serve as focal points for love, respect, prayers, gratitude, and hope. Not only do memorials such as these remind us of the victims and circumstances, they also hold the intentions of the people who visit, and invoke peaceful energies to help neutralize the traumas that took place there. Some people put up shrines at roadsides where fatal auto accidents occurred. When you visit the grave of a beloved friend or relative, and perhaps lay flowers or mementos there, you are showing reverence at a shrine created to honor that person.

CALLING THE FOUR QUARTERS/DIRECTIONS

Now let's put together some of the things you've learned in the previous chapters to do a more advanced form of circle casting. Many magickal traditions "call the quarters" as part of casting a circle. Not everyone uses the same words or gestures, however. Wiccans probably won't perform this practice in exactly the same way as ceremonial magicians do.

Before you cast your circle, erect four altars, one at each of the compass points. Decorate them as described earlier, with objects and symbols that represent the elemental energies of each direction. Of course, you'll want to cleanse, purify, and consecrate them first. Make sure you have everything in place before you actually cast the circle. Then once you and everyone else who will participate are inside it, you can light a candle at each altar and call in the quarters.

An Invoking Ritual

Some people invoke angels when calling the quarters. As we first discussed in Chapter 4, usually Raphael is associated with the east, Michael with the south, Gabriel with the west, and Uriel with the north. The deities are invoked in this order and released in the opposite order. Or, you might choose to invite gods, goddesses, animal totems, or other spirits to whom you feel a special connection or who have links to the purpose of your spell/ritual.

The following description is eclectic and generic, but nonetheless functional. As you call out to the four directions, visualize beams of pure white light stretching into the sky and connecting you at each of those directions to the powers of the universe. In time, you may wish to customize the ritual, adapting it to the season or your intention—you can even design your own entirely:

1. Begin at the east. Light a yellow candle here and face outward, with your back to the center of the circle. Call out to the forces of the east, saying, "Beings of Air, Guardians of the East, Breath of Transformation—Come! Be welcome in this sacred space. I/we ask that you stand firm to guard and protect, refresh and inspire me/us. Support the magick created here by conveying my/our wishes on every wind as it blows across the earth."

2. Move clockwise to the south and light a red candle. Invoke the deities of the south by saying, "Beings of Fire, Guardians of the South, Spark of Creation that banishes the darkness—Come! Be welcome

in this sacred space. I/we ask that you stand firm to guard and protect, activate and motivate me/us. Support the magick created here by conveying my/our wishes to the sun, the stars, and every beam of light that embraces the earth."

3. Continue to the west, light a blue candle, and call out, "Beings of Water, Guardians of the West, Rain of Imagination—Come! Be welcome in this sacred space. I/we ask that you stand firm to guard and protect, heal and nurture me/us. Support the magick created here by conveying my/our wishes to the dewdrops, rain, and the waves as they wash across the world."

4. Walk to the north, light a green candle, and say, "Beings of Earth, Guardians of the North, Soil of Foundation—Come! Be welcome in this sacred space. I/we ask that you stand firm to guard and protect, support and provide for me/us. Support the magick created here by conveying my/our wishes to every grain of sand, every bit of loam that is our world."

5. Move into the center of the circle and intone, "Ancient One, the power that binds all the elements into oneness and source of my/our magick—Come! Be welcome in this sacred space. I/we ask that you stand firm to guard and protect, guide and enhance all the energy created here. May it be for the good of all. So mote it be."

Once you've established your circle and feel the presence of the beings you've invited to join you in your sacred space, continue with your magick spell or ritual.

Closing the Circle and Releasing Magickal Energies

Releasing the sacred space is as important as erecting it. At the end of your workings, release the sphere you've created, thank the powers who've assisted you, ask them to keep guiding the energy you've raised. Bid them farewell until the next time:

1. Begin in the north quarter and move counterclockwise (as if you're unwinding something). See the beams of light that connected you to the rest of the universe slowly evaporating back into the Void.

Just because they leave your sacred space doesn't mean they're gone (energy can't be destroyed—it only changes form). They simply return to their source at the four corners of creation and attend to their tasks.

2. At the north point, say, "Guardians, Guides, and Ancestors of the North and Earth, I/we thank you for your presence and protection. Keep me/us rooted in your rich soil so my/our spirit(s) grow steadily, until I/we return to your protection again. Hail and farewell!" Then extinguish the candle.

3. Move to the west and say, "Guardians, Guides, and Ancestors of the West and Water, I/we thank you for your presence and protection. Keep me/us flowing ever toward wholeness in body, mind, and spirit, until I/we return to your protection again. Hail and farewell!" Then extinguish the candle.

4. Continue on to the south and say, "Guardians, Guides, and Ancestors of the South and Fire, I/we thank you for your presence and protection. Keep your fires ever burning within my/our soul(s) to light any darkness and drive it away, until I/we return to your protection again. Hail and farewell!" Then extinguish the candle.

5. Go to the east and say, "Guardians, Guides, and Ancestors of the East and Air, I/we thank you for your presence and protection. Keep your winds blowing fresh with ideas and hope, until I/we return to your protection again. Hail and farewell!" Then extinguish the candle.

6. In the circle's center say, "Great Spirit, thank you for blessing this space. I/we know that a part of you is always with me/us, as a still small voice that guides, protects, and nurtures me/us. Help me/us to listen to that voice, to trust it, and trust in my/our magick."

7. Before leaving the circle, some witches like to join hands and offer a closing chant, such as, "Merry meet, merry part, and merry meet again."

Calling the Quarters: An Alternative

Your invocation can be as simple or eloquent as you wish. Use your imagination. Here's a simpler and quicker technique if you're short on time. Stand in the center of the circle, facing east, while you say aloud:

Before me Raphael, guardian of the east.
Behind me Gabriel, guardian of the west.
To my right Michael, guardian of the south.
To my left Uriel, guardian of the north.
Be here now.

At the end of the spell or ritual, remember to release the energies you've called in and thank them for assisting you.

Working with the quarters and the spirits is a lot like being in an evolving relationship with someone you respect and admire. If you treat these entities accordingly, you will rarely be disappointed.

Chapter 10

THE WITCH'S TOOL KIT

If you were building a house you'd use a saw, hammer, carpenter's square, drill, and many other tools. Witches use special tools in their work, too. You've heard of magick wands, of course, but you might not be familiar with some of the other items in the witch's tool kit. And some objects you think you recognize may have magickal purposes that you wouldn't have guessed.

THE SYMBOLISM OF MAGICK TOOLS

In many cases a tool's symbolism is an important part of its magickal value and determines its function in casting spells. Its shape and/or the material from which it's made could be factors as well. The pentagram, the tool most often associated with witchcraft, is a good example. The five points of the star symbolize the five "points" of the human body: the head, arms, and legs. The circle surrounding the star represents wholeness, union, and boundaries, which is why magicians cast circles around themselves when doing spells. Thus, the pentagram's symbolism suggests one of its most popular uses: protection.

Da Vinci's Pentagram
Remember the pen-and-ink drawing artist Leonardo da Vinci did in 1490, called *Vitruvian Man?* Although the Renaissance master intended it as a diagram showing the ideal human proportions, it you look at it from a witch's perspective you'll notice it also depicts a pentagram.

Masculine and feminine symbolism appear in many magick tools. Don't think "man" or "woman" here; we're talking about energy forces. The wand, athame (ritual dagger), and sword are obviously phallic in shape. The shape of the chalice, cauldron, and bell represent the womb. Masculine tools activate, direct, and project energy; feminine tools hold, nurture, and give form to energy. Both forces are necessary in life and in magick.

The four primary magick tools—the wand, chalice, athame, and pentagram—also symbolize the four elements we've talked about in earlier chapters—fire, water, air, and earth, respectively. Each functions in accordance with its element's nature and brings its elemental force into play during a spell or ritual. For example, if your objective is to stabilize your finances, you might use the pentagram (symbol of earth) in your spellworking. If you want to fan the flames in a romantic relationship, the wand (symbol of fire) could have a role in your spell.

Are Magick Tools Really Necessary?

Witches and other magicians will tell you that tools are good helpmates to magick, but they are not necessary to the success of any spell or ritual. A tool is only something to help you focus your mind. Without your will and directed energy, the potential in any tool will remain dormant. A witch might talk about quartz crystals possessing energy-enhancing power, but until a crystal is charged and activated, that ability "sleeps" within. You awaken it. A focused will is all that any effective witch needs for magick. Everything else just makes the job easier.

THE MAGICK WAND

The best known of all magic tools is the wand, which gained even greater recognition through the Harry Potter stories. Although the scene in which Harry receives his wand is amusing, it's not accurate—the magician selects the wand, not the other way around. Until you fill your wand with power, it's just an ordinary rod.

The idea of using a magick wand to turn your boss into a toad or to make your rival vanish may be tempting, but that's not how it works. A wand's main purpose is to direct energy. If you want to send energy to a

The Modern Guide to Witchcraft

person, place, or thing, just aim your magick wand in that direction and *presto*—there it goes! You can also attract energy with a wand—point it at the sky to draw down power from the heavens, or at the ground to draw up the energy of Mother Earth. Magicians often cast protective circles around a designated space by using a wand to direct energy.

According to tradition, a wand should be at least 6" long, but only as big as is comfortable for you to handle. Early wands were wooden, cut from the branch of a tree the magician considered sacred (favorites included yew, rowan, and willow). Today, however, you can find wands made of metal, glass, and other materials as well—modern witches and wizards often prefer something with a little bling. Some magicians like to adorn their wands with gemstones and crystals, symbols, ribbons, beadwork, feathers, or painted images. Others opt for simplicity. If you decide to work with a magick wand, the decorations you choose should be ones that you find meaningful and that help you to focus your mind.

The wand corresponds to the element of fire. In the tarot, it appears as the suit of wands (sometimes called rods or staves). Therefore, you might select adornments that resonate with a fiery nature such as carnelians, red ribbons, or touches of gold or iron.

THE PENTAGRAM

As mentioned previously, a pentagram is a five-pointed star with a circle around it. The correct way to display it is with one point upright, two points down, and two out to the sides to represent the human body. Magicians use the pentagram for protection. You can wear one for personal safety. Hang one on your front door to guard your home, or place one in your glove compartment to protect your car. You can even put one on your pet's collar to shield her from harm. Some witches like to decorate their pentagrams with gemstones and crystals, or to combine it with other symbols, whereas others choose to keep it simple.

In rituals, a magician might draw pentagrams in the air as part of the circle-casting process. With a wand or athame he traces the symbol at each of the four directions to provide protection. Sometimes participants in a ritual mark pentagrams on their foreheads with essential oils (amber, basil, and pine are good choices) as additional safeguards. You can inscribe pentagrams on candles, paint them on stones, embroider them on mojo pouches and clothing—just about anyplace. You might even want to get a pentagram tattoo.

The pentagram corresponds to the element of earth. In the tarot, it appears as the suit of pentacles (sometimes called coins or discs). Thus, you may wish to decorate your pentagram with earthy gems: onyx, aventurine, turquoise, jade, or tiger's eye. (We'll talk more about gemstones and magick in Chapter 12.)

Texas Pentagrams

If you travel to Texas, you'll spot pentagrams everywhere—on houses, clothing, and jewelry, laid out in paving stones in a town square or above a courthouse's entrance—although most people don't realize the symbol's true meaning. Back in the late 1800s, the Texas Rangers (the lawmen, not the baseball team) began wearing Texas Star badges featuring a five-pointed star inside a circle. And who knows? Those pentagrams may have saved some lives.

THE ATHAME

This ritual dagger is never used for practical purposes (such as chopping vegetables) and certainly not to harm someone. Rather, a witch symbolically slices away negative energy or cuts through psychic obstacles with this magick tool. You can also cast a protective circle with it instead of a wand.

An athame is usually a double-sided knife about 4–6" long (although some witches and Wiccans prefer athames shaped like a crescent moon). It doesn't have to be sharp, however, because you probably won't cut anything physical with it. You can decorate your dagger with gemstones and crystals or other adornments if you like. Some people engrave or paint magick symbols on their athames. The choice is yours. Remember, however, that your athame is a weapon of the "spiritual warrior" and tradition says you shouldn't work with a knife that has drawn blood.

The athame corresponds to the element of air. In the tarot, it appears as the suit of swords (sometimes called daggers). Therefore, you might like to decorate your athame with air symbolism: aquamarine or fluorite, feathers, yellow ribbons, or the glyphs for Gemini, Libra, and/or Aquarius.

THE CHALICE

The most famous chalice of all is the legendary Holy Grail. As you might suspect, a chalice is used for drinking beverages—but not your everyday kind, such as a Coke with lunch. Your chalice should only hold ritual brews and magick potions. In some rituals a ceremonial drink is passed among participants, which is why chalices often have long stems that are easy to grasp.

A chalice may be made of any material: metal, crystal, glass, ceramic, even wood. Some people like to decorate their chalices with gemstones and crystals, or other adornments. You might choose to add symbols, words, and images that hold meaning for you. Ritual or high magicians traditionally paint their chalices to look like a crocus with eight petals, in blue and orange.

Site of the Grail

The Chalice Well in Glastonbury, England, is a sacred site for Celts and followers of Goddess religions. Many people believe it is the final resting place of the Holy Grail. For 2,000 years, this well has been in constant use and has never been known to run dry. A symbol of the life force, the well is revered as a gift from Mother Earth to her children.

The chalice corresponds to the element of water. In the tarot, it appears as the suit of cups (sometimes called chalices or bowls). Consider inscribing your chalice with the astrological symbols for the water signs Pisces, Cancer, or Scorpio, or adorning it with "watery" gems: pearls, aquamarines, sapphires, or coral.

CANDLES

Candles are essential ingredients in many spells. They symbolize the fire element and spirit, the energizing force that activates spells and rituals. In addition, they provide a focal point for your attention, helping you to still your mind. Their soft, flickering light creates an ambiance that shifts you out of your ordinary existence.

Witches usually keep on hand a supply of candles in a range of colors. Colors hold symbolic meanings and affect us psychologically and emotionally, so not surprisingly witches use them in lots of spells. If you're doing a love spell, for example, burn a red or pink candle that represents passion, affection, and the heart. Prosperity spells call for green, gold, or silver candles, the colors of money. Some formal rituals involve carefully placing candles in specific spots and moving them according to prescribed patterns.

Birthday Magick

Most people are familiar with a very simple and popular candle spell: making a wish and blowing out candles on a birthday cake. Because your birthday is a high-energy day, this is a good time to do magick spells as well as to eat cake and ice cream.

INCENSE AND ESSENTIAL OILS

For thousands of years, aromatic oils, gums, and resins have been used for both medicinal and cosmetic purposes, as well as in sacred rituals. Scents affect the limbic system, the portion of the brain associated with memory, emotions, and sexuality, which is why certain smells reawaken memories or stimulate the libido. Take a whiff of a certain perfume, of sea air, or of fresh-baked apple pie and, instantly, memories unfold. Because aromas immediately trigger moods, impressions, and associations, they can be assets in spells and rituals.

Essential Oils

Essential oils are extracted from plants rather than concocted from synthetic substances, as is the case with most modern perfumes. From the perspective of magick, essential oils are preferable to other scents because they contain the life energy of herbs and flowers.

Magicians use essential oils in many ways. Dressing candles is one popular practice. To dress a candle, choose an oil that relates to your intention. Pour a little oil in your palm and rub it over the waxy surface to add the properties of the scent to the candle. When the candle burns, the essence is released into the atmosphere to help manifest your intent. If you choose to make your own candles, you can incorporate essential oils into the mix.

Some essential oils can irritate skin or cause allergic reactions. A few oils are toxic. Research the oils you want to use before applying them to your skin or adding them to a ritual bath. Don't ingest the toxic ones!

Essential oils can also heighten the power of an amulet or talisman. Rub a little oil onto the charm or put a drop on a piece of paper and place it inside the charm. Magicians sometimes anoint their tools with essential oils to charge them. Of course, wearing fragrant oils is probably the most common way to enjoy them. You can even draw symbols on your body with essential oils to provide protection or to attract desired energies—and of course, for seduction.

Essential Oils and Their Magical Properties	
Acacia	Meditation, purification
Almond	Vitality, energy booster
Amber	Protection
Basil	Protection, harmony
Bay	Love spells, prophetic dreams
Bayberry	Money spells
Cedar	Prosperity, courage, protection
Cinnamon	Career success, wealth, vitality
Clove	Healing, prosperity, increased sexual desire
Eucalyptus	Healing, purification
Frankincense	Prosperity, protection, psychic awareness
Honeysuckle	Mental clarity, communication
Jasmine	Love spells, passion, to sweeten any situation
Lavender	Relaxation, peace of mind, healing, purification
Mint	Money spells
Musk	Love spells, vitality, to stimulate drive or desire
Patchouli	Love spells, protection, career success

Pine	Purification, protection, strength
Rose	Love spells, to lift spirits
Rue	Protection
Sage	Cleansing, wisdom
Sandalwood	Connection to the higher realms, knowledge, safe travel
Vervain	Money spells, fertility
Ylang-ylang	Aphrodisiac, love spells, to heighten passion or feminine power

Incense

In Latin, *incense* means "to burn." For centuries, churches and temples have used incense to clear the air and to send prayers to the deities. In Buddhist belief, burning an offering of incense invokes the Buddha into a statue of the holy being. The best incense is made from pure gums and resins, without synthetic binders.

Witches use incense to purify sacred space. Sage is the most popular herb for this purpose, but you can burn pine, frankincense, or eucalyptus if you prefer. As we discussed earlier, a witch may cast a protective circle by lighting a stick of incense and walking around the area in a clockwise direction, allowing the smoke to mark the space. You can also charge charms with incense by holding the amulet or talisman in the smoke for a few moments.

OTHER MAGICK TOOLS

Over time you may add to your magickal collection. Some of the spells in the following chapters use various tools for special purposes. Brooms sweep unwanted energies from a ritual space. Bells, gongs, drums, and rattles raise positive energy and disperse bad vibes. Magicians also use them to signal the steps in rituals. Swords, like athames, banish harmful forces and slice through obstacles. Staffs (or staves), like wands, direct energy.

The Cauldron

"Double, double, toil and trouble; / Fire burn, and cauldron bubble." Probably the best-known image of the witch's cauldron comes from

Shakespeare's play *Macbeth*, in which three crones stir into a cauldron all sorts of ghastly ingredients to brew up a magick potion. Contemporary witches still brew potions in cauldrons, but they don't use fillet of a fenny snake, lizard's leg, or howlet's wing to create a hell-broth, as the Bard's witches did.

A cauldron is a handy tool, especially if you don't have a fireplace, balefire pit, or barbecue grill, because you can build a small ritual fire in a cauldron. (Don't use regular barbecue charcoal if you're building a fire inside—the carbon monoxide can be deadly!) You can also concoct magick brews or cook ceremonial meals in it. Some people put flowers, water, crystals, or other objects in a cauldron during rituals. Because the cauldron represents the womb, it can nurture your intentions—write a wish on a slip of paper and drop it in the cauldron to slowly develop. A traditional cauldron is made of iron, but yours might be fashioned from ceramic, copper, stainless steel, stone, or another fireproof material.

Oracles

Oracles let you gaze into the future or to see things that lie beyond your ordinary range of vision. Pendulums and crystal balls provide glimpses into the unknown. Beautifully illustrated tarot cards are the most popular tools for reading the future—artists have created literally tens of thousands of different decks over the years. But divination isn't the tarot's only purpose. Some of the spells in Part II of this book use these cards in talismans, visualizations, and lots of other ways, as you'll soon see. (If you want to learn more about the tarot, see my book *The Everything*® *Tarot Book*.) Runes, too, can guide your path into the future; they also play roles in many spells. As you gain skill in working with these oracles, you may discover new applications for them in your magickal work.

CLEANING AND CHARGING YOUR MAGICK TOOLS

Before you use a tool for magickal purposes, it's a good idea to clean and purify it. This removes unwanted energies, as well as dust and dirt. In most cases the easiest way to do this is to wash the item with mild soap and water. Some people like to cleanse their tools in a running stream or sacred pool, but when that's not available ordinary tap water will suffice. If you prefer, you can "smudge" your tools by holding them in the smoke from burning sage for a few moments.

Four Elements Charging Technique

The next step is called "charging." A magick ritual in itself, charging consecrates your tools for your purposes and transforms that stick of wood or wineglass into a magickal object. One popular method for doing this involves the four elements: earth, air, fire, and water. Mix a little sea salt in water (or use ocean water, if available) and sprinkle it on the tool as you say to it: "With earth and water I charge you to do my will." Then, light incense and hold the tool in the smoke for a few moments while you say: "With fire and air I charge you to do my will." (Make sure to dry and rub down metal tools after sprinkling them with salt water so they don't tarnish or corrode.)

Charging with Essential Oils

Another technique calls for anointing your tools with essential oils. Rub a little essential oil—a single oil or a blend of several—on the tool while you say: "With this oil I charge you to do my will." The following table suggests appropriate oils for charging each tool.

Magick Tool	Charge with These Essential Oils
Wand	cinnamon, sandalwood, clove, musk, patchouli, cedar
Pentagram	mint, pine, amber, basil, fennel, anise
Athame	carnation, lavender, ginger, honeysuckle
Chalice	rose, ylang-ylang, jasmine, lily of the valley

These suggestions are just that: suggestions. You may decide to design a more elaborate or personal ritual for charging your magick tools. If you want to let your chalice bask in moonlight for twenty-eight nights or bury your pentagram beneath an oak tree for a week, by all means do it. Go with whatever feels right to you. The purpose, after all, is to make these tools yours, so the more personal the ritual the better.

The Modern Guide to Witchcraft

CARING FOR YOUR MAGICK TOOLS

How do you protect your expensive jewelry? Your heirloom silverware? Your favorite designer clothes? Devote the same care to storing your magick tools. If you have an altar, you may wish to display your tools on it. Many witches, however, prefer to store their tools safely out of sight, partly to prevent other people from handling them and partly to avoid uncomfortable questions. It's traditional to wrap your magick tools in silk, which protects them from dust and dirt as well as ambient vibrations. Alternately, you may choose to put them in velvet pouches, wooden boxes, or other containers and stash them in a drawer, trunk, closet, or cabinet. Like any precious possession, you want to safeguard them from damage and keep them from falling into the wrong hands.

Precautions and Protocols

When caring for and working with your magick tools, here are a few precautions and protocols to remember:

- Don't let anyone else use your tools or handle them, except perhaps a magickal partner with whom you work regularly.
- If someone else does touch a tool, smudge or wash it to remove that person's energy.
- If you do tarot readings for other people, use a different deck than the one you use to read for yourself. Keep a third deck for spells. The same goes for rune sets.
- Clean and smudge all tools before you begin using them to perform magick. After that, you needn't cleanse them unless someone else handles them. (Of course, if you drink or eat from a chalice or cauldron you'll want to wash it before storing it.)
- Use your tools for working magick only, not for mundane purposes.

Treat your magick tools with care and respect, and they'll serve you for a lifetime.

Acquiring Magick Tools

When you buy a car, you want to know something about its history. The same holds true for magick tools. If you purchase new items, you can check out the seller's reputation, get info about the craftspeople who actually made the objects, and read users' reports online. However, if you buy vintage items, well, tracking down their pedigrees can get a bit tricky. Antique chalices and swords may be exquisitely beautiful, reflecting a level of craftsmanship we no longer see today. But remember, magick tools used by someone else may hold that person's energy for a long time. This is especially true if the objects contain gemstones. Cleansing, purifying, and consecrating practices can remove old energies you wish to delete, but it's always a good idea to check out your tools' histories if possible before you start using them.

Once I found a handsome old knife in an antique shop, and thought it would make a fabulous athame—until the salesperson told me that it had previously been used as a bris knife. *Not* the energy I wanted tainting my ritual dagger!

You can also fabricate your own magick tools if you have skills in woodworking or metalsmithing. In earlier times, people fashioned wands from sticks of wood, and you can too. Choose a branch that has fallen from the tree, perhaps in a storm or as part of the natural aging process. Or, request permission from the tree to cut a twig and, after cutting, make an offering to the tree as a thank you. Unless you're a skilled glassblower, you're unlikely to create your own chalice from scratch. You can, however, buy special paints in crafts stores to decorate the glass with meaningful images. Even if you purchase new items from a metaphysical store, you may still want to add your own personal touches to make your tools uniquely yours.

Displaying Your Tools

As we've already said, some witches like to display their primary tools on their altars, along with candles to provide illumination, statues or deity representations, other items required for a particular spell or ritual, and maybe food and drink. If you like to have your book of shadows on hand when you do a ritual, you need room for it on the altar as

The Modern Guide to Witchcraft

well, which can make things a bit crowded. Just know that you're free to move things around as you require, which may mean setting up a secondary altar or, as we discussed in the previous chapter, four shrines within your sacred space. Do whatever you find comfortable and convenient. If you choose to leave your primary tools out on your altar, be sure to display all four for balance.

YOUR GRIMOIRE OR BOOK OF SHADOWS

A grimoire is a witch's journal of spells and rituals. Here's where you keep a record of the magick you perform, the ingredients and tools you use in spells, and your results. It's a bit like a cook's personal collection of favorite recipes.

From Days of Old

Originally, a grimoire referred to a book of spells and incantations used for calling forth spirits. Grimoires date back to the ancient Middle East, and later made their way through Europe during the Medieval and Renaissance periods.

Early grimoires were handwritten on parchment or paper, and perhaps bound in richly tooled leather or wood. Today, many witches still enjoy the process of recording spells and rituals by hand in beautifully bound journals. However, a grimoire or "book of shadows" keyboarded into your computer serves the same purpose. Most modern grimoires are written by individuals for their own use and generally they contain strictly personal records intended only for the author's purposes. However, sometimes a grimoire (or sections of it) may be passed down or copied from a master book. In such cases, the title of the original book is usually kept secret.

One of the most influential grimoires, *The Gardnerian Book of Shadows*, is attributed to Gerald Gardner and Doreen Valiente. This highly regarded book is a compilation of rituals that the authors blended and incorporated with original and modern elements between 1949 and 1961. *The Book of the Sacred Magic of Abramelin the Mage*, a fifteenth-century French manuscript translated by S.L. MacGregor Mathers in

1900, which includes spells for raising the dead and becoming invisible, had a major impact on contemporary ceremonial magick. Another amazing and rare grimoire, *The Magus*, composed by Francis Barrett in 1801, also covers astrology, alchemy, and Qabalistic knowledge, and remains an important source of information for magicians. You can see these texts online at *www.sacred-texts.com*, but be advised, they're not light reading.

Your Magickal Journey

Both a grimoire and a book of shadows hold spells, but a grimoire is intended to instruct, whereas a book of shadows is more of a personal record of a spiritual journey. Your book of shadows will not only include spells and incantations, but your observations, insights, and experiences as well. It might also contain dreams, poems, invocations, revelations, inspiration, and lore. If you like, you can draw in it, press flowers between its pages, add photographs—whatever tells of your journey.

Some people argue that a book of shadows more closely resembles a diary or a journal. Purists insist that a grimoire should be entirely instructional, full of information and practical application—no personal musings or little doodles in the borders. Fortunately, no "official" criterion exists for creating a book of shadows, so feel free to write in it whatever suits your purposes. Take the knowledge that is the gift of your elders and ancestors and combine it with your own practices and beliefs to create a new, useful work that is rooted in your tradition but remains unique and original. It's your journey, your story, and each book will be as individual as its author.

Traditionally, a witch keeps her book of shadows private—just as you'd keep your diary secret. You may, if you choose, share what you've written with people you trust, such as your teacher, a magickal partner, or an apprentice. The second part of this book is an open grimoire with spells for love, abundance, career success, health, and more. In the beginning, I recommend doing the spells as they're written. Later, when you have more magickal knowledge under your belt, you may enjoy adding your own touches or concocting original spells from scratch.

Chapter 11

PLANT MAGICK

It's reasonably safe to say that every plant has been used at one time or another for magickal purposes, especially in spellcraft. A Greek myth explains that the daughters of Hecate (one of the patronesses of witchcraft) taught witches how to use plants for both healing and magick, and throughout history witches have practiced herbalism. According to green witchcraft, all plants contain spirits. To work effectively with plants, witches communicate with them at a spiritual level, not just a physical one.

To practice plant magick you must first reconnect with nature. You can't honor something you don't feel an intimate connection with, and you certainly can't call on the energies of plant spirits without spending time with plants. If you live in the concrete jungle, this may present some challenges. But even in the heart of the city, you can find parks, botanical gardens, greenhouses, or garden centers where you can commune with plants.

Every plant is unique, with its own special energies and applications. Rowan, for instance, hung above a doorway protects your home from harm. Mugwort improves psychic awareness. Here are some ways you might choose to work with the magickal properties of plants:

- Watch plant behavior for omens and signs.
- Gather loosened leaves and petals for magick potions.
- Use plant matter in amulets and talismans.
- Add plant matter to incense and candles.

- Blend herbs for poultices and healing teas.
- Make fragrant potpourris to place in your closets and dresser drawers.
- Press pretty flowers in your book of shadows.
- Place live plants in various parts of your home or yard to encourage personal growth and well-being.

As any good cook will tell you, the key to great food lies in the ingredients and how the cook combines them. The same holds true for spells. If you think of a spell as a magick recipe, you begin to understand why the components (that is, the ingredients) are so important. If you don't measure the components correctly, add them to the mix at the right time, and give them enough time to "bake" properly, the magick goes awry.

So what constitutes a good spell component? Anything that's essential to the recipe—anything that builds the energy until it's just right. All the ingredients must mesh on a metaphysical level. Of course, the witch herself is the key component of any spell, adding a word, a touch, or a wish.

"But there are some things I know for certain: always throw spilt salt over your left shoulder, keep rosemary by your garden gate, plant lavender for luck, and fall in love whenever you can."

—SALLY OWENS, *PRACTICAL MAGIC*

In this chapter you'll learn about the magickal powers of many types of plants and how to use them in spellcraft. The lists that follow are by no means comprehensive, but provide enough information so that you can eventually design your own spells. You don't need to run out and buy everything on these lists; select a few staples that seem suited to the kinds of spells you want to cast—you can always add more later, just as a cook adds to her spice collection. As you become more proficient with spells, you'll compile your own lists of what works and what doesn't.

TREE MAGICK

Since ancient times, mythology and legends have talked about magickal trees. Early Greek myths said that certain trees could predict the future.

The Druids considered trees sacred, and liked to perform their rituals outdoors in groves of oak trees. The Celts believed that the sacred World Tree connected the upper, middle, and lower worlds. The Buddha gained enlightenment while sitting beneath a Bodhi tree.

Trees are the pillars of our world. They anchor our ground and seem to hold up the sky. They form the backbone of the green witch's practice. Although witches and herbalists tend to focus on herbs, they also work with wood, often when they want to create stability or permanence. Traditionally, magicians crafted their wands and staffs from wood. Sticks and twigs form the basis of many protective amulets; rounds cut from the cross-section of branches can be carved with magick symbols and carried as talismans. Witches also combine sacred woods in ritual fires, particularly at Yule. (You'll learn more about these practices later.)

The following list describes the magickal uses of trees, plus some associated lore. These trees grow in various areas of North America and elsewhere in the world. Depending on your purposes, you can use the bark, leaves, and/or inner wood:

- Apple: Apple trees grow in many parts of the Northern Hemisphere. Their widespread availability and fruitfulness link them with abundance, love, longevity, creativity, and fertility. Folklore associates the apple with the afterlife, fairies, and the otherworld. In Greek mythology, Paris awarded Aphrodite a golden apple because she was the most beautiful of the goddesses. If you cut an apple in half, you'll notice its seeds form a pentagram inside—a sure sign of its magick power.
- Ash: Some European cultures consider ash to be the World Tree. Magickally, ash is associated with water, strength, intellect, willpower, protection, justice, balance and harmony, skill, travel, and wisdom. Plant ash trees in your yard to protect your home and family.
- Birch: The traditional witch's broom is made of birch twigs. Magickally, birch has cleansing, protective, and purifying properties. Lore connects it with children, and cradles were often made of birch wood.
- Cedar: A precious wood that many cultures recognize as magickal and powerful, cedar has been known throughout the ages for its protective

qualities as well as its ability to repel insects and pests. Aromatic cedar was often given as an offering. Magickally, cedar is associated with healing, spirituality, purification, protection, prosperity, and harmony. Build a cedar fence around your home to attract abundance.

- Elder: Elder is also known as witchwood. Supposedly, bad luck will befall anyone who does not ask the tree's permission three times before harvesting any part of it—that's good advice when you're cutting any tree, not just elder. Folklore associates the elder with the crone aspect of the Goddess and with witches, thus elder wood is rarely used to make furniture or as firewood for fear of incurring their wrath. Herbalists prize elder for its many medicinal properties and use it as a laxative and diuretic, to treat irritated skin, sprains and bruises, and to loosen chest and sinus congestion. Magickally, elder wood is associated with protection (especially against being struck by lightning), prosperity, and healing.

- Hawthorn: Also known as May tree, mayflower, thorn, whitethorn, and haw, the hawthorn shrub often served as a boundary between properties. *Haw* is an old word for hedge. If a hawthorn grows together with an oak and ash tree, folklore says that the fairies dance among the trees. Like oak, the hawthorn's hard wood produces great heat when burned. Magickal associations include fertility, harmony, happiness, the otherworld, and protection.

- Hazel: European folklore links the hazel tree with wisdom. Thor, Brigid, Apollo, and other deities and mythological figures were associated with the hazel. Witches use both the nuts and branches in spells for luck, fertility, protection, and wish granting.

- Honeysuckle: Also known as woodbine or hedge-tree, the honeysuckle is associated with liminal or transitional (in-between) states. The scent of honeysuckle flowers is strongest in the evening, the time between day and night. Magickal associations include psychic awareness, harmony, healing, prosperity, and happiness.

- Maple: Used for furniture and other woodcrafts, maple also gives us sweet maple sugar and syrup. Magickally, maple relates to love, prosperity, life and health, and general abundance.

- Oak: A favorite of the Druids, oak's hardness and durability make it ideal for building homes, ships, and furniture. These qualities also link it magickally with strength, courage, longevity, protection, and good fortune. Traditionally, the Yule log is oak. Acorns, the fruit of the oak tree, are symbols of fertility. When found growing in oak trees, mistletoe was considered to be particularly potent by the Druids and important in their magickal work. Of course, today we think of mistletoe as something to kiss beneath—a nice application of its energies.
- Pine: Often pine is added to soaps and cleaning products. In magick, pine's cleansing properties make it useful for purification, clearing the mind, healing, prosperity, and protection from evil. Amber, one of the most beloved "gems" for magickal jewelry, is fossilized pine sap.
- Poplar: Also known as aspen, poplar's magickal associations include prosperity, communication, exorcism, and purification.
- Rowan: Rowan is also known as quicken, witchwood, and mountain ash (although technically not a true ash, it is so called due to the similarity of the leaves). A favorite of many witches, rowan's magickal associations include protection from evil, improving psychic powers, divination, healing, creativity, success, and transformation.
- Willow: The white willow, also known as the weeping willow, has long flexible branches and often grows near water. Folklore connects the willow with the Goddess and feminine cycles. Magickal associations include love, tranquility, intuition, harmony, protection, growth and renewal, and healing. Willow has traditionally been a favorite wood for magick wands and dowsers' rods.
- Witch hazel: Also known as snapping hazelnut because its seedpods spontaneously crack open, witch hazel has long been used in poultices for bruises and swelling, and for its astringent properties. Magickal associations include protection, healing, and peace.
- Yew: Yew is poisonous, which may be one reason it is associated with death. A European tree with hard, unyielding wood, it figures prominently in the lore of witchcraft and nature magick. Witches also connect it with spirits and the otherworld.

Some people have difficulty with the idea of cutting live wood away from a tree or bush because they don't know how to do it properly. When you use fresh wood, you capture a lot of life energy, which may be exactly what you're looking for in your ritual or spellwork. Deadfall is wood the tree has discarded as no longer useful, which may not be the kind of vibrant, living energy you're looking for. It depends on your personal view and the type of spell you're doing.

If you plan to cut fresh wood, you must first ask the tree or bush for permission. If you sense that the tree is okay with this, proceed with care and respect. Leave an offering for the tree as a "thank you."

Tree Attunement Exercise

Pick a tree. Stand next to it. Hold one hand about an inch or two away from the bark. Extend your awareness and feel the energy of the tree. Next, touch the bark. Explore how the tree feels to your hands. Bend close and smell the tree. Close your eyes and listen to the sounds the tree makes in response to the environment. Look closely at the tree and see the different textures, colors, and markings. If it has fruit you know to be safe, taste it.

Repeat these exercises with different kinds of trees. Compare and contrast your experiences. What are the similarities between the trees? What are the differences? After you've finished, make notes in your book of shadows.

FLOWER POWER

Flowers are the pretty parts of plants that hold essential reproductive information—in other words, they're the plants' sex organs. As such, the flower of a plant carries a tidy bundle of energy. In natural magick, the flower is often the part used. Flowers can be dried whole and woven into wreaths, pressed into a magickal collage, or made into potpourri or sachets. To fine-tune a spell, or cover all the bases if your objective is multifold, combine two or more flowers that offer the properties you seek. Here are some ways you might like to use flowers in spells:

- Fill mojo bags with dried petals.
- Add fragrant flower petals to candles.
- Wear floral essential oils that suit your purposes.
- Brew healing flowers, such as chamomile, in teas.
- Blend healing plant oils into lotions, salves, and ointments.
- Decorate your altar with flowers that relate to your intention.
- Plant flowers in a magick garden to attract nature spirits.

Do dried flowers carry a different energy than fresh flowers do? Yes and no; the intrinsic energy remains, but its expression is different. For certain rituals or charms you may want the vibrancy of fresh flowers, whereas amulets and talismans work better with dried flowers, whose energies tend to be slower acting and longer lasting.

In some cases, you might choose a particular flower for its physical properties especially if you're doing healing. Chamomile, for instance, has calming qualities that soothe mind and body. More often, however, you're looking for the symbolic value of the botanicals you use in spells. Roses, as you know, symbolize love. The following list includes flowers witches commonly use in magick, but it certainly isn't exhaustive. If you have a green thumb, you can grow your own plants for magick work. But you can find most of what you'll need at a nursery or large supermarket:

- Carnation: Also known as gillyflower, the carnation has a wonderful healing energy and makes an excellent gift for the sick. Use carnations magickally for protection, strength, energy, luck, and healing.
- Daffodil: Also known as narcissus and asphodel, the daffodil figures into charms for love, luck, and fertility.
- Daisy: We've all plucked the petals from a daisy and chanted, "He loves me, he loves me not." Not surprisingly, the daisy is commonly associated with love and flirtation, and is used in love spells.
- Gardenia: This fragrant flower brings tranquility, harmony, love, and healing. Add gardenia petals to a healing sachet or a talisman for love.
- Geranium: Grown indoors or out, geraniums carry strong protective energy, especially those with red flowers. Use rose-colored geraniums in spells for fertility, love, and healing.

- Hyacinth: Both grape and wild hyacinths have a lovely scent and a vibrant energy. Hyacinths are named for the youth of Greek legend, whose accidental death the god Apollo commemorated by creating the flower. Hyacinths are magickally associated with love, happiness, and protection.
- Iris: The iris's three petals are said to symbolize faith, wisdom, and valor. Witches use this lovely spring flower for purification and blessing, and to increase wisdom. You can grind the root, called orrisroot, and add it as a scent fixative in potpourri. Irises also play a role in love spells, especially when you want peace and harmony in a relationship.
- Jasmine: Also known as jessamine, jasmine possesses a heady but delicate scent that is usually stronger at night. Because of this, it is often associated with the moon and feminine energy. Magickally, jasmine relates to love, spirituality, harmony, and prosperity. Use it in spells for seduction and sensuality.
- Lavender: In aromatherapy, lavender calms body, mind, and spirit, and encourages relaxation and sleep. Magickally, lavender is associated with peace, tranquility, love, purification, and healing. Use it to restore harmony after a disagreement with a loved one.
- Lilac: The fragrant flowers of this shrub are usually white or a shade of purple. Magically, lilacs are used for protection and banishing negative energy.
- Lily: In general, lilies are associated with protection and removing hexes. Some cultures connect lilies (especially white ones) with death and the afterlife.
- Lily of the valley: This tiny cascade of white or cream-colored bell-shaped flowers has a delicate scent. Magickally, it enhances concentration and mental ability. You can also use it in spells to encourage happiness.
- Pansy: Also known as heartsease, love-lies-bleeding, love-in-idleness, and Johnny-jump-up, the pansy is a hardy, cheerful-looking plant with multicolored flowers, akin to the violet. Magickally, it is used for love spells, divination, communication, and happiness.
- Poppy: Although the red poppy is a gentle narcotic, the white poppy is toxic and the source of opium. Magically, the poppy is associated with fertility, prosperity, love, sleep, and invisibility.

The Modern Guide to Witchcraft

- Rose: Throughout history, the rose has been one of our most beloved flowers. Folklore and literature have made the rose synonymous with love, and witches often use it in love spells. Magickally, roses also play roles in healing, divination, peace, harmony, psychic ability, and spiritual growth. Note the rose's color to understand its uses. (We'll talk more about color symbolism later.)
- Snapdragon: Witches link snapdragons with protection, particularly from illusion or deception. Plant white snapdragons along the perimeter of your home to protect it.
- Sunflower: The sunflower is, of course, associated with the sun. Use it magickally to bring happiness, success, and health. Because the plant has an abundance of seeds, it also relates to fertility. Bring sunflowers to a celebration or a summer solstice ritual to shine light on the event. Germinate the seeds and then plant them to attract abundance.
- Tulip: The tulip's chalice or cuplike shape represents a vessel to hold prosperity and abundance. Use tulips in spells for money, love, and happiness.
- Violet: Use this delicate flower in spells for love, peace, hope, harmony, good luck, fertility, and abundance. In charms and sachets, violets help to maintain tranquility and encourage peace between people. Combine violet with lavender in an herbal pillow to help a child sleep and prevent nightmares.

Caution: May Be Poisonous

Some beautiful flowers with strong magickal powers are poisonous—even deadly. Wolfsbane—a.k.a. aconitum, monkshood, and "the queen of poisons"—is a plant you probably want to steer clear of, or at least handle with extreme care (like wearing rubber gloves when you touch it). This pretty plant has deep blue flowers and witches value its magickal protective powers, but eating it or getting the juice from its root into a cut on your hand could stop your heart—literally. Lovely foxglove, or digitalis, is also toxic. Though long known for its healing properties, it can also cause a wide range of problems, even death. Essential oils are delightful, aromatic ingredients in spells, but some can irritate sensitive skin. Of course, you don't want to put anything you aren't sure of in food or beverages. Even plants that seem benign may cause allergic reactions in some people.

MAGICK HERBS

Generally, a plant referred to as an herb possesses some sort of medicinal or culinary value. Witches, however, use the term "herb" as a catch-all for the bits of trees, flowers, spices, and all sorts of plants, and use them for healing, food preparation, and of course, doing magick. The following list of herbs isn't all-inclusive, but describes many herbs that you might want to use in your spellworking. Quite likely, these herbs already sit in your kitchen's spice cabinet.

- Allspice: A common staple in the kitchen spice rack, allspice incorporates flavors such as clove, cinnamon, and pepper. Allspice berries make wonderful additions to prosperity blends and spells for increasing energy, love, healing, and luck.
- Angelica: Also known as archangel or angel's herb, this fragrant plant has been used for centuries to improve digestion. Witches use it magickally for protection and purification.
- Basil: Commonly found in spice racks and in kitchen gardens all over Europe and the Americas, basil is used magickally for prosperity, success, peace, protection, happiness, purification, tranquility, and love.
- Bay: Also known as bay laurel, it crowned the victor of games in ancient Greece and Rome. Witches use it to enhance success, wisdom, and divination. Write a wish on a bay leaf and burn it, or sleep with it under your pillow for prophetic dreams.
- Calendula: A type of marigold, calendula is used medicinally to treat skin irritations, such as eczema, bruises, scars, and scrapes. Use it in magick spells to bring happiness, prosperity, love, psychic powers, and harmony.
- Caraway: The seed of the caraway plant protects against negativity. It's also a good antitheft herb—add it to protection amulets or charms in your home.
- Chamomile: Therapeutically, chamomile aids digestion and soothes stomach problems, calms stress, and eases headaches. Magickally, it brings prosperity, peace, healing, harmony, and happiness.
- Cinnamon: This multipurpose herb possesses a great amount of energy, and a pinch can be added to rev up a spell's power. Use it in spells and charms for money, success, vitality, love, and purification.

The Modern Guide to Witchcraft

- Clove: The small dried bud of the clove plant is associated with protection, purification, mental ability, and healing. Add three cloves to an amulet or talisman to keep the charm's action pure and focused for a longer period of time. A sachet of rosemary, angelica, sage, three cloves, and a pinch of salt tied shut with red ribbon is a good all-purpose amulet to hang above a door or in your car for protection.
- Comfrey: Also known as knitbone, comfrey is renowned as a magickal healing herb, as well as for protection during travel and prosperity.
- Dill: Use either dill seed or weed to attract good fortune, tranquility, prosperity, passion, or protection.
- Ginger: When added to spells, ginger boosts their power. Use ginger to jump-start a romance, stimulate finances, and increase the potential for success in just about anything. Medicinally, it helps calm the stomach, fight colds, and suppress nausea.
- Marjoram: Also known as wintersweet, marjoram is similar to oregano, but sweeter and milder. The ancient Greeks crowned newly married couples with marjoram. Use it magickally to bring happiness, protection, love, and joy, particularly in family environments.
- Mint: Mint comes in many varieties and it's easy to grow in a garden or on the kitchen windowsill. It helps ease headaches, stimulates the appetite, and aids digestion. Use it magically for prosperity, love, joy, fertility, purification, and success.
- Mugwort: Also known as artemisia and sailor's tobacco, mugwort helps to open your mind before you try divination. Witches associate it with prophetic dreams, relaxation and tranquility, protection, banishing, and consecration.
- Nutmeg: Medicinally, nutmeg quells nausea and soothes digestive problems (although it can be toxic in large doses). Magickally, it boosts psychic abilities, happiness, love, and money.
- Parsley: The ancient Greeks made victors' crowns from parsley to celebrate success. Witches use the herb magickally for power, strength, passion, purification, and prosperity.
- Rosemary: You can use rosemary as a skin tonic applied externally and as a hair rinse to add shine to dark hair and soothe itchy scalp. Magickally, it provides protection, improves memory, and brings wisdom.

- Sage: Sage is perhaps the most popular herb for purification. Witches also use it in spells for protection, wisdom, health, and longevity.
- Verbena: Also known as vervain, enchanter's herb, and herb of grace, verbena helps calm headaches, eases stress, and makes a relaxing bedtime tea. Magickally it is associated with divination, protection, inspiration, abundance, love, peace, tranquility, healing, prosperity, skill in artistic performance, and reversing negative activity. Make a blessing/protection oil by infusing the fresh plant in light olive oil or grape seed oil. Add the dried herb to a charm bag to encourage success.
- Yarrow: Also known as milfoil, millefeuille, yarroway, or bloodwort, yarrow is a common garden herb whose leaves have traditionally been made into poultices to staunch blood. Witches use it for courage, love, and healing.

Don't overlook other greens for spellworking. Moss, for instance, is tenacious and grows even where you wouldn't think anything could survive. Use it in spells for patience, perseverance, and toughness. Ferns have connections with invisibility. Witchy folklore says that you should collect ferns before midnight on the eve of the summer solstice if you don't want to be seen. No, you won't actually vanish, but you can go about your business in secret. Grass, because it's so adaptable, can help you be more flexible and let things take their course. In Part II, you'll learn to tap the magick in plants to make amulets, talismans, and all sorts of charms.

Chapter 12

CRYSTALS AND GEMSTONES

Long before people began prizing gems for their monetary value, they used them as magick charms. In early societies, only rulers, members of royal families, priests, and religious leaders wore gems. The ancient Egyptians used stones for healing, protection, and other purposes, both physical and spiritual. According to Nancy Schiffer, author of *The Power of Jewelry*, our ancestors believed gemstones were "capable of human feelings and passions so that they could express jealousy and shock."

Many researchers believe crystals may have been sources of power and magick on the lost continents of Atlantis and Lemuria, and that crystals were used in building the pyramids and Stonehenge.

TAPPING THE MAGICK OF STONES

Today, we wear precious and semiprecious gems mostly because they're so pretty. Witches, however, realize that crystals and gemstones can also be used for spellworking, divination, shamanic journeying, meditation, and dowsing. Stones also play important roles in healing, and although witches connect some stones with longevity, none of them holds the elixir of life like the fabled Philosopher's Stone.

Birthstones resonate with the qualities of the zodiac signs to which they correspond. Originally people wore birthstones to enhance, balance, or moderate their own personal characteristics. By the way, you should look at your birth sign, not the month of your birth, to discover your true birthstone. If you're an Aquarian, for example, your birthstone is garnet, regardless of whether you were born in January or February.

You can include crystals or gemstones in virtually any spell to increase, focus, stabilize, or fine-tune your spell's potency. Here are some suggestions:

- Wear them to enhance your own personal energy field.
- Put them in amulets or talismans.
- Set them near the windows and doors of your home to provide protection.
- Meditate with them.
- Infuse magick potions with them.
- Dowse with a gemstone or crystal pendulum.
- Display them on your altar to attract positive energy.
- Offer them to deities or nature spirits in return for assistance.
- Gaze into them to see the past or future.

Like plants, crystals and gemstones are living entities, although they resonate at a slow rate that most people can't perceive. However, their slow, concentrated energy enables them to keep working their magick for a long period of time.

MAGICKAL POWERS OF DIFFERENT STONES

As you might suspect, different stones possess different qualities and serve different functions in spellworking. A general rule of thumb is that clear stones are best for mental and spiritual issues, translucent or milky stones for emotional situations, and opaque stones for physical matters. You can use gems alone or in combination with other substances to produce the results you desire.

A stone's color or pattern, too, can provide clues to its abilities. Pink gems, such as rose quartz and morganite, are perfect for love spells. Jade, aventurine, and other green stones can benefit money spells. Since ancient times, people have valued stones with eyelike markings as protection charms against the "evil eye" and all sorts of misfortune.

The Modern Guide to Witchcraft

The following guidelines for stones and their magickal properties are simply a place to begin. In time, you'll develop your own ideas about which stones to use for which spells:

- Agate: A grounding stone, agate helps stabilize situations. Add it to a money mojo if you're having trouble holding on to money. Use it when you need extra strength or determination. Agates come in lots of colors, and the color influences the stone's powers. Green moss agate, for instance, has healing and calming qualities. Like all green stones, it works well in prosperity spells and also attunes you to nature spirits.
- Amber: Although it's not really a stone—it's fossilized pine sap— amber is highly prized by witches. Lore tells us that amber came from the tears of a setting sun, and as such it's still considered a solar/fire stone. A powerful protection gem, you can wear it or place it in an amulet to protect your home, car, business, etc.
- Amethyst: A purple quartz, this spiritual gem helps you to deepen meditation, remember dreams, and improve psychic ability. Want to attract divine assistance? Offer a favorite deity a pretty amethyst in return for her help.
- Aquamarine: A gift of the sea goddess, this lovely blue stone stimulates imagination and creativity. It can also increase intuitive awareness, mental clarity, and connection with your higher self. Use it when you want to work with the spirit world.
- Aventurine: This green stone with gold flecks in it is ideal for attracting wealth or abundance.
- Bloodstone: A green opaque stone with flecks of red, witches associate it with health (especially of the blood) and physical protection. You can also use it in spells for good luck, success, and courage.
- Calcite: Calcite comes in lots of colors, giving it a variety of potential magickal applications. Witches consider it a stone of purification and healing—use it to detoxify a situation. It also encourages spiritual growth, calms the mind, and aids intellectual processes.
- Carnelian: This milky red-orange stone is linked with success. It can also stimulate passion, sexual energy, courage, and initiative.

- Chrysocolla: In relationships and domestic situations, chrysocolla helps remove disruptive energies and restore stability. It can also help you deal with changes and heal emotional pain.
- Citrine: A yellow variety of quartz, citrine is a great stone for banishing nightmares and improving psychic abilities. Because it's also known for its cleansing properties, you can use it to clean your other stones and magick tools, or to clear the air after an argument or disturbance.
- Diamond: A popular stone for engagement rings, a diamond deepens commitment and trust, especially in a love relationship. It also enhances strength and bravery, and attracts victory.
- Emerald: Emeralds promote clairvoyance and can be used for divination. Witches also connect them with emotional healing, growth, love, and resourcefulness.
- Fluorite: Available in various colors, fluorite helps remove stress and negative energy. When things seem confused or disorganized, use fluorite to restore order. It also improves concentration, intuition, and mental clarity.
- Garnet: During the Middle Ages people wore garnets to drive away demons. Witches still consider garnet a stone of protection. It also increases love and passion, courage, and hope.
- Hematite: A dark silvery-colored stone, hematite is often used to ground unbalanced energy and to stabilize a spell. The stone also deflects negativity and is thus associated with defense, healing, and justice.
- Jade: A popular stone for prosperity magick, jade can also be used in spells to enhance beauty, increase fertility, and inspire love. Witches connect it with health and longevity, too.
- Jasper: Jasper comes in various colors and patterns, and each has its own distinctive properties. Use red jasper in love spells to stir up passion. Brown jasper aids physical healing; poppy jasper breaks up blockages that prevent energy from circulating harmoniously.
- Lapis lazuli: The most coveted lapis is a deep bluish hue, with almost no white flecks in it. Use it to increase your psychic ability and attract magickal insights. It's also a good stone to hold while meditating to

deepen your focus. Some of the best lapis comes from Chile, where it's often carved into animal figures. Shamans there use it in their spiritual practices.

- Malachite: This green stone is popular for prosperity magick. Long considered a stone of protection, it wards off evil and lets you sense forthcoming dangers or problems. It strengthens your connection to nature, and green witches use it for earth healing.
- Moldavite: This greenish stone came to us as a result of a meteor collision with the earth nearly 15 million years ago. A high-energy stone, it improves your ability to communicate with spirits, deities, and extraterrestrials. Use it to gain insight into your purpose in this lifetime.
- Moonstone: Ruled by the moon, this milky stone comes in various pastel colors and has long been used to aid dream recall. It also calms emotions, increases intuition, and benefits all sorts of female health conditions.
- Obsidian: Sacred to Hecate, the patroness of witches, obsidian is a favorite stone for scrying mirrors. Most likely, that's what the wicked queen in *Snow White* gazed into when she asked, "Who's the fairest of them all?" Obsidian also boosts strength—physically and emotionally—and can help break down blockages. Use snowflake obsidian—a black stone with whitish spots—for protection.
- Onyx: Use this black stone to banish negative energy and ground magick spells. It encourages self-confidence and determination. Onyx also helps you break deeply ingrained habits, whether physical or emotional. Wear onyx when facing adversaries in figurative or literal battles.
- Opal: This milky whitish stone encourages psychic ability and visions. Witches also use it in spells for love and seduction. In shamanic magick, it keeps potential enemies from seeing you. Opals can aid female health conditions too.
- Pearl: Ruled by the moon, pearls were considered sacred to the goddesses Isis and Freya. Use pearls in spells for love, happiness, and emotional balance. They can also aid intuition, fertility, and creativity.

- Peridot: Believed to repel evil and malevolent magick in earlier times, peridot is still used as a stone of protection. It can also help to neutralize toxins, physically and emotionally.
- Ruby: Rubies stimulate the emotions, passion, love, and sexuality. They also open your heart to divine love. Wear rubies for courage or to aid blood disorders. Folklore says they protect against vampires.
- Sapphire: Linked with Neptune, the sea god, this stone increases spiritual knowledge and connection with the Divine. Witches use it in spells for wisdom, insight, and prophetic vision; it also deepens meditation and can help you understand omens and signs. Star sapphires bring hope and clarity of purpose.
- Tiger's eye: A glossy, satiny, brown stone with bands of gold, tiger's eye is used for strength, courage, good fortune, and prosperity. Early Roman soldiers carried these into battle to keep them safe. The stone boosts self-confidence and gives you the freedom to follow your own path.
- Tourmaline: This stone comes in a variety of colors, including green, black, pinkish, and watermelon (a combination of red and green). The colors influence the stone's properties. Tourmaline clears negative energies and brings balance. Put one near your computer to dissolve electromagnetic fields. Green tourmaline aligns you with nature spirits; pink harmonizes the emotions; watermelon attracts love and friendship.
- Turquoise: A powerful stone of protection, turquoise is especially good for keeping you safe while traveling. Witches also use it for prosperity. Its healing properties help ease mental tension and emotional anxiety. Native Americans consider turquoise a sacred stone.

If you wish, you can combine several stones to address various aspects of a spell. Let's say your goal is to find a job that pays well and brings you into contact with interesting people—aventurine plus watermelon tourmaline should do the trick. In a love spell, you might seek both passion and affection, in which case you'd choose rose quartz and carnelian. After a while, you'll start to intuit which stones are right for your intentions. Stones play such an important role in magick that you'll probably

The Modern Guide to Witchcraft

want to spend time familiarizing yourself with their many properties. Judy Hall's books provide extensive information about how to use stones for a wide range of purposes.

QUARTZ CRYSTALS

Quartz crystals are the most versatile of all stones. Actually, many of the stones we've already talked about are mainly quartz with other minerals mixed in, such as the iron in aquamarine that turns it blue. If you only want to work with one stone, a beautiful clear quartz crystal can do it all. Crystal balls, in particular, are one of the most famous magick tools. You've seen crystal balls on TV and in movies, maybe even in real life, and you know witches use them to predict the future, a practice known as scrying. It is possible to view stuff you couldn't see otherwise by gazing into a crystal ball. But crystals can do oh so much more.

Quartz crystals are a combination of silica and water formed under certain conditions of pressure, temperature, and energy. These crystals possess amazing abilities to retain information, amplify energy, and transmit vibrations. That's why they're often used in watches, computers, laser tools, television and radio equipment, and many other familiar objects. Their properties also make crystals ideal for healing, storing knowledge, sending energy and thought patterns, and increasing the power of any substance they come in contact with. People who work with crystals believe they are actually unique life forms that possess innate intelligence and many diverse powers.

Quartz crystals come in various colors and shapes, both of which affect the crystal's characteristics and abilities. Let's take a look at some of the most common ones witches use.

Clear Quartz

Clear quartz crystals will probably become one of your go-to magick tools—and one of your favorites. An easily obtained stone, it looks like ice. Many have small inclusions that add to the crystal's properties. For example, those little silvery "plates" you see in some crystals are like tiny tablets where you mentally "write" your wishes. Those fine lines that look like sparkly threads, called rutiles, give the crystal a speedy quality that helps spells work faster.

You can wear crystals, put them in amulets and talismans, affix them to other magick tools, meditate with them, focus them in certain areas to promote healing, keep one in your glove compartment for protection, and on and on. Basically, they work in three ways:

1. They boost the powers of other substances. Let's say you're making a money talisman. You might put some dried mint leaves and an aventurine in a silk pouch, and then add a small clear quartz crystal to kick the power up a notch.
2. They hold on to thoughts, information, vibrations, energies, etc., for a long time. Many witches use clear quartz as protection amulets. You can "program" your crystal by either thinking or whispering your intention into it—tell it to keep you safe at all times and in all situations. Then wear it or carry it with you for safety.
3. They focus and direct energy. Want to send healing vibes to someone? First program a crystal with healing thoughts, then aim its pointed end toward that person. You can also draw power from the heavens by aiming the point at the sky and envisioning a beam of energy flowing down and into your crystal.

Caution: *Never* drill holes into your crystals—you'll kill them. If you decide to wear a quartz crystal as jewelry, make sure the stone is surrounded by wire, a band, or some other type of fastener, not pierced.

Rose Quartz

A favorite of many witches, rose quartz looks like a frozen strawberry daiquiri. It ranges in color from palest pink to deep rose, and a single crystal may contain a variety of shades, striations, and cloudy wisps. Both its color and its milky quality connect it with the emotions, and indeed, rose quartz is one of the best stones to use when doing magick for emotional issues. For witches, this crystal is synonymous with love. Use it in spells to attract romance, affection, and friendship.

But rose quartz can do more than bring romantic love. Its gentle, soothing energy also encourages emotional healing and balance. A stone of peace, it can help family members or coworkers get along together harmoniously. After a disagreement, rose quartz can smooth troubled waters and restore calm. It also can help you learn to love yourself better by increasing your self-esteem and self-acceptance. People who have suffered loss and grief can benefit from wearing rose quartz too.

Smoky Quartz

Smoky quartz ranges in color from palest gray to brownish gold to almost black. Its earthy tone connects it to security, permanence, and patience; it also increases strength and determination. Witches often use this crystal for grounding and stability. If you're dealing with a chaotic situation or upsetting changes, if everything around you seems to be spinning out of control, smoky quartz can help bring matters into balance. Its energy is slower than that of clear quartz, so it can help you reach long-term goals. Because it's associated with materialization, you can use it to bring ideas down to earth and make dreams come true.

If you're facing obstacles or blockages of some kind, smoky quartz can help you to slowly overcome them. It bolsters courage and strength, without bravado. If you need endurance to accomplish a task, smoky quartz is your friend. If you have a problem that you just can't deal with right now, you can give it to a smoky quartz crystal to hold for you until you feel ready to work through it.

Abundance Crystals

Some quartz crystals contain bits of greenish material, which magicians relate to prosperity and growth. These green inclusions may appear as specks of color scattered throughout the crystal or as slabs of green within the otherwise clear crystal. In some cases, it looks as if a smaller green crystal is actually growing inside the larger whitish one. Because we often associate green with money, healthy live plants, and growth, you can use these crystals to improve your finances or attract abundance of any kind.

CARING FOR YOUR STONES

By nature, crystals and gemstones hold on to thoughts, emotions, and information programmed into them for a long time, even for centuries. You've probably heard of the Hope Diamond, a forty-five carat blue diamond that for more than a century supposedly bore a curse that brought death and misfortune to the people who owned it. Although you probably have nothing to fear from the stones you acquire, nonetheless it's a good idea to cleanse and purify them before you use them for magickal work.

Wash them in running water, with mild soap if you like, while you envision the crystals cleansed by pure white light. This removes any unwanted vibrations as well as dust. You can also purify crystals energetically by gently rubbing them with a piece of citrine. It's a good idea to clean your crystals before using them in a magick spell or ritual. You also should wash them if they've been exposed to any strong emotions or unsettling events.

If you prefer, try one of these methods for cleaning a crystal:

- Leave it in sunlight or moonlight for a specific period of time, say twenty-four hours or a week—it's your call. Do what you feel is necessary.
- Bury it in a small dish of dirt for a time.
- Hold the stone in the smoke of burning sage or purifying incense.
- Immerse the stone in water for a time. Holding it in a running stream or the ocean's waves will purify it faster, but leaving the stone in a small bowl of water will work too. Don't worry; you cannot remove the innate energy of a stone, so it's impossible to over-purify.

Each time you use a stone for a magickal purpose, it is important to purify it. You'll also want to purify your stones if someone else handles them, so that person's energy doesn't interfere with your own in spellworking.

Some people like to display their crystals and stones on their altars or elsewhere in their homes—especially the really big, beautiful, and powerful ones. Others prefer to wrap them in silk or velvet and store them in a safe place. It's really up to you. Clear quartz crystals, in particular, love to sit in the sun, but amethysts can fade if exposed to bright sunlight. You may choose to designate certain stones for certain purposes. Witches often place stones in various places around their homes and workplaces—rose quartz or carnelian on your bedside table to attract love, aventurine or abundance crystal in your store's cash register to increase sales, and so on.

The relationship you establish with your stones and crystals will be unique. Treat your crystals and gemstones as valued partners. In time, they'll become your good friends. *Never* abuse your stones! Show them respect and they'll gladly work with you for a lifetime.

PART II

OPEN

GRIMOIRE

Chapter 13

CHARMS, AMULETS, AND TALISMANS

Myths, legends, and literature from cultures around the world mention talismans and amulets, tokens and totems. Our ancestors designed them to attract love, ward off evil, and bring health, wealth, and happiness. Museums display collections of artifacts believed to have served as power objects for Stone Age people. The early Egyptians placed charms in the tombs of royalty to ensure safe passage into the world beyond. Ancient Greek soldiers carried amulets into battle to protect them. Aztec priests used gemstones to invoke deities and for prophesying.

Is It Okay to Design Your Own Spells?

A lot of people who are new to magick often ask if it's okay to create their own spells. The answer is a resounding *yes*. After all, someone, somewhere had to come up with the first spell, and hundreds of thousands of spells have been created since then! It's probably a good idea in the beginning to use tried-and-true spells, such as the ones offered in the following chapters, until you get the hang of it. Once you feel confident in your knowledge and ability, use your imagination to come up with original spells that suit your purposes.

Good luck charms are as popular today as they were in ancient times. Even people who don't believe in magick often give special significance to certain objects, regardless of whether those objects have any monetary value. Is it just superstition, or do these items really work? Find out for yourself. In this chapter, you'll learn how to create charms, amulets, and talismans for love, money, career success, healing—whatever you choose.

THE LAW OF SIMILARS

To understand how spells work, you need to understand the Law of Similars. According to this law, colors, shapes, and various characteristics of a plant, stone, or other object give clues to an item's magickal function. For example, red stones might be used in magickal cures for blood problems; a heart-shaped leaf might be part of a love spell. Advertising certainly understands how symbolic images affect the subconscious in specific ways. It's no accident that Coca-Cola formed its bottles like a woman's figure, or that TV commercials show phallic-shaped champagne bottles spewing foam.

One of the ways witches apply the Law of Similars is with "poppets" or dolls made to represent people. You can fabricate a poppet from cloth, straw, wood, wax—whatever you prefer. You can even buy readymade poppets online. The magick happens when you do something to the doll that symbolizes your intention and the result you want to achieve.

I suspect you're probably thinking of voodoo dolls now. Voodoo priests supposedly inflict pain on a doll and that pain is magickally transmitted to the person whom the doll represents. Creepy, but that's not how you probably want to use this type of magick.

Instead, let's say you want to send healing energy to a friend who's broken her leg. First, you make a poppet to stand in for your friend. You might want to decorate the doll to look like your friend, dressing it in clothes your friend might wear or adding hair the color of your friend's—even pasting on bits of her real hair if she'll let you trim it. Then you bandage the doll's leg and send loving, healing energy to your friend in the form of a chant, thought, or visualization. Imagine your friend's leg is completely well. That's it. No pins, no blood, no harm. In later chapters, you'll find spells that rely on the Law of Similars to do their thing—even one using a doll.

CHARMS

Early charms were spoken spells. In a time when few people could read or write, witches used verbal spells. The word charm comes from a Latin term, *carmen*, that means "incantation" or "song." A charm is like a poem, and many charms rhyme or have a distinct rhythm, making it easier for the witch to commit them to memory—no need to carry a huge grimoire around, no scrolls to get damaged in the rain en route to the market!

Uttering chants, affirmations, and incantations serves two purposes: to focus your mind during spells and rituals, and to send your objectives out into the universe. If you like, you can incorporate other actions and symbolism into a verbal charm. For example, a witch might wait until the first night of a full moon to speak her charm, then recite it three times each night thereafter. The full moon represents fullness, completion, and coming into manifestation. The number three represents the body-mind-spirit connection. Witches often use the number three because it brings magickal thoughts into three-dimensional reality.

Here's an example of a simple verbal charm:

Leaf of ash,
I do thee pluck
To bring to me
A day of luck.

Abracadabra

One of the oldest and best-known written charms is the Gnostic spell that uses the word Abracadabra (no, we're not pulling a rabbit out of a hat). In the original Chaldean texts, Abracadabra translates as "to perish like the word," and it was customarily used to banish sickness. The process was relatively simple. Abracadabra was written in the form of a descending triangle on parchment, which was then laid on the afflicted body part. Then the parchment was stuck in the cleft of a tree and left there so that as time and the elements destroyed it, the magick would begin its work.

Okay, it's not a literary masterpiece, and your charms don't have to be either. The important thing is that a charm expresses your wish or goal, and that it's easy to remember. Repeat it often to give it more energy and to make the magick work faster. If you wish, you can add a physical action to the spoken charm. As you speak the word "pluck," take a leaf from a tree whose properties match your intention (see Chapter 11), and then carry it with you all day to attract good luck.

Affirmations

Affirmations are positive statements that you create to produce a result. Witches use them in all sorts of spells, both spoken and written. The important things to remember when designing an affirmation are:

- Keep it short.
- Be clear and precise.
- Only include images and situations that you desire.
- Always use the present tense, as if the condition you seek already exists.

Here are some examples of the right and wrong ways to create affirmations:

> *Right:* I am healthy in body, mind, and spirit.
> *Wrong:* I don't have any illnesses or injuries.
> *Right:* I now have a job that's perfect for me.
> *Wrong:* I want to get a better job.

See the difference? If you aren't exactly sure of all the details, it's okay to leave some things up to the universe to work out. The previous example, "I now have a job that's perfect for me," covers the bases without being specific.

Incantations

Incantations differ from affirmations in that they are usually written as rhymes. The catchy phrasing makes it easy to remember. You don't have to be a Wordsworth or Dickinson to create an effective incantation.

The Modern Guide to Witchcraft

Just follow the same rules for designing an incantation as you did for an affirmation.

Here's an example of a simple love incantation:

As the day fades into night
I draw a love that's good and right.
As the night turns into day
We are blessed in every way.

The uses for affirmations and incantations are limited only by your imagination. Write one on a slip of paper and insert it into a talisman or amulet. Put it under your pillow at night. Repeat it regularly throughout the day, such as while you're in the shower or driving to work, and especially just before you go to sleep. Write it on a sheet of colored paper, decorate it with images that resonate with you, and post it in a place where you'll see it often. Be creative!

Using Colors in Magick Spells

Colors contain lots of symbolic associations. Blue, for instance, reminds you of the sky; green suggests foliage, grass, and healthy crops; orange is the color of fire and the sun. So deeply rooted are these connections that witches can use color to influence the mind and produce magickal results. When you're doing spells, remember these color correspondences and let them increase the power of your magick.

COLOR SYMBOLISM	
Color	Correspondences
Red	passion, anger, heat, energy, daring
Orange	confidence, activity, warmth, enthusiasm
Yellow	happiness, creativity, optimism, ideas, communication
Green	health, fertility, growth, wealth
Light blue	peace, clarity, hope
Royal blue	independence, insight, imagination, truth
Indigo	intuition, serenity, mental power, dreamwork

COLOR SYMBOLISM	
Color	**Correspondences**
Purple	wisdom, spirituality, connection with higher realms
Pink	love, friendship, sociability
White	purity, clarity, protection
Black	power, wisdom
Brown	stability, practicality, grounding in the physical world

Black, a color witches frequently wear, has many negative connotations to the general public, including death and mourning. To witches, however, black is a color of power, for it contains all the other colors. It's also reminiscent of mystery and the night, the time when witches often gather to work magick. In spellworking, black is associated with the planet Saturn and used for banishing, endings, and inner strength.

AMULETS

People often confuse charms, amulets, and talismans. Sometimes they use the word "talisman" to refer to both amulets and talismans, or the word "charm" to describe all three. Since ancient times, magicians have created these spells and, as a witch, you probably will, too, so you need to know the difference. A charm can either attract something to you or repel something. An amulet's main purpose is protection, or to prevent something from happening. It wards off unwanted magick and/or harmful situations, such as an auto accident or robbery. An amulet serves as a magick "shield" that blocks danger—it doesn't go on the offensive.

What Can You Use as an Amulet?

The early Greeks called amulets *amylon* meaning "food." This suggests that people used food offerings to ask gods and goddesses for protection—the petitioners might have even eaten or carried a small bit of that food as a token. Many items found in the natural world have been made into amulets, including plants, carved stones, and metal objects. Amulets were also commonly chosen for their shapes or where they were found. For example, our European ancestors often carried "holey stones" (any stone with a hole going through it) to guard against malicious fairies (who would get trapped in the hole). A crystal found near a sacred well known for its healthful qualities might be carried as an amulet to protect the bearer's well-being.

Amulets can be worn, placed with valuable items, affixed on pet collars, hung in windows, planted in gardens, or put anywhere you want them to provide protection. A horseshoe hung above a doorway is a familiar example of a protective amulet.

Amulets from Around the World

Brass ring (Lapland): Worn on the right arm to keep ghosts away

God figurines (Assyria): Buried near the home to protect all within

Lapis lazuli eyes (Egypt): Placed in tombs to safeguard the soul's journey

Metal rattles (Ancient Rome): Tied to children's clothing for overall protection

Miniature carved canoes (Iroquois): Protection from drowning

Monkey teeth (Borneo): For strength and skill

Peach stone (China): Protection against evil

Spruce needles (Shoshone): To keep sickness at bay

Amulets and talismans can consist of a single gem or object. Amethysts, for instance, have long been worn as amulets against drunkenness, because they increase self-control. Going to a big party this weekend? You might want to put on those amethyst earrings, just as a precaution. Or, an amulet may contain several items—just make sure that each item relates to your intention and holds special meaning for you. How about the amethyst earrings *and* some amber perfume (for protection against unwanted advances or accidents), but leave off the garlic necklace unless you think vampires might crash the party.

Creating an Amulet

After you've gathered all the ingredients for your magick amulet, go through the steps outlined in Chapters 8 and 9 for cleansing, purifying, and casting a circle. The ancient magi believed that when making amulets, you must work with the components in a precise order—the primary or most important ingredient should come first. Let's say, for example, you want to create a protection amulet for a relative who's going on a trip and you've decided to use a brass disc as your base. Start with that disc, then attach stones, beads, feathers, or other items to it in their order of importance. If you plan to carve magick symbols on the disc, begin with one for safety while traveling. Then inscribe another for ongoing protection while your relative is away, and finish with a symbol for a safe return. Just as early witches did, you'll probably want to recite affirmations or incantations over the amulet while you're fabricating it. When you've finished, open the circle as described previously and give the amulet to your relative.

Witches often make amulets (and talismans too) by filling cloth pouches with magick ingredients. If you're working with loose herbs and/or tiny objects, this is a good way to go. Choose a pouch of a color that relates to your intention: pink or red for love, gold or silver for money, etc. Insert the most important ingredient, say a small quartz crystal or other stone. Then add the rest of the items—flower petals, herbs, symbols written on paper—in the order of their significance. Tie the pouch with three knots to seal in your magickal components. Once you've sealed an amulet or talisman, don't open it.

How long will your amulet last? Because amulets remain passive until something external happens that creates a need for their energy, they can stay inert for a long time. However, once the magick energy has been activated and spent, the amulet has served its purpose. After showing gratitude, you can retire it: Burn it in a ritual fire, bury it, or otherwise dispose of it in a respectful manner.

A Talking Amulet

Disney jumped on the witchy bandwagon with a magick necklace, a big purple gemstone amulet fit for a princess, to wit, the princess Sofia. You can purchase a talking version of the playful amulet for your favorite little girl, complete with twelve action cards she can insert into the "amulet" to get insights from the stone.

TALISMANS

A talisman is designed to attract something its owner desires. Gemstones and jewelry have long been favored as talismans. The Chinese, for example, prize jade and wear it to bring health, strength, and good fortune. For centuries, women of many cultures have worn lockets that contain snippets of their lovers' hair as talismans.

You can also combine several items that relate to your objective (see Chapters 11 and 12 for suggestions). Slip the selected items into a cloth or leather pouch and wear it as a talisman. Or you could place meaningful items in a wooden box and set it on your altar to attract the object of your desires. If you know feng shui (a type of Chinese magick that focuses on harmonizing you and your environment) put the talisman in the part of your home that relates to your intention. A talisman can be made for yourself or for someone else. It's usually best to fashion a talisman while the moon is waxing (between new and full) because the waxing moon encourages increase and development.

Many old stories say that spirits lived in talismans and whoever possessed the talisman could command the spirit to do specific tasks. Remember Aladdin's lamp that held a powerful genie? The genie had to grant Aladdin three wishes. That's a mythological example of a talisman. For our purposes here, think of talismans as magick tokens created for a particular purpose.

What Goes Into a Talisman?

You create a talisman essentially the same way as you make an amulet, using one or more ingredients that relate to your objective. When choosing your ingredients, pay attention to both the purpose of the spell and your own associations with the objects themselves. If you (or the person you're making the talisman for) plan to carry it around, small, lightweight ingredients are essential. If you plan to wear an amulet or talisman, you'll need to design it with comfort, convenience, and beauty in mind.

Tokens as Talismans

You're enjoying a peaceful walk at a place that has special meaning for you, when you spot a pretty pebble lying on the ground. You pick it up, study its markings for a moment, rub its smooth surface, and then slip it into your pocket. From time to time, throughout the day, you touch the stone fondly. Back home, you place the stone on the mantel or coffee table, where it continues to bring pleasant thoughts. Perhaps you carry it with you on future sojourns.

This token now holds the positive energy you've given it. It has all the makings of a lucky talisman. In fact, many simple talismans are nothing more than ordinary objects that have been infused with meaning by their owners—the good feelings and thoughts associated with such objects are what give them their power. Objects found in this manner, and especially those that come from sacred sites, are ideal to use as talismans.

Because they actively send out energy to attract something you desire, talismans "burn out" faster than amulets do. If you don't get what you want in a reasonable amount of time, you might need to "feed" your talisman to reinforce its strength. You can do this by dabbing a little essential oil on it. Essential oils are extracted from plants and contain the life energy of herbs and flowers. Choose an oil from a plant that relates to the purpose of your talisman (see Chapter 11 for ideas).

TIMING SPELLS

If you're launching an ad campaign, applying for a job, or running for a political office, timing can be crucial to your success. The same holds true for magick. By performing a spell or ritual on an auspicious date, you increase the likelihood of accomplishing your goal quickly and effectively. In timing spells, the moon's cycle is usually the most important factor.

When casting spells, pay particular attention to these four significant lunar periods: the new moon, full moon, waxing, and waning phases. As we discussed in Chapter 4, each has its own unique energy that can help or hinder the power of your spells.

Superstition attaches all sorts of strange and scary things to the full moon especially. Despite all that nonsense about werewolves, the full moon is a high-energy period and it can be a great time to connect with

The Modern Guide to Witchcraft

the Goddess, nature spirits, and the earth. If you're interested in astrology, you'll also want to pay attention to the moon's passage through different zodiac signs—it changes signs about every two and a half days. Find a good book about astrological signs and choose a sign that relates to your intention—Libra for love, Sagittarius for travel—in order to boost the energy of your spell.

THE DAYS OF THE WEEK

Before powerful telescopes allowed astronomers to see beyond the range of the human eye, only seven heavenly bodies could be observed from earth: the sun, moon, Mercury, Venus, Mars, Jupiter, and Saturn. Early people believed that gods and goddesses inhabited these bodies, and named them for those deities.

Each god or goddess was said to possess particular characteristics and oversee certain aspects of life on earth. Venus, for instance, guided love and relationships. Mercury ruled communication and commerce. According to ancient tradition, each deity's power reigned supreme on one of the seven days of the week. By scheduling activities on a day when the deity who ruled your particular interest was in charge you could increase your chances of success.

When doing magick spells, the same holds true in modern times. Love spells, for example, can benefit from the energy of Venus if you perform them on Friday. The following table shows which days and deities govern which areas of life.

MAGICK DAYS		
Day of the Week	**Ruling Planet/Deity**	**Areas of Influence**
Monday	Moon	fertility, creativity, home and family matters, intuition
Tuesday	Mars	contests/competition, courage, strength/vitality, men
Wednesday	Mercury	communication, commerce, intellectual concerns

MAGICK DAYS		
Day of the Week	**Ruling Planet/Deity**	**Areas of Influence**
Thursday	Jupiter	growth/expansion, prosperity, long-distance travel
Friday	Venus	love, partnerships, the arts, women
Saturday	Saturn	limitations, authority, endurance, stability, protection
Sunday	Sun	public image, confidence, career pursuits, health/well-being

The Modern Guide to Witchcraft

Chapter 14

PROSPERITY SPELLS

Living gets more expensive every day. Each time you fill your car's tank with gasoline or buy groceries at the supermarket, it costs more. Most people's salaries aren't keeping pace with the rising cost of living and economic forecasts sound pretty grim. What's a person to do? When the going gets rough, witches start conjuring up some cash. Whether you're just trying to pay your bills or want a little extra to buy something special, magick can help.

WHAT DOES PROSPERITY MEAN TO YOU?

Do you define prosperity as a dollar amount, a cool million, for instance? Or do you think of it as a state of being, such as living comfortably? Does *abundance* mean having more of everything or having enough of everything? These distinctions may seem trivial, but before you begin doing prosperity spells, you need to be absolutely clear in your own mind about what these concepts mean to you.

If you're like most people, your beliefs about money and prosperity were instilled in you long ago, perhaps by your parents, a religious institution, or the society in which you lived. If these old attitudes are preventing you from having the abundance you desire, you'll have to get rid of them and replace them with new ideas.

If you were to conduct an informal survey among your friends, you might be surprised to discover how differently people view prosperity. Their responses would probably cover a wide spectrum: to have more money; to be in a better job; to enjoy a happy marriage or romantic relationship; to write a best-selling novel or screenplay; to own a house; to be self-employed; to be able to travel.

How about you? Finish the following sentences to see what your true feelings are. Don't try too hard or think about it too long.

1. I am happiest when . . .
2. My wildest dream is to . . .
3. Given the choice, I would most like to spend my time . . .
4. I thoroughly enjoy . . .
5. I would love to . . .
6. I now spend my free time . . .
7. I feel a sense of accomplishment when . . .
8. My greatest passion is . . .
9. One of my favorite hobbies is . . .

This list describes what makes you happy—and happiness is what "abundance" is all about. You can have all the money in the world, but if it doesn't make you happy, what good is it?

Write Your Wish List

Take a few minutes to define what prosperity and abundance mean to you today, right now, in this moment. Make a list of ten things that would make you feel prosperous if you had them. Now find an object that represents each entry on your list. Select these objects with care— you're going to use them to work magick.

Let's say that your wildest dream is getting your pilot's license. Perhaps you haven't yet accomplished this goal because you didn't have enough money for lessons or an airplane. Any number of objects might represent your dream: a model airplane, a photograph of the type of plane you would like to fly, or a child's plastic toy plane. The point is to choose something that immediately connects you to the feeling of flying.

When you've collected all ten items, put them in a place where you'll see them often: your desk, a windowsill, or your altar. Each time you

The Modern Guide to Witchcraft

look at them, you'll be reminded of your dreams of abundance and your intention to attract prosperity into your life.

Creating a Prosperity Consciousness

Do you think you're worthy of prosperity? Do you believe you are inherently valuable? Do you trust the universe to provide for you and always give you whatever you need? Or do you constantly worry about paying bills and fear poverty? Do you believe that money is the root of evil? Do you think you can't be both rich and spiritual?

Prosperity consciousness means you wholeheartedly believe you deserve to have whatever you desire. You know that your good fortune doesn't take away from anyone else's—the universe's warehouse of goodies is infinite. You welcome wealth of all kinds into your life. You use money to enrich your life and the lives of others. If you don't have a prosperity consciousness, you'll need to develop it before you can successfully do spells for prosperity.

Each time you notice yourself saying or thinking something that undermines your prosperity consciousness, such as "I can't afford that," cross it out in your mind's eye by drawing a line through it. Then rephrase the statement in a positive way.

We talked about affirmations in Chapter 13. Affirmations are good tools for reprogramming your ideas. Write down one or more affirmations related to prosperity and repeat them often. Say your affirmation(s) aloud at least a dozen times a day, until your subconscious gets the message. Here are a few suggestions:

- My life is rich with abundance of all kinds.
- I have everything I need and desire.
- All my bills are paid, and I have plenty of money to spare and share.
- I am happy, healthy, wealthy, and fulfilled in every way.

Try not to concern yourself with how you're going to get the money. Just trust that opportunities will begin to present themselves to you if you continue to say the affirmation and believe in yourself.

Timing Prosperity and Abundance Spells

For each of the spells in this chapter, I've noted the best time to perform the spell. In most cases, you'll be more successful if you do spells for prosperity and abundance while the moon is waxing. The seeds you plant with your spell will grow along with the moon. As the moon's light increases, so will your wealth.

Taurus is the zodiac sign of money, material goods, and physical resources. Therefore, an ideal time to do prosperity spells is when the moon and/or the sun is in Taurus. If your spell involves other people's money, insurance, taxes, inheritance, or litigation, you might be better off casting a spell when the moon and/or sun is in Scorpio.

The best days of the week for doing prosperity magic are Thursday and Friday, the days ruled by Jupiter and Venus respectively. These planets encourage growth, abundance, and good luck.

SO MANY BILLS, SO FEW FUNDS

Stop dreading those bills—that's the key to this spell's success. Instead, try looking at your bills in another light. Your creditors have provided goods or services up front, because they're confident you'll be able to pay. Now it's time for you to believe in yourself.

INGREDIENTS/TOOLS:
- A piece of green paper or paper designed to resemble money
- A pen that writes gold or silver ink
- A black ribbon
- A stick of peppermint incense
- An incense burner

BEST TIME TO PERFORM THE SPELL:
- Whenever you pay your bills

Gather together all bills that are due, plus your checkbook and a pen. Collect the listed ingredients. Cast a circle around the area where you will perform the spell. Cut the green paper into a rectangle the size and shape of paper currency and write $1,000,000 on it. Use the pen with gold or silver ink to write the following affirmation on the green paper: "I always have more than enough money to pay all my bills. My prosperity increases every day in every way."

After you've finished writing checks to cover your bills, stack the receipts and place the piece of green paper on top of them. Tie up everything with the black ribbon. Fit the stick of incense into its burner and light it. Hold the envelopes containing your checks in the smoke for a few moments. Put aside any fears and imagine you have everything you need, when you need it. Open the circle. Repeat this spell every time you pay your bills.

SPELL FOR UNEXPECTED EXPENSES

When you least expect it, often at the most inopportune time, the dishwasher breaks or your car's air conditioner dies. Here's a spell to generate extra cash to cover those emergency expenses.

INGREDIENTS/TOOLS:
- A ballpoint pen
- Three candles, one green, one gold, and one silver
- Three candleholders
- Enough coins (any denomination) to form a circle around all three candles
- Matches or a lighter

BEST TIME TO PERFORM THE SPELL:
- Preferably during the waxing moon, but in an emergency you can do this spell as necessary

Collect the ingredients needed for this spell. Cast a circle around the area where you will do your spell. Using the ballpoint pen, carve the word "money" on the green candle. Inscribe the gold candle with the word "abundance" and write "now" on the silver candle. Set the candles on your altar or another place where they can burn safely. Position them so they form a triangle, with the green and gold candles at the base and the silver one at the apex of the triangle.

Next, with the coins make a circle around the candles. Be sure all the coins are face up and that each coin touches those on either side of it. Light the candles and call upon your favorite spiritual helper—a guardian angel, totem animal, or other deity—and ask for assistance in acquiring the money you need.

Allow the candles to burn down completely, but don't leave the burning candles unattended. If you must leave the circle before the candles finish burning, extinguish them and light them again later to continue the spell. When the candles have burned completely, open the circle and thank the deity for helping you.

MAGICK MONEY OIL

This versatile magick potion has many possible applications. Rub it on candles to increase their power. Dab it on talismans. Anoint gemstones, crystals, or magick tools with it. Rub a little on your body. However you use it, this money oil helps you attract all forms of abundance.

INGREDIENTS/TOOLS:
- A green glass bottle with a lid or stopper
- A small piece of tiger's eye or aventurine
- 4 ounces of olive, almond, or grape seed oil
- A few drops of peppermint essential oil
- Gold or silver glitter

BEST TIME TO PERFORM THE SPELL:
- During the waxing moon, preferably on Thursday

Wash the bottle and gemstone with mild soap and water, then dry them. Gather all the listed ingredients. Begin by casting a circle around the area where you will do your spell. Pour the olive, almond, or grape seed oil into the bottle. Add the peppermint essential oil and glitter. Drop the tiger's eye or aventurine in the mixture, then

The Modern Guide to Witchcraft

put the lid or stopper on the bottle and shake three times to charge the potion.

Open the circle and apply your Magick Money Oil in whatever manner you choose. This magick oil can be incorporated into many of the spells in this chapter.

Oil Your Candles for More "Octane"

You can increase the power of the candles by rubbing Magick Money Oil on them before you burn them. Or, pour a little oil of cedar, sandalwood, mint, clove, or cinnamon—scents associated with money—in your palms, then rub the oil on the candles. Some witches say you should start at the middle of the candle, and if you wish to increase or attract something, rub the oil toward the top of the candle—just don't get oil on the wick. If you want to decrease or repel something, such as cutting expenses, start at the center and rub oil down toward the candle's base.

GOTTA HAVE IT SPELL

Whether you've got your eye on a pair of designer shoes, a new computer, or a sports car, this spell helps you obtain whatever your heart desires. You can magickally manifest big things as easily as little ones. The only limits are in your own mind.

INGREDIENTS/TOOLS:
- A clear quartz crystal or an abundance crystal (one that contains a greenish mineral called chlorite)
- A picture or other likeness of the object you've "gotta have"
- Essential oil of cedar (or the money oil from the previous spell)

BEST TIME TO PERFORM THE SPELL:
- During the waxing moon, preferably on Thursday

Collect the ingredients needed for this spell. Wash the crystal in mild soap and water. Cast a circle around the area where you will do your spell.

Hold the crystal in your left hand while you gaze at the picture of the item you've "gotta have" and imagine yourself already owning it. Really get your feelings and senses involved in the visualization—wearing the shoes, driving the car. The more vivid you can make the experience the better.

When your mind starts to drift, dab four dots of essential oil on the picture, one at each corner. Let the scent strengthen your intention to acquire the object you desire. When you feel confident that you'll receive your heart's desire, open the circle. Place the picture on your altar, desk, or another place where you'll see it often. Set the crystal on top of the picture to increase the power of your spell. Look at the picture regularly, reaffirming your intention, until the object materializes.

SIMPLE CAULDRON SPELL

The cauldron symbolizes abundance. In spells, it holds your intention along with whatever ingredients you use in your spells for a period of time, to let the spell brew. This is the easiest possible money spell you can do with your cauldron, but don't let that fool you into thinking it isn't powerful!

Put one penny in your cauldron every day. As you do, say aloud, "I invest in my financial well-being. Every day brings greater abundance to me." When the cauldron is full, take the pennies to your bank or donate them to a charity of your choice.

GOODBYE DEBT SPELL

The cauldron represents creativity and fertility; cedar is associated with wealth. Combine the two with the action of fire, and you've got a potent spell.

INGREDIENTS/TOOLS:
- A large iron cauldron (or a cooking pot if you don't have a cauldron)
- Cedar wood chips, sticks, or shakes
- The five of pentacles from a tarot deck you don't use for readings
- A shovel or trowel

The Modern Guide to Witchcraft

- During the waning moon

Place the cauldron in a spot where it's safe to build a fire. Cast a circle around the area where you'll do your spell. Put the cedar inside the cauldron. Set fire to the wood, and when you have a small blaze going, drop the tarot card into the flames. The five of pentacles signifies debt and poverty; as the card burns, envision your debts disappearing as well. Let the fire burn down completely, then collect the ashes. Open the circle. On the next new moon, bury the ashes someplace far away from your home.

BURIED TREASURE SPELL

Instead of hunting for a pirate's hidden chest of gold doubloons, in this spell you symbolically stash treasure in order to "prime the pump" so greater riches can flow to you.

INGREDIENTS/TOOLS:
- A small mirror
- A tin box with a lid
- Nine coins (any denomination)
- A magnet
- A shovel

BEST TIME TO PERFORM THE SPELL:
- During the waxing moon, preferably on a Thursday

Gather all the listed ingredients. Begin by casting a circle around the area where you will do your spell. Place the mirror in the bottom of the tin box, with the reflective side up. Lay the coins, one at a time, on top of the mirror while you envision each one multiplying. Attach the magnet to the inside of the box (on the lid or a side) and visualize it attracting an unlimited number of coins to you. Put the lid on the box and open the circle.

Take your "treasure chest" and the shovel outside and dig a hole beneath a large tree. Bury the box in the ground near the tree's roots. When you've finished, say this incantation aloud:

"By the luck of three times three
This spell now brings great wealth to me.
The magnet draws prosperity.
The mirror doubles all it sees.
My fortune grows as does this tree
And I shall ever blessed be."

YOUR GOOD LUCK COIN

Find a coin minted in the year of your birth (or in a year that has special significance for you). It can be any denomination—even a coin from another country if that country has positive associations for you. Say the following incantation aloud to give the coin its magickal power:

"By these words, my will, and coin,
Magick and good fortune join."

Carry the coin with you or place it where you need the most luck—your home, business, or elsewhere.

CRYSTAL ABUNDANCE SPELL

Some quartz crystals contain bits of greenish mineral matter in them. These are known as "money crystals" or "abundance crystals." If possible, use one of these in this spell. Otherwise, a clear quartz crystal will work fine.

INGREDIENTS/TOOLS:
- 1 quartz crystal
- An image that represents abundance to you

The Modern Guide to Witchcraft

BEST TIME TO PERFORM THE SPELL:
- On a Thursday when the moon is waxing

Select a magazine picture or download an online image that symbolizes prosperity to you. It might be an object or condition you desire, such as a new home, a sports car, or a European vacation. Lay the picture face up on a windowsill where the moon's light will shine on it.

Wash the crystal in warm water with mild soap to cleanse it of any unwanted energies. Dry the crystal, then hold it to your third eye (between your eyebrows) while thinking about your intention. Doing this sends the image into the crystal. Then set the crystal on the picture. Make sure the crystal's point faces toward the inside of your home, to draw what you want to you. Leave the crystal in place overnight. In the morning, remove the crystal and picture and give thanks for the bounty you are about to receive.

MONEY TALISMAN

If you like, you can decorate the pouch for this talisman with beads, tiny charms, embroidery, or symbols that represent wealth to you.

INGREDIENTS/**T**OOLS:
- 1 strip of paper
- A pen that writes green, gold, or silver ink
- Peppermint essential oil (or the Magick Money Oil from earlier in this chapter)
- 1 green pouch (preferably made of silk or velvet)
- 1 coin (any denomination)
- Cedar chips
- 3 whole cloves
- 1 pinch of cinnamon
- 1 gold or silver ribbon 9" long
- Incense burner
- Pine or sandalwood incense
- Matches or a lighter

• During the waxing moon

On the strip of paper, write this affirmation: "I now have plenty of money for everything I need and desire. Riches come to me from all directions." Dot the corners of the paper with essential oil, then fold it three times and slip it into the pouch. Add the coin, cedar, and herbs to the pouch.

Tie the pouch with the ribbon, making three knots. Each time you tie a knot, repeat your affirmation. When you've finished, say, "This is now accomplished in harmony with Divine Will, my own true will, and with good to all." Fit the incense into the burner and light it, then hold the talisman in the incense smoke to charge it. Carry the pouch in your pocket or purse. If you prefer, take it to your workplace to help you earn more money.

TAROT SPELL TO INCREASE YOUR INCOME

The vivid colors and images on tarot cards make them a wonderful addition to any spell. Even if you don't understand all the symbols on the cards, your subconscious will register them. The candles' colors are meaningful, too. Green is the color of paper money in some countries, and also reminds us of healthy, growing plants. White represents clarity and protection.

INGREDIENTS/TOOLS:
• 1 green candle and 1 white candle
• 2 candleholders
• An object that represents your desire
• 1 deck of tarot cards
• Matches or a lighter

BEST TIME TO PERFORM THE SPELL:
• During the waxing moon

Cast a circle around the area where you will perform this spell. Put your candles at opposite ends of your altar. Between them, place an object that signifies your desire to increase your income. This could be one of the items that you chose at the beginning of this chapter to symbolize the intentions on your wish list. It could also be a coin, a dollar bill, a piece of jewelry, or something else that suggests wealth.

From your deck of tarot cards, select the ace of pentacles (sometimes called coins or discs), which represents new financial undertakings and opportunities. Place it in front of the white candle. In front of the green candle, put the ten of pentacles. Sometimes called the "Wall Street" card, the ten symbolizes a financial windfall. In the middle, between the two candles, place the nine of cups—the "Wish" card—and the Star card, which symbolizes hope.

Light the candles and say:

"The money I spend
and the money I lend
comes back to me
in multiples of three."

See money flowing to you from all directions. The more vivid you can make your visualization, the faster your wish will manifest. End the spell by extinguishing the candles and giving thanks. Open the circle. Allow everything to remain on your altar overnight.

KEEPING TRACK OF YOUR SPELLS

Whenever you do a spell, record all the details in your book of shadows. That way, you can perform the spell again at a later date, adjust it, or adapt it to other circumstances. Following is a list of the basic information you should include about any spell or ritual you perform:

1. Name and type of spell. Write this at the top of the page.
2. Date and time you did the spell. If it's an original spell, you may also wish to add the date and time you composed it.

3. Who else was present, if anyone.
4. Moon phase. Add the moon sign if you know it, as well as other pertinent astrological information.
5. Weather. This is more important than you might think, as weather can affect your feelings as well as the place where you choose to perform your spell.
6. Location. Did you do the spell in the living room, backyard, etc.?
7. Your health. Your energy level and overall health can impact your spells. If you are female, also note where you are in your menstrual cycle.
8. Purpose of the spell. This may be obvious from the name of the spell, but a heading such as "Simple Cauldron Spell" might require a little more information about why you did the spell.
9. A complete list of the tools and ingredients used. This is vital for future reference and if you choose to repeat the spell.
10. Deities invoked, if any.
11. The entire text of the spell or ritual. You can write this down before the ritual, and just work from your text, if necessary.
12. How long it took to complete the spell.
13. The immediate reaction you felt to the ritual.
14. Short-term results. What did you notice over the first few days or weeks following the ritual?
15. Long-term results. What sort of changes have you observed over the following months or years?

You may choose to add other information you consider relevant, interesting, etc. Add drawings, poems, or other jottings if you like. Of course, you can always come back later and put in notations about things you thought of afterwards, dreams, discussions you may have had with fellow witches, and so on. It's your book to work with however seems best for you.

Chapter 15

LOVE SPELLS

Witchcraft and spellcasting are inseparable. Witchcraft, as you already know, is the practice of using your will, mind, emotions, and perhaps special tools to bring your intentions into being—magick is what happens during that process. Magick spells don't have to be complicated to be successful. If anything, the simpler the better—unless lots of details and drama enable you to create the magickal ambiance you desire. Some spells need nothing more than the witch's presence to activate them.

In myth, song, and poetry, love and magick are often linked. When we speak of falling in love we use such terms as enchanted, charmed, bewitched, under a lover's spell—and it often feels that way. But as Shakespeare wrote in his delightful play about magick and love, *A Midsummer Night's Dream,* "The course of true love never did run smooth." Therefore it's probably no surprise that the most frequently cast spells are—you guessed it—love spells.

Love spells, however, can be tricky and more than a few witches have performed questionable spells for romantic reasons. It's easy to let your heart rule your head. Before you do the spells in this chapter, give some thought to what you really want in a relationship and what your motives are for casting a spell. Do you really want to use magick to snag a guy who's not that into you? If your girlfriend is cheating on you, do you really want her back?

DEFINING WHAT YOU WANT

What's your reason for doing a love spell? Are you trying to attract a new romantic partner? Looking for your soulmate? Hoping to rekindle the spark in an existing relationship? The more specific you can be, the greater your chances of success.

Keep in mind that a love spell's primary purpose isn't to use magick to manipulate someone into falling in love with you. Its purpose is to balance your own energy so you attract the partner who is right for you. A relationship results from the interaction of two people, two individual forces—yin and yang—that merge to form a sum greater than the parts.

You'd think this should be easy, but for many people it's not. Your ideas may be influenced by the expectations of your family, your friends, or the culture in which you live. Your perceptions about your ideal mate might be conditioned by television and movies, books and magazines, and all sorts of societal stereotypes. The reasons a man in Zimbabwe marries could be quite different from those that unite a couple in Sweden. Even you and your best friend may not agree on what constitutes a good relationship.

Your Love List

Before you do any love spells, make a list of the qualities you seek in a partner. The act of compiling this list will prompt you to really think about your needs, desires, hopes, and priorities, and to put energy and intent behind the process of creating what you want. In a sense, your list becomes a spell. Like an affirmation, you state your intentions—what you intend to find in a partner—and focus your mind toward achieving your goal.

Your list can be as long and as detailed as you choose. As you write your list, be sure to state your desires in a positive way and in the present tense. Here are some examples:

- I now have a partner who respects and values me.
- I can trust and rely on my partner at all times and in all situations.
- My partner and I support and encourage each other's goals.
- My partner and I share a spiritual path.

- My partner and I have many common interests and enjoy one another's company.
- I now have a mate who is willing and able to enter into a committed, loving, primary partnership with me.

Be specific. Consider every angle. Cover all your bases. You might want to let a trusted friend read your list and provide feedback, so you don't overlook anything. You don't want to write a long and detailed love list that described all the qualities you seek in a mate, and then realize too late that you left out something important. I once drew up a list of things I wanted in a partner, and one qualification was "likes to travel." I should have stated "likes to travel *with me*" because the man I attracted loved to travel—and did, a lot—he just preferred to travel alone.

Timing Love Spells

Astrologers connect Venus with love and relationships, and Venus rules the zodiac signs Taurus and Libra. Libra is the sign of romantic partnerships and marriage, so you'll get an energy boost if you perform a love spell when the moon and/or the sun is in Libra. Taurus is connected with the physical side of love, so if you want to improve your sex life, consider doing your spell when the sun and/or moon is in Taurus.

If you're trying to attract a new partner, do a spell on the new moon. If you want to increase the joy or passion in an existing relationship, or to nudge a budding affair into full bloom, do your spell when the moon is waxing. To end an unfulfilling relationship, do magic while the moon is waning.

SPELL TO GET NOTICED

Does it sometimes seem like you're invisible? If you aren't getting the attention you seek, perhaps you need to boost your personal power. This spell helps you raise energy and project it into your environment, so that the person you've got your eye on will notice you.

- A clear quartz crystal
- A drum or gong

BEST TIME TO PERFORM THE SPELL:
- During the full moon

Collect the ingredients needed for this spell. Wash the quartz crystal with mild soap and water, then pat it dry. Cast a circle around the area where you will do your spell. Stand (or sit) in the center of the circle with the drum or gong. Place the crystal nearby.

Begin playing the drum or gong. Feel the vibration breaking down the invisible wall around you that has prevented that certain person from seeing you clearly. Now imagine you are drawing energy up from the earth, into your body. Envision it as a brilliant silver light moving up your legs and spine, until your entire body is filled with a silver glow.

Continue playing the drum or gong as you now imagine drawing energy down from the heavens. Visualize this as golden light flowing into the top of your head, down your spine, until your whole body is alive with a golden glow. Pick up the crystal and hold it to your heart. Strike the drum or gong one time as you imagine the mixture of silver and gold light radiating outward from your heart. As it flows through the crystal the light is magnified tenfold and spreads out, filling the room. Strike the drum or gong again as you send the light further, into the environment outside. You can project this powerful light as far and wide as you choose.

When you feel confident and secure in your newfound radiance, open the circle. Pick up the crystal and carry it with you at all times. It will retain the energy of the spell and continue resonating with it, enhancing your personal power wherever you go.

Clean Up Your Love Life

In the ancient Chinese magick system known as feng shui, everything in your home has symbolic value. If your love life is stuck, stressful, or nonexistent, take a look at your bedroom. Is it full of clutter? Does it feel unwelcoming? Get rid of old stuff that you don't need or use anymore—old stuff represents emotional baggage and things from your past that may be holding you back. Faded, worn-out objects represent a love life that's lost its sparkle. Broken items indicate broken dreams or a physical breakup. Organize what you choose to keep so your bedroom is neat and orderly.

SPELL TO ATTRACT A NEW LOVER

This is your chance to put to work that love list you so carefully compiled earlier. Use your magick to attract the perfect partner.

INGREDIENTS/TOOLS:
- Ylang-ylang, rose, or jasmine essential oil
- 1 rose-colored candle
- List of qualities you seek in a partner
- Matches or a lighter

BEST TIME TO PERFORM THE SPELL:
- The first Friday after the new moon

Cast a circle. Pour a little oil in your palm, and then rub it over the entire candle (except the wick). Set your list on your altar or other surface, and set the candle (in a candlestick or other fireproof container) on top of the list. Light the candle.

As the scent of the heated oil wafts into the air, vividly imagine your lover. Feel this person's presence right there in the room with you. How does this person look, act, speak, and dress? See as much detail as possible. What type of work does he or she do? What are his or her passions? Continue the visualization for as long as you like, making your mental images as rich as possible.

When you've spent as much time as you feel is necessary, snuff out the candle's flame and open the circle. Repeat this spell two more times before the full moon. On the night of the full moon, release your wish by allowing the candle to finish burning down completely. Express thanks for the love you are about to receive.

TURN UP THE HEAT

Has the spark gone out of your relationship? This spell uses spices to add spice to your love life, along with fire to heat up things between you and your partner.

INGREDIENTS/TOOLS:
- A fireplace, balefire pit, barbecue grill, hibachi, or other place where you can light a fire safely
- Matches or a lighter
- A piece of paper (hot pink or purple preferably)
- A pen that writes red ink
- Cayenne pepper
- Mustard seeds (or dry mustard)
- Ginger (freshly grated or powdered)

BEST TIME TO PERFORM THE SPELL:
- During the waxing moon, preferably on Tuesday

Collect the ingredients needed for this spell. Cast a circle around the area where you will do your spell. Build a small fire in a safe place.

On the paper, write what you find enticing about your partner and what you desire from him or her. Be as descriptive and explicit as you like—no one but you will read what you've written. When you've finished, draw the runes *Gebo*, which looks like an ✕, and *Teiwaz*, which looks like an arrow pointing up, around the edges of the paper. These two symbols represent love and passion respectively.

Place the spices on the piece of paper and fold it to make a packet that contains them. Visualize you and your lover in a passionate embrace. As

The Modern Guide to Witchcraft

you hold this image in your mind, toss the packet of spices into the fire. As it burns, your intention is released into the universe.

When you feel ready, open the circle.

MAGICK BALM TO HEAL A BROKEN HEART

She rejects your love. He finds someone else. We've all suffered with broken hearts. This spell eases the pain of losing the one you love and helps your heart begin to heal.

INGREDIENTS/TOOLS:
- A small piece of rose quartz
- A glass jar or bottle, preferably green, with a lid or stopper
- 3 ounces of olive, almond, or grape seed oil
- 6 drops of rose, jasmine, or ylang-ylang essential oil
- ¼ teaspoon dried chamomile leaves

BEST TIME TO PERFORM THE SPELL:
- Begin on the new moon and continue for as long as necessary

Collect the ingredients needed for this magick balm. Wash the rose quartz and the jar with mild soap and water. Cast a circle around the area where you will do your spell. Pour the olive, almond, or grape seed oil into the jar. Add the essential oil and inhale the fragrance, allowing it to relax your mind. Crush the chamomile leaves very fine and sprinkle them in the oil. Add the rose quartz. Cap the jar and shake it three times to blend and charge the ingredients. Open the circle.

Before going to bed, pour a little of the magick balm into your palm and dip your index finger in it. Then rub the oil on your skin at your heart. Feel it gently soothing the pain. Take several slow, deep breaths, inhaling the pleasant scent, letting it calm your thoughts and emotions. Repeat each night and each morning until your sadness diminishes.

Note: You can also try taking a flower essence called "Bleeding Heart," available online: *www.flowersociety.org* and in some large health food stores.

LOVE TALISMAN

This good luck talisman can help you attract a new lover or improve your relationship with your current partner. If you choose rich fabric, and perhaps add some beads, embroidery, or other decorative touches you can fashion a talisman that's pretty enough to wear.

INGREDIENTS/TOOLS:
- 1 strip of pink paper
- 1 pen with red ink
- 1 pink or red pouch, preferably made of silk or velvet
- 2 dried rose petals (a deep pink color is best)
- A pinch of cocoa
- 2 apple seeds
- 1 piece of rose quartz
- 1 small pearl
- 1 purple ribbon at least 6" long
- Red wine or apple juice
- 1 ritual chalice or cup

BEST TIME TO PERFORM THE SPELL:
- On the first Friday after the new moon

Cast a circle. On the strip of paper, write an affirmation such as, "I now have a lover who's right for me in every way and we are very happy together" if you want to attract new love. If you want to improve an existing relationship, write something like, "[Partner's name] and I are very happy together and everything is good between us." Fold the paper three times and slip it into the pouch. Add the rose petals, cocoa, apple seeds, and gemstones.

Tie the pouch with the ribbon, making six knots to tie in the ingredients and your magickal energy. Six is the number of give and take, and it signifies compatible energy between two people. Each time you tie a knot, repeat your affirmation. When you've finished say, "This is now accomplished in harmony with Divine Will, my own true will, and for the good of all."

Pour the wine or apple juice into your ritual chalice or cup and swirl it around three times, in a clockwise direction, to energize it. Dip your finger in the wine or juice, and then dot the talisman with the liquid to charge it. Drink the rest. Open the circle. Carry the pouch in your pocket or purse, or wear it. If you know feng shui, you can place the talisman in the relationship sector of your home.

SPELL TO REV UP YOUR SEX LIFE

Do you or your significant other work such crazy hours that you never have time for each other? Do you lack privacy in your home because of the kids, roommates, etc.? Are your schedules so frantic that you both constantly seem to be moving in opposite directions? If so, this spell might be just what you need.

INGREDIENTS/TOOLS:
- Sea salt
- Ylang-ylang oil
- Jasmine oil
- Aromatherapy diffuser/burner
- 4 red candles
- Matches or a lighter
- Your favorite music

BEST TIME TO PERFORM THE SPELL:
- During the full moon or on a Tuesday

A full moon on a Tuesday is best for this spell, although a full moon on any day of the week is good too. But don't worry if nature doesn't suit your schedule and you find you're in the mood some night when there isn't a full moon—you can still get good results. First, draw a bath and sprinkle sea salt into the water. Sea salt is an excellent psychic and spiritual cleanser. Soak as long as it takes to relax fully—not just your muscles, but down to the very center of your being. You and your partner can bathe together or separately, whichever you prefer.

When you're completely relaxed, dry off and put on loose and comfortable clothing (a sensuous silk robe is best). Cast a circle. If you have set up an altar, put several drops of both oils into an aromatherapy diffuser. Light the candle beneath it. (If you don't have an aromatherapy diffuser/burner, you can rub a little of each oil directly on the candles.) As soon as the fragrance begins to fill the air, place a candle in each of the four directions, beginning in the east and moving clockwise.

As you light each candle, say: "Goddesses of the [east, south, west, north], bestow your blessings, your power, your love, on [partner's name] and me, to make us one. So mote it be."

When you're finished, open the circle and put the candles, still lit, into the bedroom or wherever you and your significant other will be. Play your favorite music. Let the candles burn out safely on their own.

GEMSTONE FIDELITY SPELL

Are you just beginning a relationship and want to make sure your partner doesn't stray? Or, do you suspect he or she is interested in someone else? Either way, this spell can deepen the feelings and commitment between you.

INGREDIENTS/TOOLS:
- An oval- or circular-shaped piece of rose quartz
- An obelisk-shaped piece of carnelian
- 1 piece of dark blue ribbon long enough to tie around the two stones
- 1 piece of white silk large enough to cover the stones
- A metal box (preferably copper, brass, or lead) with a lid, large enough to contain the two gemstones
- A shovel

BEST TIME TO PERFORM THE SPELL:
- When the moon is in Capricorn or on a Saturday

The gemstones have two symbolic meanings in this spell. Not only do they represent you and your partner, but rose quartz is a stone of love and affection, and carnelian brings passion. The ribbon's color—dark blue—indicates strength, sincerity, and permanence; the white cloth offers protection.

In the morning, wash the gemstones with warm, soapy water, and then stand them side by side on your altar so that they are touching. Imagine one symbolizes you, the other your beloved (it doesn't matter which gem you choose to represent which person, although rose quartz has a feminine/yin resonance and carnelian a masculine/yang one). Tie the stones together with the ribbon, making two knots, while you visualize you and your partner connected by a strong bond of love and devotion. Cover the gems with the white cloth and leave them until evening.

Once the moon has risen, wrap up the gemstones in the white silk cloth, and then place the package in the box. Take the box outside and bury it in the ground, preferably beneath an oak or apple tree.

AMULET TO BLOCK UNWANTED ATTENTION

Some people just won't take "no" for an answer. If someone seems determined to push his or her way into your life and won't leave you alone, this amulet helps you repel unwanted attention and establish clear boundaries.

INGREDIENTS/TOOLS:
- A piece of amber
- A piece of onyx
- Pine incense
- An incense burner
- Matches or a lighter
- A piece of paper
- A pen with black ink
- A black pouch, preferably silk or leather
- Dried basil leaves
- Anise or fennel seeds
- An ash leaf

- A white ribbon 8" long
- Salt water

- During the waning moon, preferably on a Saturday

Collect the ingredients needed for this spell. Wash the amber and the onyx with mild soap and water. Cast a circle around the area where you will do your spell. Fit the incense in its burner and light it.

Envision yourself safe and sound, completely surrounded by a sphere of pure white light that no one can penetrate without your permission. On the paper, write the word "Protection." Draw a circle around the word and fold the paper so it's small enough to fit into the pouch.

Add the botanicals and stones to the pouch. Tie it closed with the white ribbon, making eight knots. Each time you tie a knot repeat this incantation aloud: "From energies I don't invite / This charm protects me day and night."

Sprinkle the amulet with salt water, then hold it in the incense smoke for a few moments to charge it. Open the circle. Wear or carry the amulet with you at all times, until the annoying person stops bothering you.

ADAPTING SPELLS

At times, you might want to adapt a spell to suit your specific needs, but where do you begin the process? Although adapting a spell is far easier than creating one, it still requires some forethought. When examining a spell, look for continuity and comprehensiveness. Ask yourself these questions:

1. Does the spell really target your goal with its words, actions, and components?
2. Does it do so on a multisensual level, engaging your senses of hearing, sight, touch, taste, and smell?
3. Does every part of the spell inspire you?

If the answer to any of these questions is no, you should try to find a substitute. For example, many old love spells call for blood as an ingredient. However, there are many health reasons why this may not be such a good idea today—plus, it might gross you out. Instead, you could substitute a red fruit juice or red wine—your intention is the most important component in the success of your spell. If you don't like some of the words in a particular incantation, there's nothing wrong with editing that poem or chant so it speaks to you. Lots of people have allergies to certain substances or just don't like the way an essential oil or incense smells—so go ahead and use something you do enjoy.

In many instances, it's great to do a love spell with your romantic partner (assuming he or she is willing and in agreement with you). You can even incorporate sex magick into your spellworking to increase the octane, so to speak—but make sure you know what you're doing before you start (my book *Sex Magic for Beginners* explains what you'll need to know to get started).

Chapter 16

SPELLS FOR SUCCESS

What does success mean to you? Some people consider themselves successful if they reach the highest ranks of their profession; others see money as a marker of success. In our celebrity-oriented society, fame is often the benchmark of success. In a broader sense, however, success means feeling a sense of purpose and joy in what you do. According to author Christopher Morley, "There is only one success—to be able to spend your life in your own way." Whether you want to ace an exam, land a great new job, or make your mark in the world, magick can help you succeed.

SETTING GOALS AND INTENTIONS

Just as travelers plot a route, companies design business plans to guide them where they intend to go. Without a road map of some sort, you can easily get sidetracked or your plans may be derailed. Some business people recommend establishing a five-year plan, whereas others opt for longer or shorter terms and update their plans periodically. Many experts suggest that entrepreneurs at least create a mission statement that describes the business's vision. You can apply this in other ways, too. Is your goal to finish college? Move to another part of the country where you'll have more opportunity? Start a home-based business?

Given what you already know about magick, you can probably see the value of setting a goal—an end result you wish to achieve. That's what you do every time you cast a spell. Once you've created an image of your goal, you can use your willpower to bring your dream into being. Your plans don't have to be etched in stone, but it's important to at least have a clear view of what you would like to accomplish. Remember, the more vivid you can make your images of your goals, the more likely they are to materialize in the way you desire.

Self-Esteem and Success

Your work life is connected with your beliefs about self-worth, prosperity, and success. If you feel unworthy, this will be reflected in your income and in your work situation. If, on the other hand, you believe you're valuable and deserving—of a raise, a promotion, or better working conditions—your self-image will be reflected in your outer-world image.

In the following brainstorming activity, you're going to take inventory of your work situation—the work you do, your bosses and other people who have power over you, your coworkers or colleagues, or your personal circumstances if you're self-employed:

1. Describe the work that you do; give specific details.
2. Is your work satisfying? Why or why not?
3. Do you get along with your boss?
4. Do you get along with your coworkers?
5. Are you passionate about your work?
6. What would you change about your work if you could?
7. Do you have moral or ethical objections to the work you do?
8. Do you feel you're paid fairly for what you do?
9. What are your professional goals for the next year? The next five years?
10. Do you have regrets about the career path you've chosen?
11. Have you gotten regular promotions and raises? If not, why?
12. Is your work life filled with struggles? If so, explain.
13. Are you earning enough doing what you do?
14. If you could choose to do anything you wanted, what would it be? Why?
15. If your passion lies elsewhere, can you imagine earning your living at it?

If your answers to the previous questions are mostly positive, then you're probably exactly where you want to be in life right now. If the answers are predominantly negative, it's time to start doing magick to change what you don't like.

"Obstacles are those frightful things you see when you take your eyes off your goal."

—Henry Ford

Write It Down

Don't just keep your goals in your head. Instead, write them down in a journal or loose-leaf binder. Writing your goals is the first step toward bringing them into the material world. The very act of putting words on paper takes them out of the realm of imagination. The tactile nature of writing, instead of keeping a folder in your computer, makes your ideas more tangible.

State your objectives in the form of affirmations. Your affirmations might be all-encompassing and general, such as "I now have a job that's perfect for me," or they may be very precise, such as "I graduate at the top of my class and [company name] hires me and pays me [$X/year]." Make a list that includes at least three and not more than ten goals. As soon as you've accomplished one objective, replace it with another.

Read through your affirmations twice daily, when you first wake up and just before going to sleep at night. Repetition imprints your goals on your subconscious and directs it to carry out your wishes.

TIMING SUCCESS SPELLS

Like other spells, the ones you do for success will be more powerful if you do them at the right time. In magick, as in other areas of life, timing counts. In most cases, you'll get better results if you do spells for work success while the moon is waxing. However, if your goal is to eliminate an obstacle or condition that's blocking your success, or you want to scale down your work-related responsibilities, do a spell during the waning moon.

Capricorn is the zodiac sign of business, goals, and public image. Therefore, an ideal time to do spells for career success is while the moon and/or the sun is in Capricorn. Virgo is connected with work, work relationships, and work-related health matters, so if your intention involves these things, do a spell when the sun and/or moon is in Virgo. If you seek status, recognition, or a promotion, do a spell while the sun and/or moon is in Leo, the sign of leadership and fame.

The best days of the week for doing success spells are Thursday, Saturday, and Sunday, which are the days ruled by Jupiter, Saturn, and the sun, respectively. These heavenly bodies govern growth, business, travel, public image, status, ambition, self-image, determination, and leadership ability. The best day(s) for doing each of the spells in this chapter is indicated for each spell.

SPELL TO CLARIFY YOUR GOAL

This spell helps you get clear about your goal. Often we think we want one thing and later on find that what we really wanted was something else entirely. So before you get to the "later on" point, do this simple spell for clarification.

INGREDIENTS/TOOLS:
- 1 dark blue candle
- 1 fireproof candleholder
- A few drops of essential oil of citrus
- Pen and paper

BEST TIME TO PERFORM THE SPELL:
- As you feel the need

Dress your candle with the oil, put it in the candleholder, and light it. As you smell the scent of citrus, write down your goal in the form of an affirmation. Keep it simple. Prop the paper on which you've written your goal up against the candleholder or lay it in front of the candle. Gaze into the candle's flame and sit quietly for a few moments, keeping

The Modern Guide to Witchcraft

your goal in mind. Imagine that you have already achieved this goal. How does it feel? Are you comfortable with it? How does it affect your family and friends? What is your life like now that you have gotten what you wanted?

The more vivid and detailed your visualization, the better. Hold the image in your mind until your mind starts to wander, then stop. Now read your goal again. Is it what you really want? If not, rewrite it. You may find that you merely need to fine-tune what you've written. If you rewrite your goal, let it sit for a day or two before you look at it again. Then ask yourself if it feels right. Chances are that it will. Once you're certain you've got it right, burn the piece of paper to release your intentions into the cosmic web.

SPELL TO GET THE RESPECT YOU DESERVE

Does your boss overlook your hard work and neglect to give you credit for what you do? Do clients and customers seem unappreciative when you go the extra mile for them? If you're feeling dissed lately, this spell can help you get the respect you deserve.

INGREDIENTS/TOOLS NEEDED:
- A ballpoint pen
- An orange candle
- A candleholder
- Cinnamon essential oil
- Dried bay leaves
- Matches or a lighter
- A piece of paper
- Colored pens, pencils, or markers
- Tape

BEST TIME TO PERFORM THE SPELL:
- During the full moon, on Sunday, or when the sun or moon is in Leo

Gather the ingredients needed for this spell. Cast a circle around the area where you will do your spell. With the ballpoint pen, inscribe a circle with a dot in its center on the candle; this is the astrological symbol for the sun. Dress the candle by rubbing the essential oil on it (not on the wick) and set it in its holder. Inhale the scent of cinnamon, letting it stimulate feelings of confidence and power. Lay the bay leaves in a circle around the base of the candle. Light the candle.

With the colored markers and paper, write the word "Respect." Add other images that represent status, honor, power, and recognition to you. (If you like Aretha Franklin, you could play her song "Respect" during the process.) While you work, imagine yourself being lauded by the people with whom you work. See them bowing down to you, offering you gifts, singing your praises, or whatever scenario pleases you. When you're happy with your design, put a dot of cinnamon oil on each corner of the piece of paper. Extinguish the candle and collect the bay leaves. Open the circle.

Take the paper and the bay leaves to your workplace. Tape the bay leaves, which represent victory and success, on your desk, computer, door, wall, or other spot in your work area; if you prefer, put them in a desk drawer or other safe place out of sight. Look at your respect drawing often—especially if someone treats you badly. Take a few deep breaths, inhaling self-confidence. Remember Eleanor Roosevelt's words: "No one can make you feel inferior without your consent."

SPELL TO ATTRACT SUPPORT

We all need encouragement and support in the work we do. This spell helps you attract someone who believes in you, sees your talent, and wants to nurture it.

INGREDIENTS/TOOLS:
- 1 ceramic pot
- Potting soil
- 9 seeds for a plant that blossoms with red or purple flowers
- Water

The Modern Guide to Witchcraft

- On a Thursday during a waxing moon

Fill your ceramic pot with potting soil and place the nine seeds at various spots in the soil. As you plant the seeds, say aloud:

> *"I plant these seeds*
> *And draw to me*
> *The one who sees*
> *What I can be.*
> *So mote it be."*

Once the seeds begin to sprout, the person who recognizes your genius should appear in your life. Until that happens, lavish your plant with tender loving care. Take every opportunity to make contacts—you never know who might become your "angel."

SPELL FOR A SUCCESSFUL START

Whether you're entering college, seeking a new job, or taking on a new project, this spell can help you make a successful start. Nothing can be as scary as the prospect of beginning something new. Most people wonder if they're smart enough, experienced enough, or talented enough to make a go of it. But if you listen to your fears, you'll never know how successful you might have been if you'd ignored them.

INGREDIENTS/TOOLS:
- A picture that represents what you are about to begin
- 1 quartz crystal

BEST TIME TO PERFORM THE SPELL:
- Nine days before the full moon

Cut out a picture from a magazine or download an online image that represents what you are about to start. Nine days before the full moon, lay the picture face up on your altar. Set the crystal on top of it. On the night of the full moon, burn the picture while you imagine yourself succeeding at your new effort, thereby releasing your intention into the cosmic web. Carry the crystal in your pocket or purse, or place it where you'll see it often to reinforce your self-confidence.

BITCHY COWORKER SPELL

There's one in every office—the coworker who makes everyone else's life miserable. The word "teamwork" isn't in his vocabulary. Her negativity drags down the rest of the staff's morale. Can a little magick sweeten this sour situation? Absolutely!

INGREDIENTS/TOOLS:
- A piece of tumbled rose quartz
- A piece of watermelon tourmaline
- A spray bottle
- Spring water
- Granulated sugar
- Jasmine essential oil
- Lavender essential oil

BEST TIME TO PERFORM THE SPELL:
- During the waning moon, preferably on Friday

Gather the ingredients needed for this spell. Wash the gemstones with mild soap and water. Cast a circle around the area where you will do your spell. Fill the bottle with spring water, then add the sugar and essential oils. Shake the bottle three times to charge the mixture.

Envision the annoying coworker surrounded by a sphere of pink light. Even though this person may be as prickly as a cactus, try to understand that negative people are filled with fear. This spell works by boosting your coworker's self-esteem, so projecting positive energy will actually defuse this person's bitchiness. Open the circle.

Take the magick potion and the gemstones to work with you. When your irritating coworker isn't around, mist his/her workspace with the water-and-oil mixture. Repeat as necessary. Hide the piece of tourmaline somewhere in the bitchy person's work area. (Tourmaline neutralizes and disperses negative energy.) Keep the rose quartz for yourself. Whenever you start feeling annoyed, rub the stone until you calm down. Before long you should notice a change in your coworker's attitude and behavior, and in your own reactions to him/her.

SPELL TO GET A RAISE

Everything seems to be going up except salaries. This spell uses growth symbolism to help you get a raise, even when the economy's bad and companies are cutting back.

INGREDIENTS/TOOLS:
- A clear glass bottle (no designs) with a lid or stopper
- Spring water
- A $20 bill (or larger denomination)
- Tape

BEST TIME TO PERFORM THE SPELL:
- During the waxing moon, preferably on Thursday or Friday

Collect the ingredients needed for this spell. Cast a circle around the area where you will do your spell. Fill the bottle with spring water. Tape the $20 bill on the side of the bottle. This infuses the water with the image of money. Cap the bottle and shake it three times to charge it.

Drink some of the magick water. As you do this, imagine you are being "watered" with wealth. See your boss calling you into his/her office and offering you a raise, or visualize yourself receiving a paycheck with a larger amount printed on it—choose an image that clearly expresses your intention. Open the circle. Continue drinking your "money water" daily—make more when you finish the first batch—and watch your income increase.

SPELL TO GET A BETTER JOB

You want to tell your boss to take this job and shove it, but times are tough and good jobs are hard to find. Instead, put your magick skills to work and get busy creating the perfect job.

INGREDIENTS/TOOLS:

- Pictures from magazines, the Internet, or other sources
- A piece of paper or cardboard large enough for you to stand on (if necessary, tape two or more sheets together)
- An orange marker
- Glue, paste, or tape

BEST TIME TO PERFORM THE SPELL:

- During the waxing moon, preferably on Sunday or Thursday

Spend some time thinking about the job you'd really like. What images come to mind? Is travel a factor? If so, a plane might be a good symbol. Perhaps a big walnut desk represents authority to you, or a TV screen suggests fame. Coins and paper currency signify money. Cut out magazine pictures that depict various aspects of your dream job or download images from the Internet.

Gather up all your images along with the other ingredients needed for this spell. Cast a circle around the area where you will do your spell. On the paper or cardboard, use the marker to draw a symbol that astrologers call the Part of Fortune. This lucky design looks like an ✗ with a circle around it. Make your drawing large enough so that you can paste all your pictures inside it. Begin attaching the pictures you've collected to the Part of Fortune. As you work, imagine yourself happy and successful in your new position.

When you've finished, lay the paper/cardboard on the floor. Remove your shoes and stand in the middle of it. Close your eyes and imagine yourself becoming one with your new job. Make the visualization as real as possible. Stand there until your mind starts to wander, then step off the paper/cardboard and open the circle. Repeat as necessary, until you land your ideal job.

SPELL TO BIND A BACKSTABBER

She spreads damaging gossip about you at work. He steals your ideas and claims they're his. It's time to bring out the big guns—magick-wise, that is. This spell ties the backstabber's hands and prevents him/her from doing further harm.

INGREDIENTS/TOOLS:
- A small figurine (poppet) made of clay, wax, cloth, wood, or another material
- A black marker
- Black cord long enough to wrap around the figurine several times
- A shovel
- A large stone

BEST TIME TO PERFORM THE SPELL:
- During the waning moon, preferably on Saturday

Collect the ingredients needed for this spell. If possible, make the figurine (known magickally as a poppet) yourself, but if you aren't handy you can purchase an ordinary doll (the plainer the better, unless you can find one that resembles the backstabber). Cast a circle around the area where you will cast your spell.

With the marker write the troublemaker's full name on the poppet. Say aloud: "Figure of [whatever material the poppet is made of], I name you [the backstabber's name] and command you to cease your attacks on me now. I bind your ill will and render you powerless against me." Wrap the black cord around the figurine several times and tie it, making eight knots. Each time you tie a knot, repeat the last sentence of the affirmation: "I bind your ill will and render you powerless against me." When you've finished, open the circle.

Take the poppet and shovel to a place near your workplace and dig a hole in the ground. If that's not feasible, go to a remote area away from trees or water (and not on your own property). Place the poppet in the hole and cover it with dirt, then put the stone on top of it for good measure.

CREATING SPELLS FROM SCRATCH

After a while, you'll probably want to design some original spells. That's great. Following these steps will help you to create spells that can be just as effective as the ones you learn from this book and from other sources:

1. Boil down the purpose of the spell to a word or short phrase.
2. Find the ingredients suited to your goal.
3. Consider the best time to cast the spell.
4. Decide if you want to include an affirmation or incantation. If so, write one according to the instructions in Chapter 13.
5. Cleanse and purify all the objects you'll use in your spell.
6. Consider the order in which you'll do what you do.
7. Write your spell in your book of shadows, along with your experiences.

What kinds of results can you expect from your spellwork? Well, that depends on you. Like a computer, spells do what you tell them to do. That's why it's important to carefully consider what you really want and to state your objective accordingly. If you perform a spell to find a perfect companion and end up with a wonderful dog, your magick certainly has worked!

Chapter 17

PROTECTION SPELLS

The modern world is a dangerous place. Turn on the TV or read a newspaper and you'll see an ongoing parade of scary scenarios: hurricanes and earthquakes, car wrecks and plane crashes, robberies, kidnappings, and murders. Disease lurks just around the corner, threatening health and well-being. Accidents happen when you least expect them. How can you protect yourself against the evils of the world?

Since ancient times, people in all cultures have used magick to safeguard themselves, their loved ones, and their property. In fact, the earliest charms were probably created for protection—from wild animals, bad weather, and malicious spirits. The early Greeks, for example, carried leaves on which they'd written the goddess Athena's name in order to ward off hexes. The Egyptians believed the Eye of Osiris would protect them on earth and in the life beyond.

Before you start doing the spells in this chapter, consider what we've discussed already about the power of the mind. You can drive yourself crazy worrying about all the bad things that *could* happen, most of which never will. As Plato expressed it, "Courage is knowing what not to fear."

Magicians say you should never put your mind on anything you don't want to occur, lest you draw that thing to you. That's what the Law of Attraction teaches, too: You attract whatever you focus your attention on. So as part of your protection magick, you might consider turning off those violent shows on TV (including the news).

BREAKING THE FEAR BARRIER

The next time fear stares you in the face, don't turn around and run. Stare back. Confront it by asking yourself: What is the absolute worst that can happen? What is this fear really saying to me?

Here are a few tips for beating your fears:

- Identify your fear: If you don't identify your fears, they will unnecessarily spill into other areas of your life. Instead recognize the bottom line, or true root, of your fears. Maybe at some time in the long-ago past, that fear served a purpose, but you've outgrown it now. Once you do this, you can come to a better understanding of your fears and start to move past them.
- Release your fear: When confronted with a fear, try finding an object to represent your fear, then take a hammer to it, and smash it. Physical exercise sometimes serves the same purpose. When you find yourself in the grip of fear, head for the outdoors, if you can, and walk fast. Better yet, run. Run until your legs ache and you're panting for breath.
- Work through it: Sometimes in life, certain situations are so painful or difficult that nothing seems to work to break the hold a particular fear has on you. In that case, you simply have to keep working with it and live through it day by day, until you can finally get beyond it.

Taking slow, deep breaths can also help to calm anxiety. While doing this, you might try simultaneously pressing a spot on the center of your torso, about halfway between your heart and your belly button. Acupressurists call this the "Center of Power." With your index and middle fingers, apply steady pressure (but not so hard that it's uncomfortable) to this spot for a minute or two whenever you feel a need to ease fear and insecurity.

PENTAGRAM PROTECTION

As we discussed in Chapter 10, a witch's pentagram is a symbol of protection. Many witches wear pentagrams as jewelry to keep them safe and sound, and you may want to do the same. You could also put one in your car's glove compartment or hang one from the rearview mirror. Put one on the door of your home to keep would-be intruders and annoyances away. Place one in your desk at work. Decorate your clothes with pentagrams—you can even buy pentagram panties online. Paint pentagrams on your toenails. Some witches get pentagram tattoos for permanent protection. Or, if your need for safety is only temporary, try drawing or painting one on your chest near your heart.

WHITE LIGHT SAFETY SPELL

You're alone at night in a bad part of town. You're hiking in the mountains and the trail is more treacherous than you'd expected. It's time for some on-the-spot magick! This quick and easy spell can be done anywhere, in any situation, to provide instant protection.

INGREDIENTS/TOOLS:
• None

BEST TIME TO PERFORM THE SPELL:
• Any time

Begin breathing slowly and deeply. If possible, close your eyes. Imagine you are in the center of a sphere of pure white light that completely encloses you like a cocoon. Visualize the light spinning clockwise around you. See the light expanding, providing a thick wall of protection that extends outward from your body in all directions. If you're in a car, plane, or other vehicle, see the white light surrounding the vehicle as well.

Say or think this affirmation: "I am surrounded by divine white light. I am safe and sound, protected at all times and in all situations." Repeat the affirmation three times. Feel yourself growing calmer and more confident as you place your welfare in the hands of a higher force.

PROTECTION AMULET

A dicey situation has you worried and you feel a need for some extra protection. Protection amulets are one of the oldest forms of magick. This one helps to shield you from potential injury or illness.

INGREDIENTS/TOOLS:

- A piece of amber
- A piece of bloodstone (for protection from physical injury)
- A piece of turquoise (for protection from illness)
- Pine incense
- An incense burner
- Matches or a lighter
- A photo of you (or another person if you're doing this spell for someone else)
- A pen or marker with black ink
- Essential oil of rosemary
- A white pouch, preferably silk
- A black ribbon 8" long
- Salt water

BEST TIME TO PERFORM THE SPELL:

- During the waning moon, preferably on a Saturday

Collect the ingredients needed for this spell. Wash the stones with mild soap and water, then pat them dry. Cast a circle around the area where you will do your spell. Fit the incense into the burner and light it.

Across the photograph write the words "I am safe" as you envision yourself completely surrounded by a sphere of pure white light. Dot each corner of the photo with essential oil. Inhale the scent of the oil and mentally connect it with a feeling of safety. Slip the photo into the pouch; if necessary, fold it so it's small enough to fit.

Rub a little essential oil on each of the stones and add them to the pouch. Tie the pouch closed with the black ribbon, making eight knots. Each time you tie a knot repeat this incantation aloud:

The Modern Guide to Witchcraft

"Anything that could cause me [other person's name] harm
Is now repelled by this magick charm."

Sprinkle the amulet with salt water, then hold it in the incense smoke for a few moments to charge it. Open the circle. Wear or carry the amulet with you at all times to protect you from harm, or give it to the person you wish to protect.

EVIL EYE AMULET

Do you feel you're under attack? Since ancient times, people in cultures around the world have used eye amulets to scare off evil of all kinds. Whether the evil force threatening you is human, animal, or supernatural, this all-seeing protection charm guards your home and its inhabitants.

INGREDIENTS/TOOLS:
- A disc of wood, ceramic, or stone about 1" in diameter
- Blue, black, and white paint
- A small paintbrush
- A white ribbon at least 1" wide and 4–6" long
- Tacky glue or something to attach the disc to the ribbon
- A small loop or hook for hanging
- Other adornments (optional)

BEST TIME TO PERFORM THE SPELL:
- On Saturday

Collect the listed ingredients. Cast a circle around the area where you will do your spell. Paint an eye with a blue iris, a black pupil, and white highlight on the disc—make it realistic or stylized, it's up to you. If you like, decorate the ribbon with symbols or designs that represent protection to you, such as pentagrams or circles. When the paint dries, attach the disc to the ribbon. Affix the loop or hook to the back of the disc. Open the circle.

Hang the amulet inside your home, near the front door. Each time you enter or leave your home, touch the eye amulet for good luck and to reinforce your sense of safety.

CIRCLE OF SECURITY

Here's another way to keep your home and everyone in it safe from harm of any kind—acts of nature as well as human menaces.

INGREDIENTS/TOOLS:
- Small clear quartz crystals
- A black cloth
- A garden trowel or shovel

BEST TIME TO PERFORM THE SPELL:
- Begin on Saturday during the waning moon

Collect the listed ingredients. If you live in a house and have a yard, you'll need enough crystals to completely circle your house. If you live in an apartment, you'll need one crystal for each window and each door to the outside. Wash the crystals with mild soap and water, then pat them dry. If you have a large area to cover and a lot of crystals, you might need to continue this spell over a period of days.

Draw or find a picture of a pentagram and lay it on your altar, or another surface. Place the crystals on it and visualize them absorbing the protection represented by the pentagram. Lay the black cloth over the crystals, covering them completely. Allow the crystals to sit overnight.

In the morning, remove the cloth. Pick up the crystals, put them in a bowl or other container, and take them outside. Beginning in the east, bury the crystals in your yard one at a time, making a protective circle that surrounds your home. Position them as close together or as far apart as feels right to you. If you live in an apartment, start at the east and place a crystal on each windowsill (inside) of your living space. Then set a crystal in a safe spot near or above each exterior door. As you work repeat this affirmation aloud:

"Crystals wise, crystals strong
Protect my home all day long.
Crystals clear, crystals bright
Keep it safe throughout the night."

You may also want to hang a pentagram on each door that leads into your home.

SPELL TO RELEASE NEGATIVITY

You already know that negative ideas and feelings attract negative situations. If you're concerned that your attitude may be drawing unwanted forces to you, this spell can help you let go of those bad vibes you've been putting out. After an unpleasant situation has occurred, perform this spell to shift the energy and prevent future problems.

INGREDIENTS/TOOLS:
- 1 piece of white paper
- 1 pen with blue ink
- White carnations in a clear glass container
- Matches or a lighter

BEST TIME TO PERFORM THE SPELL:
- During the waning moon

Write the following intention on the paper:

I now release [name the situation]
And create new, positive energy to carry me forward.
I trust this is for my highest good
And affirm my commitment to this new path.

Place the paper beneath the vase of flowers. Leave it there until the flowers wilt. When you throw out the flowers, burn the paper to complete the releasing process.

GUARDIAN ANGEL CHARM

Are you facing a challenge that seems bigger than you can handle? According to many spiritual traditions, everyone has a personal guardian angel who provides guidance and protection when you need it. This magick charm reminds you that your angelic helper is always near at hand.

INGREDIENTS/TOOLS:
- A small silver or gold hanging charm in the shape of an angel
- A white cord or ribbon 18" long
- Essential oil of amber

BEST TIME TO PERFORM THE SPELL:
- On Saturday

Collect the listed ingredients. Cast a circle around the area where you will do your spell. Slide the charm on the cord or ribbon and tie a knot to make a pendant necklace. As you tie the knot, visualize yourself safe, happy, and healthy. Say the following incantation aloud:

"Guardian angel, be with me.
Keep me healthy, safe, and free.
Guide my steps so I can see
What I must do. Blessed be."

Put a dot of amber essential oil on the angel charm. Inhale the scent and let it calm your nerves. You may sense your guardian angel nearby. Imagine yourself placing your concerns in the angel's hands, knowing that everything will be taken care of. Slip the necklace over your head and wear it for protection. Open the circle.

BASIL BATH

Locks on your doors and windows may deter human threats, but what about psychic ones? If you fear that someone is sending you "bad vibes" try this herbal protection spell.

The Modern Guide to Witchcraft

INGREDIENTS/TOOLS:

- A large pot
- Two quarts of water
- A large bunch of fresh basil

BEST TIME TO PERFORM THE SPELL:

- On Saturday, preferably when the sun and/or moon is in Capricorn

Heat the water in the pot. Add the basil and let it simmer for several minutes. Allow the brew to cool. Strain the basil out and set it aside to dry—save it to use in other spells.

Run a nice, hot bath. As the tub fills, slowly pour in the basil-infused water. If you like, you can add Epsom salts or sea salts—salt has protective and purifying properties, too. While you're doing this, say the following affirmation aloud:

"I am now protected at all times,
In all situations,
Always and all ways."

Soak in the bathwater for as long as you like. During this time, imagine yourself at peace, surrounded by pure white light, and sheltered from all harm.

PET PROTECTION SPELL

It's a dangerous world out there for animals, too. As anyone who's ever had an animal companion knows, the threat of cars, other creatures, and entrapment loom large and can endanger our beloved pets. This spell helps protect Fluffy or Fido from harm.

INGREDIENTS/TOOLS:

- A collar for your pet
- Sage incense, or loose sage
- A marker that will write on fabric or leather
- Amber essential oil

- Any time

Purchase a new collar, made of leather or fabric, for your pet. Cast a circle around the space where you'll be working. Light the sage and hold the collar in the smoke to cleanse it of unwanted energies. On the inside of the collar, write: "[Pet's name] is safe and sound at all times." Draw a pentagram at the end of the statement. The pentagram, as you know, is a symbol of protection. On the outside of the collar, write your name and phone number; or, get a pet tag made that includes this information and attach it to the collar.

Put four drops of essential oil on the collar, one at each end, on both sides of the collar. Open the circle. Place the collar in the sun for one day to charge it. Then fasten the collar on your pet to keep him safe.

(To be extra safe, ask your vet about having a tiny computer chip permanently implanted in your pet's skin that will identify him to city pounds, veterinarian's offices, and other agencies with scanners that can read such chips. See *www.homeagain.com* for information.)

WORDS OF POWER

Many spells, including those in this chapter, use affirmations or incantations. That's because words have power, as witches and magicians of all stripes know. Spiritual and occult literature frequently mentions the power of the human voice. For millennia people have been reciting magick words as a way of asking supernatural forces for assistance. This is usually done by calling out the deities' names. Speaking someone's name is said to be an act of power, giving the namer influence over the named.

Magicians recognize the power inherent in some words and, therefore, incorporate those words into spells and rituals. For example, if a witch wants to banish a spirit, he might order it to leave by saying, "Be gone." Many witches end spells with the words "So mote it be." This phrase (like "so be it") seals a spell.

You may choose to speak an incantation as part of a ritual or spell. Incantations, like prayers or blessings, can also be recited at mealtime or before going to sleep. If you prefer, write your incantation on paper and display it in a spot where you'll see it often. You might enjoy adorning your words with colorful pictures and framing your artwork—or even stitch an old-fashioned sampler like our great-grandmothers did. The more energy you put into your creation, the more effective it will be. Creating incantations is fun—use your imagination. In the process, you may even discover a talent for poetry that you never realized you had.

Chapter 18

SPELLS FOR HEALTH AND HEALING

Before we had modern surgery, pharmaceuticals, and state-of-the-art medical equipment, people turned to medicine men and wise women when they suffered health problems. These healers practiced magick to remedy diseases. Their knowledge of the spirit world and the healing energies in plants made them respected members of their communities. Today, healing remains a primary focus for many witches. Sometimes miraculous cures that baffle conventional doctors can be achieved through the same magickal practices that are used to attract wealth or love.

Holistic healing teaches that the mind and body are linked, and that our thoughts and emotions can produce illness or good health. This is most obvious in the case of stress, which we know can cause all sorts of problems, from headaches to digestive complaints to heart conditions.

The idea certainly fits in with what you know about magick and your ability to produce outcomes with your mind.

In magick, healing involves two steps:

1. Cleansing and/or purifying of the negative presence
2. Replacing the negative presence with something positive

In other words, you first need to clear away whatever is causing the problem, whether that's a virus, an emotional issue, or something else.

After you've accomplished this, you have to put into place something that will prevent the problem from coming back. That might mean a change in attitude, diet, or lifestyle. You may also want to do a protection spell to safeguard yourself or another person in the future.

Body Talk

Pay attention to the words you use to describe health conditions—they reveal the link between body, mind, and spirit. Is a situation at work giving you a "pain in the neck"? Are you having trouble "digesting" an idea? Eye problems may indicate you don't want to see something. Arthritis suggests you are emotionally or mentally inflexible. "Body talk" provides clues to an ailment's cause.

TAKING INVENTORY OF YOUR HEALTH

Just as doctors ask questions before they treat a patient, you'll have more success with healing spells if you understand your "patient" before you try to heal him or her. That's true even if the patient is you. By taking inventory of your health, you'll have a clearer idea about which spells will work best for you. Ask yourself these questions:

- Most of the time, is your energy high or low?
- In general, how would you describe your health?
- Have you noticed any particular patterns to your health?
- Describe your beliefs about illness and health.
- Are there certain times of the year when your health is better or worse?
- Do you worry a lot about your health?
- When was your last visit to a doctor? Why did you go?
- Do you have regular checkups?
- Do you have chronic health problems? If so, what are they?
- Do you get several colds a year?
- How much sleep do you need each night?
- When do you feel happiest and healthiest?
- Do you experience major fluctuations in your moods?

- Do you consider yourself a basically optimistic person?
- Have you ever sought "alternative" treatments for an illness or disease?
- Does anyone in your family have a chronic illness? If so, what?

Pay special attention to your answers for questions concerning your beliefs about health and illness. It may be that the three colds or the flu you get every year are directly related to your belief that getting three colds a year or coming down with the flu during the winter is normal. Read your answers several times. If you find that you hold negative or limiting beliefs concerning health, then changing these beliefs will do more for you than any spell.

THE HUMAN ENERGY FIELD

"Your body is designed to heal itself," writes Donna Eden in *Energy Medicine*.

In fact, we have all the tools we need to heal ourselves. It begins with an awareness of the subtle energies that give our bodies life. In China, this energy is called *chi* or *qi*. In India and Tibet, the energy is known as *prana*. The Sufis call it *baraka*. It runs through pathways in our bodies called meridians and is focused in seven major centers, or *chakras*, which extend from the base of the spine to the crown of the head.

Chakra literally means disk or vortex. Imagine a swirling circle of energy of various colors and you'll have a pretty good idea of what it looks like. When your energy is balanced, you're healthy. When your energy centers are unbalanced or blocked, you get sick. Each energy center has a particular function and relates to certain organs and physical systems in your body.

Before it shows up as a physical problem, illness exists in the body's energy field. When a medical intuitive, psychic healer, or shaman looks at an energy field, he or she can read your psychological as well as your physical health history. However, you don't have to be psychic to pick up information about your own health or someone else's. Sometimes your first impression, going "from the gut," is enough. The more you develop your intuitive ability, the better you'll get at receiving this sort of information—and knowing what to do with it.

The following list of the chakras and the parts of the body associated with them is based on medical intuitive Caroline Myss's system:

ENERGY CENTERS (CHAKRAS) AND HEALTH		
Chakra	**Location**	**Organs and Body Systems**
1	Base of spine	Immune system, rectum, feet, legs, bones
2	Below navel	Sexual organs, large intestines, appendix, hips, bladder
3	Solar plexus	Abdomen and stomach, upper intestines, liver, kidneys, gallbladder, pancreas, middle vertebrae, adrenal glands
4	Chest center	Heart, lungs, shoulders, arms, circulatory system, diaphragm, ribs, breasts, thymus gland
5	Throat	Throat, neck, thyroid, parathyroid, trachea, esophagus, mouth, teeth, gums, hypothalamus
6	Middle of forehead	Eyes, ears, nose, brain, nervous system, pineal and pituitary glands
7	Crown	Skeletal system, skin, and muscular system

HEALTH SPELL CAVEATS AND CAUTIONS

You know someone who's suffering, and you know a little magick could help that person. Shouldn't you do a healing spell for her? Well, *maybe*. Physical pain is a red flag that something needs attention—not just the obvious symptom, but the underlying root of the problem. Perhaps the discomfort your friend feels is actually helping her get in touch with the deeper issues involved. If so, it may be a necessary and beneficial part of her healing process.

Respecting another person's free will is also important when you're doing magick. You can't change anyone else unless he wants to change.

As well, you may not fully understand the issues involved in another person's disease. Perhaps an injury is forcing an overachiever to slow down, work less, and spend more time with his family. Unless someone asks for your help, proceed with caution and reserve.

Finally, it's important to acknowledge that magick spells, no matter how powerful and well intentioned, aren't a substitute for professional medical care. Although you've perhaps heard of shamans who can cure broken bones by tying charmed sticks to the damaged limb, in most cases it's wise to have the bone set by a qualified doctor. You may have personally witnessed miraculous healings for conditions that orthodox medicine couldn't cure. But if you break a tooth, you'll probably be grateful for the skills of a competent dentist. Combine humility, patience, and common sense with magickal belief, for both your own good and everyone else's.

TIMING HEALTH SPELLS

Healing spells will be more powerful if you do them at the right time. It's usually best to do spells to increase vitality or repair damage to bone or tissue while the moon is waxing. But if your goal is to eliminate or reduce something, do a spell during the waning moon. Spells to lose weight, for example, should be done while the moon wanes.

The full moon is a high-energy day, and many people experience peak vitality at this time. However, the full moon can also increase stress and bring emotional or psychological issues out into the open. The three days prior to and including the new moon tend to be low-energy days. It may take longer to recover from an illness or injury during this period—don't push yourself too hard.

Virgo is the zodiac sign of health, so you may wish to do healing spells while the moon and/or the sun is in Virgo. The sun is connected with vitality, and Mars with physical strength. Therefore, you could do a healing spell when the sun and/or moon is in Leo or Aries, depending on your intention.

Spells to limit the spread of disease or to reduce problems associated with a condition should be done on Saturday. Spells to bolster strength and vitality are best done on Tuesday, Thursday, or Sunday.

Don't undergo surgery or other medical procedures unless you absolutely have to while Mercury is retrograde (meaning the planet looks as if it's moving backwards in the sky), as mental errors are more common at this time. If you have tests done while Mercury is retrograde and the results are unfavorable or inconclusive, consider having the tests redone. Mercury goes retrograde every four months for three weeks at a time; you can check online astrology sites such as *www.astro.com* to see when.

INGREDIENTS FOR SCENT-SATIONAL SPELLS

In recent years, aromatherapy—healing with scent—has entered the mainstream. But witches and healers have known about this practice for thousands of years. The ancient Chinese and Indians used these oils for both healing and spiritual purposes. Scented oils played an important role in the Egyptians' mummification process. And remember the frankincense and myrrh that the wise men gave Jesus at his birth?

This following list gives some common magickal correspondences for essential oils. If you're applying aromatics to your skin, be careful—some of these strong scents may cause irritation, and some people may be allergic to certain oils. Dilute them in a "carrier" oil such as olive, grape seed, or jojoba. Don't ingest them either. Although some are edible, others are toxic.

Aromatic	Correspondence
Almond	vitality, energy booster
Amber	protection
Apple	happiness, especially in love
Basil	protection, harmony
Bay	strength, prophetic dreams
Bayberry	money spells
Cedar	prosperity, courage, protection

Aromatic	Correspondence
Cinnamon	career success, wealth, vitality
Clove	healing, prosperity, to increase sexual desire
Eucalyptus	healing, purification
Frankincense	prosperity, protection, psychic awareness
Gardenia	harmony, love
Ginger	cleansing, balance, awareness
Honeysuckle	mental clarity, communication
Jasmine	love spells, passion, to sweeten any situation
Lavender	relaxation, peace of mind, purification
Lilac	psychic awareness
Mint	money spells
Musk	love spells, vitality, to stimulate drive or desire
Narcissus	self-image
Patchouli	love spells, protection, career success
Pine	purification, protection, strength
Rose	love spells, to lift spirits
Rosemary	memory retention, banishing
Sage	cleansing, wisdom
Sandalwood	connection to the higher realms, knowledge, safe travel
Thyme	work with fairy folk
Vanilla	increases magickal power
Vervain	money spells, fertility
Violet	attraction
Ylang-ylang	aphrodisiac, love spells, passion, feminine power

Aromagick is one of the loveliest types of spellcasting. As you work with scents, consider both their mystical and physical effects. Combine two or more to "customize" your spells.

Aromagick Oils

An essential oil is prepared directly from the plant, which means that it carries the original energy of the plant. Synthetic scents and perfumes don't. Essential oils tend to be more expensive than perfume oils, but because they're stronger you only need a drop or two.

Here's an easy recipe you can use to make a versatile oil blend to boost energy, health, and happiness. If you'll only use it magickally, say to dot on talismans or to add to a ritual bath, you needn't dilute the essential oils. However, if you plan to apply the blend directly to your skin, be sure to mix the essential oils into a carrier oil.

Awake and Alive Oil
- 1 part rosemary oil
- 1 part mint oil
- 1 part orange oil
- ½ part lemon oil
- ½ part thyme oil
- 20 parts carrier oil (depending on how you'll use it)

Wash a plain glass jar and let it dry. Then one by one, pour the oils into the container. Swirl them together. Empower the oil blend by holding it in your hands and visualizing your personal energy flowing from your hands into the oil. Cover the jar and label it: Write down the date, the ingredients, and the proportions. Store the oil in a cool, dark place.

Magick Healing Baths

For thousands of years, people have soaked in water for therapeutic reasons. Many spas such as those at Saratoga Springs, New York, Ojo Caliente in New Mexico, and Hot Springs, Arkansas, still attract visitors who seek healing through water cures (or hydrotherapy). The ancient Greek physician and Father of Medicine, Hippocrates, believed that "the way to health is to have an aromatic bath and scented massage every day."

You can put a couple spoonfuls of fragrant dried herbs inside an old sock or stocking, tie a knot in it, and toss it under the running water as you fill the tub. The result in an infusion brewed directly in your bath. Or, you can add essential oils to your bathwater. You'll probably only need a few drops if you're using the oils "neat," more if you've blended them in a carrier oil. In the beginning, add only a small amount because your skin may be sensitive to the oils. Mixing essential oils into Epsom salts and adding those to your bathwater is another good way to get their therapeutic benefits—use about ¼ cup of the scented salts in a bath, and store them in a glass container. You may also enjoy positioning scented candles at the corners of your bathtub and bathing by candlelight.

SIMPLE CHAKRA BALANCING SPELL

To do this spell you only need your imagination and willpower. Witches and healers link each of the chakras we talked about earlier with a color—it's sort of like having a rainbow running through your body.

- First (root) chakra: Red
- Second (sacral) chakra: Orange
- Third (solar plexus) chakra: Yellow
- Fourth (heart) chakra: Green
- Fifth (throat) chakra: Blue
- Sixth (brow or third eye) chakra: Indigo
- Seventh (crown) chakra: Purple

Sit in a quiet, comfortable place and breathe slowly, deeply. Focus your attention on the first chakra, and send beautiful, clear red light there. Do this for a minute or two, until you feel warmth at this energy center. Then shift your attention to the second chakra and focus orange light there. Repeat, moving up through your body, sending the appropriate-colored light to each chakra. By the time you reach the top of your head, you'll feel more relaxed and balanced in body, mind, and spirit. Try to do this every day to maintain personal harmony and well-being.

CASTING A HEALTH SPELL FOR ANOTHER PERSON

Once you've got the okay to go ahead and cast a spell for someone else, use sympathetic magick to provide healing.

INGREDIENTS/TOOLS:
- Something that represents the other person
- Sprig of sage

- Eucalyptus oil
- 1 gold candle
- 1 purple candle
- 2 fireproof candleholders
- Oil burner
- Matches or a lighter

BEST TIME TO PERFORM THE SPELL:
- As needed

Find an object that represents the person for whom you're casting the spell. It could be a photograph of the person or an item that belongs to her, such as a piece of clothing or jewelry. Smudge your work area and the object that will stand for the other person with the smoke of sage. Cast a circle. Set the item in the middle of your work area or on your altar, and position a candle on either side of it. Place the oil burner behind it.

Pour several drops of eucalyptus oil into your burner. Light it, and then light the candles. After a moment of reflection during which you bring to mind the person's face and being, say:

"As the oil and candles burn,
Illness gone and health return,
For my [state relationship and the person's name]
Who is yearning and deserving."

Extinguish the oil burner. Open the circle and let the other two candles burn down naturally.

ENERGY ELIXIR

If you're like most people, you hit a slump late in the afternoon. When you need a quick pick-me-up that's all natural and caffeine and sugar free, drink this magick Energy Elixir to boost your vitality and clear your mind.

INGREDIENTS/TOOLS:

- A clear glass jar with a lid
- A small piece of rutilated quartz crystal
- Spring water
- A few drops of essential oil of peppermint or spearmint
- A few drops of essential oil of lemon
- A few drops of essential oil of sweet orange
- The Strength card from a tarot deck

BEST TIME TO PERFORM THE SPELL:

- Any time

Collect the ingredients needed for this spell. Wash the jar and the quartz crystal with mild soap and water, and let them dry. Cast a circle around the area where you will do your spell. Fill the jar with spring water. Add the essential oils, then the crystal. Cap the jar and shake it three times to charge it.

Lay the Strength card face up on your altar, table, or another surface. Set the jar on the card and leave it for at least ten minutes, so the water can absorb the energy of the image.

Remove the crystal, with your fingers, spoon, or tongs. Open the circle. Sip this supercharged elixir whenever you need an energy boost.

SPELL TO QUELL THE COMMON COLD

It's cold and flu season, and you're definitely feeling below par. A little herbal magick plus some TLC can relieve those miserable symptoms fast and make you feel better all over.

INGREDIENTS/TOOLS:

- Spring water
- Hyssop leaves and/or flowers
- An aqua beeswax candle with a cotton wick
- A candleholder
- Matches or a lighter

- As needed

Brew a strong tea from the hyssop leaves and/or flowers. Strain the herb residue from the water. Fill a bathtub with comfortably hot water and add the tea to it. Fit the candle in its holder and light it. Get into the tub and soak for as long as you like, inhaling the soothing scent of hyssop.

Focus your mind on loving thoughts and feelings. Envision yourself surrounded by love. As you inhale, imagine you are bringing love into your body. See and sense love circulating through your entire body, from head to foot. Spend several minutes doing this. Let the loving energy gently nourish you, strengthening your system so it can throw off the cold.

Remain in the tub for as long as you like. After you get out of the bathwater, extinguish the candle. Repeat this pleasant ritual whenever you like.

GREEN LIGHT SPELL TO SPEED RECOVERY

An illness or injury has sidelined you temporarily. This simple spell uses the color green, symbolizing health, to aid your recovery. Repeat it often and you'll be back in the game soon.

INGREDIENTS/TOOLS:
- A green light bulb or green filter that will color the light from an ordinary lamp
- A green ribbon long enough to tie around the afflicted body part

BEST TIME TO PERFORM THE SPELL:
- During the waxing moon to promote new tissue growth or to increase vitality; during the waning moon to eliminate an unwanted condition or to decrease unpleasant symptoms

Tie the ribbon comfortably around the part of your body that is injured or ailing. Make sure it doesn't interfere with an open wound or other skin damage. As you tie it, say aloud: "I am radiantly healthy and whole, in body, mind, and spirit." Shine the green light on the afflicted area for a few minutes, while you visualize yourself completely healed. *Don't* think about the injury or illness; imagine the end result you desire instead.

Repeat this "green light" treatment several times a day. Leave the ribbon in place until the condition is healed, then remove it and burn it.

HEAVEN AND EARTH HEALING SPELL

This spell draws upon the powers of heaven and earth to help heal any condition. You can do it for yourself or for someone else (remember to ask that person's permission first). Even if the other person is not physically present, you can still send him/her healing energy in this manner.

INGREDIENTS/TOOLS:
- A magick wand

BEST TIME TO PERFORM THE SPELL:
- Any time

Cast a circle around yourself. If you are doing the spell for another person who is physically present, cast the circle around both of you. Stand in the center of the circle with your feet about shoulder-width apart. Close your eyes. Hold the wand over your head with both hands, with your arms outstretched and straight. Point the tip of the wand at the sky and say aloud: "With this wand I draw down the healing force of the heavens." In your mind's eye see light flowing into the wand, making it glow brightly.

Open your eyes and point the tip of the wand at the afflicted part of your body (or the other person's). If the person for whom you are doing this spell is not physically present, aim the wand toward his/her location. Envision the light you collected from the heavens flowing into the injured or ailing body part, zapping it with healing rays.

When you sense that all the light has been transferred from the wand to the body, point the wand at the ground. Close your eyes and say aloud:

"With this wand I draw up the healing force of Mother Earth." In your mind's eye see light flowing into the wand from the center of the earth, making it glow brightly.

Open your eyes and aim the tip of the wand at the afflicted part of your body (or the other person's). Envision the light you collected from the earth flowing into the injured or ailing body part, zapping it with healing rays until all the light has been transferred from the wand to the body. When you've finished, thank the forces of heaven and earth for assisting you and open the circle.

SPELL TO EASE DIGESTIVE COMPLAINTS

This spell combines both physical and magickal healing to soothe problems with digestion.

INGREDIENTS/TOOLS:
- 1 glass cup
- A blend of chamomile tea and peppermint tea
- 1 piece of paper
- 1 pen with green ink
- Tape

BEST TIME TO PERFORM THE SPELL:
- Any time

On the paper, write the words *balance, harmony, peace, love,* and *acceptance.* Tape the paper to a clear glass cup, so that the words face in. Then brew some tea, combining chamomile and peppermint, and pour it into the glass cup. Let the tea sit for a few minutes to allow the words to imprint their message into the liquid.

Sip the tea slowly, feeling its soothing warmth in your stomach. Envision healing green light entering your stomach and abdomen, calming the upsets in your digestive tract. Feel yourself relaxing. Repeat this spell one or more times daily, until your problem improves.

STRESS-BUSTER RITUAL

You may not be able to avoid stress, but you can keep it from getting you down. This relaxing ritual helps you release stress and stay calm in the presence of everyday annoyances.

INGREDIENTS/TOOLS:

- Soothing music (new age or classical is best, either instrumental or chanting, without a catchy rhythm or lyrics)
- A tumbled chunk of amethyst
- A tumbled chunk of rose quartz
- A blue candle
- A candleholder
- A ballpoint pen
- Essential oil of lavender, vanilla, sweet orange, or ylang-ylang
- Matches or a lighter

BEST TIME TO PERFORM THE SPELL:

- Any time

Collect the ingredients needed for this spell. Wash the stones with mild soap and water, and then pat them dry. Start the music you've chosen. Cast a circle around the area where you will do your spell. With the ballpoint pen write the word "Peace" on the candle. Dress the candle by rubbing it with essential oil (not on the wick). Fit the candle in its holder and light it.

Hold one gemstone in each hand. Sit in a comfortable place and close your eyes. Begin breathing slowly and deeply. Inhale the soothing scent and allow it to calm your mind. Rub the smooth stones with your fingers. Feel the stones neutralize stress, irritability, and anxiety. Focus on your breathing. If your mind starts to wander, gently bring it back and say or think the word "peace."

Spend at least ten minutes this way, longer if you wish. When you feel ready, open your eyes and extinguish the candle. Open the circle. Let the music continue playing or shut it off. Carry the stones with you and rub them whenever stress starts to mount.

MAGICK HERB GARDEN

Early healers grew their own herbs to cure all manner of illness. You, too, can grow a magick herb garden and have fresh, healing herbs available when you need them for teas, poultices, lotions, and balms—and of course, for spells. If you don't have space for an outdoor garden, plant herbs in flowerpots or window boxes. Plant whatever you think you'll need for your magickal and healing work. Start with a few and add to your garden as your skills and needs expand.

Here are some suggestions:

- Lavender (for relaxation)
- Peppermint (for nausea and stomach ailments)
- Echinacea (for colds and flu)
- Dandelion (for skin disorders)
- Comfrey (for congestion and stomach complaints)
- Garlic (to clean wounds and prevent infection)
- Basil (for insect stings and bites)
- Aloe (for burns, constipation, and diverticulitis)
- Blackberry (for diarrhea, colds, and sore throats)
- Raspberry (for female complaints)
- Chamomile (for digestive disorders, nervous conditions, and insomnia)
- Calendula (for rashes, eczema, and skin irritations)
- Parsley (to cleanse the kidneys and liver)
- Rosemary (for headaches and insomnia)
- Sage (to staunch bleeding; for sore muscles)
- St. John's Wort (for bronchitis, low spirits, and lung congestion)
- Verbena (for coughs, breathing difficulties, and fevers)

BEST TIME TO PLANT:
- During the waxing moon, preferably when the sun or moon is in Taurus

Do some research to determine which plants to use for which health problems. Familiarize yourself with the magickal properties of the herbs you choose, too. (You'll find some information in Chapter 11.)

The Modern Guide to Witchcraft

Consider every step of your gardening process—planting, watering, tending, and harvesting—as a magickal act. Invite the nature spirits to assist you. Talk to your plants and thank them for helping you, especially when you harvest them.

AN ATTITUDE OF GRATITUDE

Gratitude is the final step in doing a spell. Always end every spell by showing gratitude to whomever you consider the source or creative power in the universe. Even before you see results, say thank you. Gratitude has two purposes in magickal work. It indicates that you fully believe your intention will materialize, and it acknowledges the help you receive from forces outside yourself.

An expression of gratitude may be as simple as saying "Thank you" at the close of a spell. Some people like to make an offering of some kind. Others demonstrate gratitude for the help they've received by giving help to someone else. How you choose to show gratitude is less important than the intention behind it. Sincerity is what really matters.

Chapter 19

SPELLS FOR PERSONAL POWER

Personal power has a lot to do with having "presence." We all know people who just seem to shine, and everyone looks at them when they enter a room. Movie stars, powerful politicians, and celebrities have it. However, you don't need to be someone in the public eye to possess presence. In fact, your job or social position rarely has anything to do with it. Presence comes from within—from being present in the moment and in harmony with yourself. Some little kids have it. Some elderly people have it. You'll meet people from all walks of life who don't even realize they have it. In some instances, a person may be born with presence, but usually it's something you cultivate and nurture over time, with the development of self-knowledge.

Remember the old adage, know thyself? To know yourself and to use what you learn requires an act of will. As you know already, your will is the crux of every visualization, manifestation, and spell you cast. You don't simply say the words or use the right herbs. You don't just go through the motions. You plunge into yourself, you delve deep to discover your true motives, needs, and desires. You bring that self-knowledge into your daily awareness. Then you commit to your path and trust the process. The spells in this chapter will help you to expand self-awareness and increase your personal power.

YOUR SELF-IMAGE

Ironically, your self-image probably isn't something you created yourself. It's a patchwork affair made up of bits and pieces you've collected from lots of other people: family members, teachers, religious leaders, friends, your culture, and the media. Like donning clothing that's *in* style, rather than in *your* style, the self-image you wear might be uncomfortable or inappropriate. Maybe you even fashioned your self-image without questioning whether or not the "garment" was right for you.

Tailoring your self-image according to someone else's ideas usually results in unhappiness or frustration. If you see yourself in this picture, perhaps it's time to take a closer look at the person you think you are, the person you'd like to be, and where the ideas you hold about yourself originated.

From what you know about magick, your thoughts about yourself and what you deserve will produce conditions that fit with your ideas. Your life is your mirror. What you see is a reflection of what you believe about yourself. If you aren't happy with your situation, you can change it by changing your perceptions of yourself.

Remember, nobody else gets to decide whether you're worthy. Only you do. Nor can anyone else limit your personal power without your consent—and that's pretty sweet.

Your Self List

Make a list of your ideas about yourself. Consider your physical qualities, mental abilities, talents, job, relationships, lifestyle, and so on. What are your strengths and weaknesses? What things do you feel comfortable with, and which would you like to change?

Look at all areas of yourself. Make "plus" and "minus" categories if you like. Are you good at managing time? Do you have pretty eyes? Are you a skilled cook? Are you compassionate, a good listener, a loyal friend? Are you overweight? Are you always late for appointments? Do you buy things you don't need to make yourself feel better? Are you impatient, judgmental, or lazy? It can help to also examine where the negative ideas you hold about yourself originated.

Feeling Powerful

Think back to a time in your life when you felt powerful. Bring to mind the feelings that you experienced then, and reconnect with them. Hold these impressions in your mind and heart for a while, and remind yourself that inside you are still that powerful person.

This is the feeling you want to tap into when you do spells. The better you feel about yourself, the more positive energy you can bring to your magick. The more confident you are that your spells will succeed, the more likely it is that they will.

Go with the Flow

Although you may think this saying implies passivity, what it really recommends is that you put yourself into the stream of cosmic energy that flows through everything in the universe. What "go with the flow" really means is "stop resisting, and relax." Swimming is a good analogy. If you relax, the water will buoy you up, but if you flail about, you could drown.

Instead of struggling to figure out everything with your rational mind, allow your intuition to kick in. Trust that the universe, your higher self, Divine Will, Source, or whatever term you prefer has everything under control—all you have to do is stop interfering with the plan. When you hook into something larger than yourself, you discover that the big picture is way more amazing than you imagined.

The flow of a river is altered constantly by the curvature of the land that contains it, as well as by weather patterns and other factors. In the same way, the "flow" in your life changes as your goals and needs change. When you allow for that, you're better equipped to seize opportunities, to face challenges, and to fulfill your potential. In short, you are empowered.

INCANTATION FOR INSPIRATION

You're in a rut. You really need to come up with some great new ideas, but you just don't feel inspired. Chanting can spark your enthusiasm. Think how a crowd's cheers raise energy and fire up a ball team. Incantations operate on the same principle.

INGREDIENTS/TOOLS:

- A piece of paper
- A pen that writes red ink
- A drum, gong, or large bell

BEST TIME TO PERFORM THE SPELL:

- On a Tuesday during the waxing moon

Collect the ingredients needed for this spell. Cast a circle around the area where you will do your spell. On the paper, write an incantation that describes what you desire. It should praise you and your abilities with positive statements and imagery. Don't worry about its literary quality—no one but you will hear it. The point is to make it upbeat and catchy.

When you're satisfied with your rhyme, read it aloud. Then strike the drum, gong, or bell. Repeat the incantation again, and again, sounding the drum/gong/bell each time. If you prefer, you can strike the drum/gong/bell after each line or after each word of the incantation. Feel the sounds stimulating your energy. Feel the blockages within you crumbling. Feel your confidence growing. Continue for as long as you like. When you feel inspired, stop and open the circle.

Inspired Dreams

Some of the greatest moments of inspiration occur while we are sleeping. For example, the 2010 movie *Inception* starring Leonardo DiCaprio is based on director Christopher Nolan's own dreams. The Beatles's hugely successful song "Yesterday" came to Paul McCartney in a dream. So did the story for Stephen King's novel *Dreamcatcher.*

TALISMAN TO MAKE A GOOD IMPRESSION

You've got to make a good impression, but you feel anxious and uncertain. Whether you're going for a job interview, giving a presentation, or meeting with someone you admire, this lucky charm helps you shine. Remember, the key to success is believing in yourself.

Ingredients/Tools:

- Sandalwood incense
- An incense burner
- Matches or a lighter
- Red nail polish or red paint
- A small brush
- A small stone
- A piece of paper
- A pen
- An orange cloth pouch, preferably silk
- Cedar chips
- Cinnamon
- Dried parsley
- A yellow ribbon 6" long
- Salt water

Best time to perform the spell:

- On Sunday, preferably when the sun or moon is in Leo

Collect the ingredients needed for this spell. Cast a circle around the area where you will do your spell. Fit the incense in its burner and light it. Use the nail polish or paint to draw the rune *Inguz*, which looks like two ✕s stacked one on top of the other, on the stone. This rune represents new beginnings, fertility, and power.

While the nail polish or paint is drying, write on the paper what you intend to accomplish. Whom do you wish to impress? What results do you desire from this meeting? As you write your list of objectives, see yourself already achieving them. When you've finished, fold the paper so it's small enough to fit into the pouch and say aloud: "This is now accomplished in harmony with Divine Will, my own true will, and for the good of all."

Put the stone, paper, cedar, cinnamon, and parsley into the pouch. Tie the pouch closed with the ribbon, making three knots. Hold the image of your success in your mind as you tie the knots. Sprinkle the talisman with salt water, then hold it in the incense smoke for a few moments to charge the charm.

Open the circle. To bring good luck, carry this talisman in your pocket or purse when you go to your meeting. Just knowing it's there will increase your self-confidence and help you make a good impression.

POWER BELT

In karate, the belt you wear signifies your level of skill and accomplishment. The belt you create in this spell is not only a badge of your ability, it actually enhances your personal power.

INGREDIENTS/TOOLS:
- Music that energizes you and that signifies power to you
- A purple cord long enough to circle your waist three times (drapery cord is perfect, but you can use any material you like)

BEST TIME TO PERFORM THE SPELL:
- During the waxing moon, preferably on Sunday

Collect the items needed for this spell. Cast a circle around the area where you will do your spell. Begin playing the music you've selected. Close your eyes and allow the music to stimulate you, making you feel stronger and more energetic. Let your breathing become deeper.

Grasp the purple cord in your hands as you see yourself drawing up silvery light from the earth. Feel the light flow up your legs, into your torso, arms, and head. Next, visualize yourself drawing golden light down from the heavens, into the crown of your head. Feel this light flow into your torso, arms, and legs until your whole body resonates with it. Imagine these two forces blending harmoniously in and around you, increasing your vitality, confidence, and personal power.

Holding on to this sensation, open your eyes and begin tying knots in the cord. See yourself capturing some of the energy you've raised into each knot you tie. Tie as many knots as you like—just make sure the cord will still fit around your waist. When you're finished tying the knots, wrap the belt around your waist and secure it. Open the circle.

The Modern Guide to Witchcraft

Wear this "power belt" to help you address whatever challenges you face. If at any time you need a quick rush of vitality or courage, untie one of the knots and release the energy it holds.

SALAMANDER COURAGE SPELL

Setbacks, disappointments, losses, or frustrating circumstances can make you feel like giving up. In this spell you draw upon the fire power of the universe and get assistance from the fire elementals we talked about in Chapter 5 to bolster your vitality and confidence.

INGREDIENTS/TOOLS:
- 9 small red votive candles
- Matches or a lighter
- A magick wand

BEST TIME TO PERFORM THE SPELL:
- During the waxing moon, preferably on Tuesday or when the sun and/or moon is in Aries, Leo, or Sagittarius

Arrange the candles in a circle around you, in a place where you can safely leave them to burn down completely. Beginning in the east, light the candles one at a time as you move in a clockwise direction around the circle (making sure that you'll be inside the circle when you're finished). When all the candles are burning, stand in the center of the circle and face south.

Call out to the salamanders, the elementals who inhabit the element of fire. Tell them you have lit these nine candles in their honor. Explain your situation and request their assistance, by chanting the following incantation aloud:

"Beings of fire
Shining so bright
Fuel my desire
Increase my might.

Help me be strong
All the day long
So I'll succeed
In every deed."

You may notice faint flickerings of light—other than the candles—in the room. Or, you might sense the energy around you quickening. It may even seem a bit warmer. That means the salamanders are present and willing to work with you.

Take up your magick wand and point it toward the south—the region where the salamanders reside. Imagine you are drawing powerful energy in through the tip of your wand. You might see the wand glow or feel it tingle. Now turn the wand and aim it at yourself. Your movements should be strong and purposeful, not wimpy. Sense the energy you've attracted from the south flowing from the wand into your body. Feel yourself growing more powerful, more confident, more alive.

Continue using your wand to pull energy and courage from the south in this manner for as long as you like. Remain in the center of the circle of candles until they have all burned down completely. Thank the salamanders for their assistance and release them. Open the circle and leave with renewed vitality and confidence.

SPIRIT ANIMAL SPELL

According to shamanic traditions, spirit animals provide power, protection, and guidance in this world and beyond. These animals can lend you their special powers to accomplish a particular task. For example, a cheetah can give you speed when you're up against a deadline. An elephant can bring you strength to overcome obstacles. Foxes are clever and can show you how to dodge difficulties. Think about various animals and their distinctive qualities. Which animal's characteristics do you need now? (See my book *The Secret Power of Spirit Animals* for more information.)

When you've chosen an animal helper, find a photograph, small figurine, or another symbol of that animal.

Ingredients / Tools:

- A black candle
- A white candle
- Two candleholders
- Matches or a lighter
- A photo, figurine, painting, or other image of the animal whose help you are soliciting

Best time to perform the spell:

- Any time

Collect all the listed ingredients. Cast a circle around the area where you will do your spell. Fit the candles in their holders and set them on your altar (or another surface, such as a tabletop). As you face the altar, the black candle should be at your left and the white one on your right. Light the candles and place the image of the animal between them.

Gaze at the animal image. Sense this animal's presence near you, not necessarily as a physical creature but as a spirit being who will accompany you wherever and whenever you need it. Breathe slowly and deeply, bringing into yourself the qualities you seek from that animal: strength, courage, speed, cunning, and so on. Feel your fear ebbing away. Ask this animal to share any suggestions that might help you. An answer may come in the form of a vision, insight, sensation, sound, scent, or inner knowing.

When you feel ready, extinguish the candles and pick up the image of your animal guardian. Open the circle. Carry the image with you to give you the power you seek.

RITUAL TO RECLAIM YOUR ENERGY

Do you feel worn out at the end of the day, especially if you have to deal with a lot of people? When you're around a difficult person, do you notice your energy diminishing? According to ancient Toltec teachings, you leave a bit of your own vitality behind with every individual you meet during the day. This ritual lets you reclaim the energy you've given away so you don't get depleted.

- None

BEST TIME TO PERFORM THE SPELL:

- At the end of each day, before going to sleep

Choose a time when you won't be disturbed; turn off the TV, silence the phone, and so on. Sit in a comfortable chair and close your eyes. Start breathing slowly and deeply. Begin recalling all the people you encountered and all the incidents that occurred during the day, one at a time.

Turn your head to the left and remember something in which you participated in some way. Inhale as you recall the thoughts and feelings you had, as well as the actions that took place. Then turn your head to the right and exhale, releasing the experience with your breath. Continue doing this until you've recapped every event of the day, from beginning to end, the little things as well as the big ones. Feel yourself relaxing and gaining strength with each memory you cast out.

Repeat this procedure every night. Daily practice keeps you from draining your natural energy resources.

SPELL TO STRENGTHEN YOUR SELF-WORTH

This spell energizes the third chakra, located at your solar plexus. Energy healers connect this chakra with confidence and self-esteem.

INGREDIENTS / TOOLS:

- 1 ballpoint pen
- 4 yellow candles
- Almond oil
- 4 candleholders
- Matches or a lighter

BEST TIME TO PERFORM THE SPELL:

- On a Thursday, Friday, or Sunday night, or during the full moon

With the ballpoint pen, carve a circle on each candle and make a dot in the center of the circle. This is the astrological symbol for the sun. Yellow, the sun's color, is also the color associated with the solar plexus chakra. Rub almond oil on the candles to dress them, and then position them in their holders. Dab a little almond oil on your solar plexus, too, to energize it.

Place the four candles at the four cardinal directions and stand at the center of the space you've defined. Starting at the east, move clockwise as you light the candles, making sure you'll be inside the circle when you're finished. After you've lit all four candles, spend a few minutes drawing the fire energy from the candles into yourself. Inhale the scent of almond oil and imagine a golden-yellow ball of light glowing in your solar plexus. Let this light expand until it fills your whole body with warmth and confidence.

Pinch your right nostril shut, inhale through the left, and hold to the count of ten. Release, and exhale through the right nostril. Repeat this five times, then switch sides. As you do this alternate nostril breathing, sense your power growing.

Spend as much time as you like in the circle of candlelight. When you're ready, extinguish the candles in reverse order from the direction you lit them and leave the circle.

SPELL TO EXPAND SELF-AWARENESS

Self-awareness is linked with personal power. Most of us underestimate ourselves and are more familiar with our weaknesses than our strengths. We may not even be fully aware of our many abilities. The more you practice witchcraft, the more you develop an appreciation for yourself and your power. If possible, do this spell outside, under the full moon.

INGREDIENTS/TOOLS:
- 1 amber-colored candle
- A candleholder
- Frankincense essential oil
- Myrrh essential oil

- An object that represents personal power to you
- 1 quartz crystal

BEST TIME TO PERFORM THE SPELL:
- Preferably on a Thursday night during a full moon

Thursday is Jupiter's day, and Jupiter encourages expansion. If you can't do this spell on a Thursday, do it during a full moon on any day except Saturday (Saturn's day).

The object that represents your personal power should be something solid and three-dimensional: a stone or figurine, for instance, versus a photograph. Select the object with care. The amber-colored candle symbolizes the sun's golden light. The crystal you're using will amplify your desire.

Pick a spot where you won't be disturbed. Dress the candle with both essential oils, fit it in the candleholder, and set it on your altar, at your right. The object that represents your personal power and the crystal should be positioned directly in front of you. Light the candle, and then open your arms to "embrace" the moon. Vividly imagine its light filling you as you say:

"This light is presence,
This light is power.
It fills me
Until I am presence,
And I am power."

Gaze at the crystal and your power object as the moon's light shines on them. Inhale the aroma of the oils for as long as you like, then snuff out the candle's flame. Carry your power object with you and touch it whenever you need a power boost.

THE POWER OF DREAMS

One way to expand your power is to learn how to gain info from your dreams. Your dreams are your friends, even if it doesn't always seem that way. Getting in touch with your dreams can help you understand what's going on during your waking hours. Dreams can help you work through problems. They may also present possibilities you might not have considered otherwise.

Dreams have fascinated us throughout history. The ancient Babylonians believed that spirits sent dreams to humans. In Egypt, people thought that dreams were gifts from the gods. The earliest known recorded dream, which belongs to King Thotmes IV, is carved on a granite tablet that rests between the paws of the Sphinx.

Often dreams give us a glimpse of the future, which can be immensely helpful to witches and others. What if you could see what's going to happen before it does? A practice called "lucid dreaming" allows you to control your dreams and direct them in the way you choose. Developing this technique while you sleep can help you direct your waking life, too.

Keeping a Record of Your Dreams

Dedicate a section of your book of shadows to dreamwork, and place your book and a pen or pencil near your bed. To get the most out of your dreams, write them down immediately upon waking—it's easier then to capture the fleeting images, before they vanish into the busyness of your day. You needn't write in complete sentences. Just make enough notes so you can come back later and revisit the dream and analyze it.

Don't make any value judgments about what you write. Just record your feelings and the images that stand out. Who appears in your dreams? Where do the dreams take place? Do you notice patterns or similarities in your dreams? Sometimes you'll realize that what takes place in your dream is a reworking of what happened during the day. The dream might even slip you a tip about how to handle something that occurred. Other times, a dream may serve as a warning to prepare you, or give you a glimpse into what lies ahead so you can take advantage of an opportunity when it comes. Always date your dreams, and include any information about what's going on in your waking life at the time that may be relevant.

The more you work with your dreams, the more they will reveal to you and the more guidance they'll provide—giving you the inside track. And, as you develop a better rapport with your subconscious, you'll discover your spellworking improves.

Chapter 20

MISCELLANEOUS SPELLS

For every desire, every worry, and every situation, there's a spell. You can use magick for the big deals in life and for all those little things as well. Whether you want to find the perfect life partner or the perfect pair of shoes to wear to an upcoming event, magick can help. And if a "readymade" spell doesn't already exist, you can always design your own or customize one to suit your needs.

The spells in this chapter address a variety of circumstances, both large and small, that show up in our daily lives. Some are so versatile they can be used in a number of different ways. A few of these spells may seem trifling, but hey, why wait until something major happens to flex your magickal muscles? Lots of witches use magick to get a parking space at a crowded shopping mall—nothing wrong with that. Every spell you do strengthens your power as a witch, so don't hesitate to use your talents whenever you have the occasion to do so.

PIECE-OF-CAKE SPELL

Things aren't going as smoothly as you'd hoped. A project is taking longer or costing more than expected; a romance has hit a snag; you have to deal with a lot of uncooperative people at work or at home. This spell uses "kitchen witchery" to sweeten a frustrating situation.

You don't have to be a gourmet cook to carry off this spell—your intention is what counts. When you've finished baking your magick cake, you may want to share it with the other people who are involved in the challenging situation, so that everyone benefits. Choose a flavor that suits your intentions: chocolate or strawberry for love; cinnamon or mint for money; almond or vanilla for peace of mind.

INGREDIENTS/TOOLS:
- A cake mix (or ingredients for making your favorite cake recipe)
- Food coloring
- A large bowl
- A large spoon
- Cake pan(s)
- Candles
- Matches or a lighter

BEST TIME TO PERFORM THE SPELL:
- Depends on your intentions

Collect the ingredients needed for this spell. Cast a circle around the area where you will do your spell, in this case your kitchen. Preheat the oven.

Follow the directions for making the cake, according to the package or your favorite recipe. As you work, focus on your objective and imagine you are sending your intention into the batter. If you like, add food coloring to tint the batter to match your intention: pink for love, green for money, and so on. Stir the batter using a clockwise motion if your goal is to attract something or to stimulate an increase. Stir counterclockwise if you want to limit, decrease, or remove something. Pour the batter into the pan(s) and bake.

When the cake has finished cooking, let it cool. Ice it with frosting in a color that relates to your intention. You may want to decorate it with symbols, pictures, and words that also describe your objective. Add candles of an appropriate color. The number of candles should also correspond to your goal: two for love, four for stability, five for change, and so on.

Light the candles and concentrate on your wish. Blow out the candles. Share the cake with other people, if you like, or eat it yourself. Each person who eats some takes the intention into him/herself and becomes a cocreator in the spell's success.

LUCKY CHARM BRACELET

When you were a kid you may have worn a charm bracelet with tiny symbols that represented your interests or achievements. The symbols on the magick charm bracelet you make in this spell, however, represent your desires and intentions. Keeping these symbols in your immediate energy field makes this bracelet work, well, like a charm.

INGREDIENTS/TOOLS:
- A silver or gold link bracelet
- Small charms that can be attached to the bracelet

BEST TIME TO PERFORM THE SPELL:
- Any time

Choose a bracelet that appeals to you and that can hold as many charms as you have wishes. You might want to wear a metal that relates to your goal. Silver embodies feminine qualities and corresponds to the moon. Its energy is receptive, intuitive, emotional, creative, and works through the power of attraction. Gold signifies masculine qualities and relates to the sun. Its energy is assertive, direct, logical, and works through the power of action.

Select charms that hold meaning for you and that depict your objectives. If your goal is to attract a lover, a heart is an apt symbol. A car or airplane might represent travel. Wear as many charms as you like. Add or remove them over time as your intentions change. Remember to wash your charms before wearing them, to get rid of any lingering energies left behind by other people who may have touched them.

SPELL TO END SHOPPING LINE WOES

Does it seem that you always get in the slowest checkout line at the store, especially when you're in a hurry? Let Sheila the Shopping Goddess put you in the fast lane.

* None

BEST TIME TO PERFORM THE SPELL:
* Any time

To make this spell succeed, you have to use your intuition—not logic. As you approach the checkout area of the store, close your eyes, clear your mind, and take a deep breath. Think or quietly say this incantation:

"Goddess Sheila so divine
Guide me to the fastest line."

Open your eyes and allow yourself to be drawn to a particular line. Don't analyze it or second-guess yourself. The shortest line may not be the fastest, and the shoppers with the fewest number of items in their carts might be the very people who'll dawdle. Trust your instincts.

BLESSING A NEW HOME

Whenever you move into a new home, it's a good idea to clear away the energies left behind by the former occupants, so they don't interfere with your comfort. This spell also blesses your home and brings happiness to you and anyone else who will share the home with you.

INGREDIENTS/TOOLS:
* Sage
* Broom
* 1 bottle of wine or apple cider
* 1 loaf of freshly baked bread

BEST TIME TO PERFORM THE SPELL:
* Before you move into your new home

Begin by smudging your home with sage to cleanse it. Then, use the broom to sweep out the former occupants' vibrations. After you've done this, pour the wine (or cider) and slice the bread. The bread and wine ensure that you will always have enough to eat and drink in your new home. Share this magick meal with all who will live in the home with you and/or any friends who will enjoy visiting you there.

SMOOTH TRAVEL SPELL

No matter why you're traveling, where you're going, or what mode of transportation you'll take, this spell smooths the way. If possible, cast the spell in a place where you can see the moon. If you're traveling with someone else, add a piece of rose quartz for him or her.

INGREDIENTS/TOOLS:
- 1 ballpoint pen
- 1 white candle
- A candleholder
- Rosemary essential oil
- Matches or a lighter
- 1 piece of tumbled rose quartz

BEST TIME TO PERFORM THE SPELL:
- At night, within twenty-four hours prior to your departure

With the ballpoint pen, draw the astrological symbol for Jupiter (the planet that rules travel) in the candle's wax—it looks a bit like the number 4. Dress the candle with the rosemary oil, fit it in the candleholder, and light it. If you wish, you can burn a little dried rosemary in a fireproof dish. Set the rose quartz in front of the candle.

Repeat this incantation while you gaze into the candle's flame and inhale the scent of the rosemary:

"By the light of Lady Moon,
I reach my destination soon.

The trip shall safe and happy be,
For all concerned, as well as me."

When you're finished, extinguish the candle and pick up the rose quartz. Rub a little rosemary oil on it and carry the stone with you while you're traveling.

NO WORRIES INCANTATION

Worrying never makes a problem better. This spell uses the power of sound plus your intention to chase fearful thoughts away and raise positive energy.

INGREDIENTS/TOOLS:
- A dark blue candle
- A candleholder
- Matches or a lighter
- A hand drum or gong
- An athame or wand
- A bell

BEST TIME TO PERFORM THE SPELL:
- At midnight, during the waning moon

Collect the ingredients needed for this spell. Cast a circle around the area where you will do your spell. Fit the candle in its holder, set it on your altar (or other surface where it can burn safely), and light it. Begin playing the drum or gong to break up negative thoughts and vibrations. Feel the sound resonating through your body, stirring up your power and confidence. When you feel ready, chant the following incantation aloud. If possible, shout it out—really express yourself!

"Doubt and fear
Don't come near.
By the dawn

Be you gone.

By this sign [with your athame or wand draw a pentagram in the air in front of you]

And light divine

Peace is mine.

I am strong

All day long.

My worries flee

Magickally.

I ring this bell [ring the bell]

To bind this spell,

And all is well."

As you chant, see your fears disappearing into the darkness, losing their strength. When you're ready, extinguish the candle and open the circle.

BUBBLE MAGICK

This is fun to do with children, but even if you're a mature adult, you can still enjoy this playful magick spell. Let it bring out the child in you.

INGREDIENTS/TOOLS:
- 1 bottle of bubbles
- A power object (a special stone, charm, animal figurine, or other token)

BEST TIME TO PERFORM THE SPELL:
- Any time, weather permitting, but during the full moon is best

On a breezy evening when the moon is full, take the power object and bottle of bubbles to a hill, field, or park—someplace wide open. Place the power object on the ground between your feet, then make a wish and blow the bubbles. Project your wishes inside the bubbles. Let your power object direct the bubbles as the breeze carries them high into the air, where the gods and goddesses will hear the wishes and grant them.

As the bubbles, with your wishes inside, rise into the moonlit sky, say the following incantation:

"My wishes travel
The whole night through
So that magick's power
Can make them come true."

Watch the bubbles float off into the sky, and trust they will make your wishes come true.

A STEP IN THE RIGHT DIRECTION

This spell might sound a little silly, but a lighthearted approach is sometimes best when dealing with everyday troubles. Don't be put off by the playful quality of the spell—it can be quite powerful.

INGREDIENTS/TOOLS:
- Nail polish
- Polish remover
- Cotton balls and/or swabs

BEST TIME TO PERFORM THE SPELL:
- Depends on your intentions

Collect the ingredients needed for this spell. Select one or more bottles of nail polish, in colors that correspond to your intentions: pink or red for love, green or gold for money, and so on. Cast a circle around the area where you will do your spell.

Assign an objective to each toe. You can give all ten toes the same intention or pick ten different goals—or any other combination. Begin painting your toenails in colors that are appropriate to your objectives. As you paint each nail, concentrate on your intention and see it already manifesting. If you like, also decorate your nails with symbols that represent your intentions: dollar signs for money, hearts for love, and so on.

Have fun and be creative. If you make a mistake or change your mind, simply remove the polish and start over.

Allow the polish to dry, and then open the circle. For the next week or so, or for as long as the polish lasts, know that each step you take will bring you closer to your goals.

SAFETY SHIELD FOR YOUR CAR

The average person drives about 12,000 miles each year. That exposes you to plenty of potential delays, accidents, and other problems. This spell protects you from harm whether you're driving your car in your own neighborhood or cross-country.

INGREDIENTS/TOOLS:
- 1 white paper square
- Colored markers
- Amber essential oil
- Tape, glue, or other adhesive

BEST TIME TO PERFORM THE SPELL:
- During the waning moon, preferably when the moon is in Gemini or Sagittarius

Cast a circle around the area where you'll be working. Cut a 4" square of paper. Within this square draw a circle. Write the word *safe* or an affirmation of your choice in the center of the circle. If you wish, add other symbols that represent safety (such as a pentagram) and travel to you. The pattern you've created is your safety shield.

Dot the four corners of the paper with amber essential oil. Open the circle. Attach the shield to the dashboard or window of your car. Each time you get into your car, look at the shield and touch it to activate its protective energies. Visualize yourself and your car surrounded by pure white light, and know that you are protected wherever you go.

MORNING RITUAL

We all engage in daily rituals. Anything that you do each day with awareness is a ritual, from your morning shower to reading in bed before you
fall asleep. These rituals provide a sense of stability and continuity in
our lives. Now that you are walking a witch's path, you'll naturally want
to include magick in your routine.

Part of your morning routine should be writing in your book of shadows as soon as you awaken. While your mind is still fresh, jot down your
dreams, first thoughts of the day, your intentions, and so on. In addition
to your writing, you may want to come up with a simple ritual that will
color the rest of your day. Maybe it's saying an affirmation or offering a
blessing. You may only need a few moments of time to transform your
morning into a more inspired experience. Here's a suggestion you might
want to try:

1. Set a small crystal, a cup or chalice of water, a stick or cone of
   incense, and an essential oil that you find pleasing on your altar.
   Take a moment to think about the types of energies that you would
   like to call upon to influence the unfolding day. Imagine your perfect
   day and try to form a very clear image of it in your mind. You may
   have a specific accomplishment in mind. See yourself achieving whatever your heart desires. Imagine yourself doing everything you do
   throughout the day in a state of joy and satisfaction.
2. Put a small drop of oil on your fingertip and touch your fingertip to
   your third eye. See yourself bathed in the lovely morning light.
3. Light the incense and let its scent waft over you. Say an affirmation
   or blessing and focus your intentions for the day.
4. Hold the cup of water up to "toast" the day. Then bring it down to
   chest level, close to your heart. Dip your fingers in the water, close
   your eyes, and place a drop of water on each eyelid. Ask that your
   perception expand so you can see with clarity in all situations.
5. Hold the crystal and project into it your intentions for the day. Ask it
   to help you stay focused on your purpose throughout the day and to
   give you strength and determination when you need them.

The Modern Guide to Witchcraft

You may choose to carry the crystal with you throughout the day.

EVENING RITUALS

Twilight is a magickal time. Behind the setting sun's brilliant colors, the mystery of night approaches. You are moving "between the worlds." You'll want to mark the end of the day's activities and your entrance into the world of dreams with a well-crafted ritual. Here's a simple four-element ritual you may wish to use:

1. Begin by reflecting on the day that has just passed. Contemplate the energies you experienced, the things that went as you had hoped, and those you would like to have changed if you had the chance.
2. Place a cup of water and a crystal on your altar. Light a candle. Ask that you receive insight and guidance while you sleep.
3. Light a stick of incense and ask that your prayers rise up with the smoke and be heard by whatever deity you choose.
4. Take a sip of water and affirm that you'll enjoy a peaceful, restful night and awake refreshed in the morning.
5. Hold the crystal to your third eye. Trust that it will protect you throughout the night and anchor your spirit as it travels in the world of dreams. Place the crystal on your bedside table or under your pillow while you sleep.

Waking and Sleeping

You might want to choose different scents, stones, and candle colors for your morning and evening rituals. For example, a clarifying, energizing scent such as citrus, eucalyptus, or carnation could help awaken you to the day's possibilities, whereas lavender or chamomile can relax you at the end of the day. Light a yellow or orange candle in the morning, a blue or indigo one in the evening. A carnelian could jump-start your vitality as you begin the day; a piece of rose quartz or amethyst soothes you so you can sleep better.

Of course, these morning and evening rituals are merely springboards to get you started. In time, you'll develop your own daily rituals that hold special meaning for you and that enrich your days and nights in countless ways. In the next chapter, we'll discuss the eight special days of the magickal year and the rituals many witches and Pagans use to celebrate them.

Chapter 21

THE SEASONS OF THE WITCH

For centuries, earth-honoring cultures have watched the sun as it traveled through the sky (at least so it seems from our vantage point here on earth). Rather than thinking of the year as linear, witches view it as a circle. You'll often hear Wiccans, in particular, refer to it as the Wheel of the Year, and they divide that wheel into eight periods of approximately six weeks each. Each "spoke" in the wheel corresponds to a particular degree in the zodiac and marks a holiday (or holy day) known as a "sabbat." These high-energy days bring special opportunities for performing magick spells and rituals.

The wheel has its roots in the old agricultural festivals that marked the beginnings, peaks, and endings of the seasons. Four of the eight holidays relate to the four great Celtic/Irish fire festivals. Called the "cross-quarter" days, because they mark the midpoint of the seasons, these festivals were known to Pagans as Samhain, Imbolc, Beltane, and Lughnassadh. The four solar festivals—Yule (winter solstice), Ostara (spring equinox), Midsummer or Litha (summer solstice), and Mabon (fall equinox)—celebrate the dates when the sun enters 0 degrees of the cardinal signs of the zodiac: Capricorn, Aries, Cancer, and Libra respectively.

Even before recorded time, our ancestors celebrated these holidays. The ancient stone circles of Great Britain, such as Stonehenge, and the passage tombs of Ireland, such as Newgrange, clearly show that the early people noted the changes in the sun's position throughout the year. The Romans marked the winter solstice with the festivities of Saturnalia; the Greeks observed the Eleusinian mysteries during the fall equinox.

It's no coincidence that many of our modern-day holidays fall close to the dates when the early Greeks, Romans, Celts, and Germanic peoples of northern Europe celebrated these special days. In fact, we still enjoy some of the same customs and festivities as our distant ancestors, as you'll soon see. The Great Wheel is turning, and a magickal journey awaits you.

SAMHAIN

The most holy of the sabbats, Samhain (pronounced SOW-een) is usually observed on the night of October 31, when the sun is in the zodiac sign Scorpio. Better known as Halloween or All Hallow's Eve, this is the holiday people usually associate with witches and magick. Most of the ways the general public marks this sabbat, however, stem from misconceptions—it's a solemn and sacred day for witches, not a time for fear or humor.

The Holiday's Significance

Considered to be the witches' New Year, Samhain begins the Wheel of the Year. Thus, it is a time of death and rebirth. The word *samhain* comes from Irish, meaning "summer's end." In many parts of the Northern Hemisphere the land is barren at this time. The last of the crops have been plowed under for compost, and the earth rests in preparation for spring.

New Year, New Resolutions

Witches often choose to shed old habits or attitudes at this time, replacing them with new ones—similar to how nonwitches make resolutions on January 1. Consider writing on a slip of paper whatever you want to leave behind when the old year dies—fear, self-limiting attitudes, bad habits, and so on. Then burn the paper in a ritual fire to symbolically destroy what you no longer need.

For witches, Samhain is a time to remember and honor loved ones who have passed over to the other side. That's why people associate Halloween with the dead. No, skeletons don't rise from graves, nor do ghosts haunt the living on Samhain, as movies and popular culture tend to portray it. You probably won't be annoyed by uneasy or vengeful spirits, and it's highly unlikely that Grandpa's bones will rattle about in your living room.

Witches may attempt to contact spirits in other realms of existence, however, or request guidance from ancestors or guardians. The origin of the jack-o'-lantern is rooted in the belief that wandering spirits and ghosts turn up on Samhain. The lantern's glow was meant as a beacon so that the spirits of the dearly departed could find their way; the terrible faces carved on the pumpkins were meant to frighten away evil spirits.

Southwestern witches sometimes combine features from the Mexican Day of the Dead with Celtic Pagan customs on Samhain. People decorate their altars to mark the sabbat, often displaying photos of deceased loved ones. During the week before Samhain, they go house to house, visiting the altars of friends and relatives, saying prayers and paying respects. You, too, might wish to honor the memories of your deceased loved ones by placing photos, mementos, and offerings on your altar during Samhain.

Because the veil that separates the seen and unseen worlds is thinnest at Samhain, it's easier to communicate with beings on the other side at this time. You might also want to pull out your tarot cards or crystal ball during Samhain, to see what lies ahead in your future.

Psychic Babies

In earlier times, babies born on Samhain were thought to possess psychic power and could predict the future. No surprise, really, if you consider that these kids are Scorpios, and people born under this zodiac sign are notoriously perceptive and intuitive.

Ways to Celebrate Samhain

What would Halloween be without colorful costumes? This practice stems from the early custom of making wishes on Samhain, similar to making New Year's resolutions. Wearing a costume is a powerful magick spell, a visual affirmation of your goals. No witch would portray herself as a hobo or ghost! Instead, try dressing up as the person you'd like to be in the coming year in order to tap the magickal energies of this sabbat.

Samhain Spell to Free Yourself

Do you feel burdened or trapped by old beliefs, habits, or relationships? Now's the time to release yourself from figurative chains that may be holding you back. This spell breaks old bonds and sets you free to enjoy a happier life.

INGREDIENTS/TOOLS:
- A ball of red yarn (cotton or wool, no synthetics)
- An athame (or kitchen knife)
- A cauldron (or pot)
- Matches or a lighter

Cut the yarn into 9" pieces. Knot the ends together, forming a circle. Give each one a label, something in your life that you feel is holding you back. Perhaps it is a past hurt or a regret that you have been dwelling on. Cut as many pieces as you need. Slip them around your wrist and tell each of them specifically:

> *"[What you want to release], I have carried you long and far.*
> *Your burden has been my teacher, and I accept your lessons.*
> *Now I summon the strength to release you,*
> *For your presence serves me no longer."*

With your athame, begin cutting through the circlets. This might take a while, as an athame isn't normally sharp—your persistence is part of the spell. As you cut away your symbolic bonds, imagine yourself separating from your actual bonds. When you finish, burn the yarn in your cauldron, saying, "You are now consumed by the flames of transformation. You no longer bind me. Away you go, so that something new and blessed in me shall grow."

When the flames die and the cauldron cools, take it outside. (If your cauldron is too heavy to carry, scoop the ashes into something smaller.)

Stand with the wind at your back and release the ashes into the air. As they blow away, prepare yourself to make a new start.

WINTER SOLSTICE OR YULE

The winter solstice occurs when the sun reaches 0 degrees of the zodiac sign Capricorn, usually around December 21. This is the shortest day of the year in the Northern Hemisphere. The word *solstice* comes from the Latin *sol stetit*, which literally means "sun stands still." Also known as Yule, the holiday marks the turning point in the sun's descent into darkness; from this point, the days grow steadily longer for a period of six months. Thus, witches celebrate this sabbat as a time of renewal and hope.

The Holiday's Significance

Pagan mythology describes the apparent passage of the sun through the heavens each year as the journey of the Sun King, who drives his bright chariot across the sky. In pre-Christian Europe and Britain, the winter solstice celebrated the Sun King's birth. This beloved deity brought light into the world during the darkest time of all.

It's easy to see parallels between the Old Religion's myth and the Christmas story. You can also see the theme expressed in the custom of lighting candles during Hanukkah and Kwanzaa, both of which fall near the winter solstice. In these religious practices, light symbolizes blessings, joy, and promise. However, the Yuletide celebration goes back even further, to the ancient Roman observance of Saturnalia, the festival of the Roman deity Mithras, which was held from December 17 until December 25. The cult of *Sol Invictus*, or "invincible sun," with which Mithras is often associated, may have predated the Romans by several hundred years.

Ways to Celebrate Yule

Before the Victorian era, Christians didn't decorate their homes at Christmas with ornamented pine trees and holiday greenery. That's a Pagan custom. Because evergreen trees retain their needles even during the cold winter months, they symbolize the triumph of life over death. Holly was sacred to the Druids. According to Celtic mythology, holly bushes afforded shelter for the earth spirits during the wintertime. The Druids valued mistletoe as an herb of fertility and immortality. It has long been used in talismans as an aphrodisiac—perhaps that's the reason we kiss beneath it today.

The Magickal Origins of the Christmas Tree

Magick trees show up in lots of contemporary stories and films; some of the best known include the Evil Talking Trees in *The Wonderful Wizard of Oz*, Treebeard in *Lord of the Rings*, the Tree of Life in *Avatar*, and Mother Willow in *Pocahontas*. But the concept of enchanted trees dates back to ancient times. In early Germanic and Norse cultures, people believed the King of the Forest made his home in a fir tree. Others thought benevolent nature spirits lived in firs. People danced around magick fir trees and decorated them with painted eggs, charms, and flowers. Quite possibly, Christmas trees have their origin in this old tradition.

Burning the Yule log is another ancient tradition by which Pagans mark the winter solstice. On the eve of Yule, witches build a fire from the wood of nine sacred trees. The central element in the Yule fire is usually an oak log, for the oak tree represents strength and longevity (although you can use any wood). The fire symbolizes the sun's return. After the fire burns down, anyone who wishes may collect ashes and wrap them in a piece of cloth. If you place the package under your pillow, you'll receive dreams that provide guidance and advice for the coming year. Tradition says you should save a portion of the Yule log and use it to kindle the fire the following year.

Harvesting your Yule log is a ritual in itself. If you live in the country in a wooded area, you may find just the right log lying dead on the ground. If you take a cutting from a live tree, do so with humility and clear intention. Ask for the tree's permission before you start cutting and leave a symbolic offering (such as a special crystal or an herbal charm) in its place. Select your Yule log long before the winter solstice because it will need some time to dry in order for it to burn properly.

The Modern Guide to Witchcraft

Before you light your Yule log, cast a circle large enough to encompass your home and call in the guardians of the four directions (as discussed in Chapter 9). If you don't have a working fireplace or wood stove, you can place four candles in fireproof candleholders at the four directions and light them instead. Adapt the basic method to fit the season, as follows:

> *"Guardians of the east, we greet the dawn of the shortest day. We beckon you to join us in our celebration of the returning light and new beginnings. May the spirits of air bless us with the winds of winter. Hail and welcome!*

> *"Guardians of the south, we honor the return of your radiant light. The lengthening of days is upon us. May the spirits of fire bless our home and hearth. Hail and welcome!*

> *"Guardians of the west, the sun retreats to you and brings us to the longest night. You spirits of water, who take many forms, bless us with your purity and grace. Hail and welcome!*

> *"Guardians of the north, yours is the place of all endings. In the depths of darkness, we dance upon the sleeping earth and ask for your blessing tonight. Hail and welcome!"*

Light candles on your table and altar. Enjoy a special Yule feast either alone or with companions as you watch the fire and candles burn. Share gifts with your companions, such as the good luck charm that follows. When you've finished, release the directions, open the circle, and extinguish the candles and fire.

Yule Good Luck Charm

Would you like to help your friends and loved ones by increasing their good luck throughout the coming year? This Yuletide custom lets you make a unique magickal gift for everyone on your list.

- A Yule log
- Matches or a lighter
- A cloth drawstring pouch for each person on your gift list
- Dried pink rose petals (for love)
- Dried lavender buds (for peace of mind)
- Dried basil (for protection)
- Dried mint leaves (for prosperity)
- Dried echinacea (for health)
- A sheet of paper
- Scissors
- A pen

BEST TIME TO PERFORM THE SPELL:

- Yule (usually December 21)

On the night of the winter solstice, build a Yule fire in a safe place and burn an oak log in it. The next morning when the ashes have cooled, scoop some into each pouch. Add the dried botanicals. Cut the sheet of paper into slips, one for each person on your list. Write a personalized wish on each slip of paper. Fold the papers three times and add them to the pouches. Tie the pouches closed and give them to your loved ones.

IMBOLC, BRIGID'S DAY, OR CANDLEMAS

This sabbat honors Brigid, the beloved Celtic goddess of healing, smithcraft, and poetry. A favorite of the Irish people, Brigid was adopted by the Church and canonized as Saint Brigid when Christianity moved into Ireland. Her holiday begins on the evening of January 31 and concludes on February 2, although some witches celebrate it around February 5, when the sun reaches 15 degrees of Aquarius. This marks the midpoint between the winter solstice and the spring equinox.

In the Northern Hemisphere, daylight is increasing and the promise of spring is in the air. We begin to notice the first stirrings of new life. Therefore, Imbolc is considered a time of hope and renewal.

The Holiday's Significance

Brigid's association with the fires of the hearth and the forge represent both the strengthening of the sun's light and creativity. Brigid is one of the fertility goddesses, and Imbolc means "in the belly." In agrarian cultures, this is the time when baby animals grow in their mothers' wombs. This holiday honors all forms of creativity, of the mind as well as the body. Illustrations of Brigid sometimes show her stirring a great cauldron, the witch's magick tool that symbolizes the womb and the receptive, fertile nature of the Divine Feminine. As the goddess of inspiration, Brigid encourages everyone, regardless of gender, to stir the inner cauldron of creativity that exists within.

Ways to Celebrate Imbolc

Witches celebrate this spoke in the Wheel of the Year as a reaffirmation of life and a time to plant "seeds" for the future. In keeping with the holiday's theme of fire, you can light candles to honor Brigid. Fill your cauldron with soil or kitty litter. The cauldron symbolizes the womb of the Goddess. Take nine tapered candles and "plant" them into the "earth" in a spiral pattern, beginning in the center and continuing in a clockwise direction. With each candle, contemplate a different aspect of Imbolc:

1. Light the candle in the middle first, picturing light penetrating winter's darkness.
2. As you light the second candle, welcome the approaching spring.
3. Think of the possibilities contained in new life and new beginnings as you light the third candle.
4. With the fourth candle, imagine your own "rebirth" and your relationship to the Divine Mother.
5. As you light the fifth candle, consider the lessons your spiritual path has taught you. Give thanks for challenges met and knowledge gained.
6. The sixth candle represents the unknown, the lessons that lie before you and all the things you have yet to learn.

7. Light the seventh candle and meditate on things you wish to change. They can be mental, physical, emotional, or spiritual. Think of how you can use your magick to make positive changes in your life.

8. The eighth candle represents the things you wish to heal. These might be physical ailments, the suffering of the planet, rifts in relationships, and so on. Make room for the healing to begin within you. Release old wounds and past hurts. Take responsibility for your health. Focus on the best possible outcomes for situations that are beyond your control or influence.

9. As you light the ninth and final candle, welcome inspiration into your life. Sing or play music. Write a poem in Brigid's honor. Paint a picture. Even if you don't think you are particularly artistic, use the energy of the season and enjoy the creative process. Fashion a special charm or a new blend of incense. Whatever your chosen method of expression, ask the Goddess to inspire you and lend her beauty to your work.

SPRING EQUINOX OR OSTARA

Pagans and witches celebrate Ostara when the sun enters 0 degrees of Aries, around March 21. In the Northern Hemisphere, the spring equinox ushers in warmer weather, days that are longer than nights, and life reawakening. Birdsong fills the air and new buds sprout on bare tree limbs; baby animals are born and the greening of the earth begins.

Christianity adopted this joyful period of the year for the celebration of Easter (which usually falls near the spring equinox). Ostara gets its name from the German fertility goddess Ostare; the word *Easter* derives from the same root. Both holidays celebrate the triumph of life over death.

The Holiday's Significance

The spring equinox marks the first day of spring and the start of the busy planting season in agrarian cultures. Farmers till their fields and sow seeds. Ostara, therefore, is one of the fertility holidays and a time for planting seeds—literally or figuratively. Because day and night are the same length on the equinoxes, these holidays also signify balance.

Ways to Celebrate Ostara

On Ostara, sow seeds that you want to bear fruit in the coming months. This is an ideal time to launch new career ventures, move to a new home, or begin a new relationship. If you're a gardener, you'll start preparing the soil and planting flowers, herbs, and/or vegetables now. Consider the magickal properties of botanicals and choose plants that represent your intentions (see Chapter 11). If you don't have room for a garden, you could plant seeds in a flowerpot to symbolize wishes you hope will grow to fruition in the coming months.

Origins of the Easter Bunny

In an old German story, a rabbit laid some sacred eggs and decorated them as a gift for the fertility goddess Ostara. Ostara liked the beautiful eggs so much that she asked the rabbit to share the eggs with everyone throughout the world.

Some popular Easter customs have their roots in Ostara's symbolism. Eggs represent the promise of new life, and painting them bright colors engages the creative aspect of the sabbat. Some cultures connect the egg's golden yolk with the sun. You might enjoy decorating eggs with magickal symbols, such as pentagrams and spirals. Rabbits, of course, have long been linked with fertility.

Decorating Eggs for Ostara

Ukrainian folk art gives us some of the best examples of ritual egg decoration. Two main types of decoration are called *krashanka* and *pysanka*. *Krashanka* (plural *krashanky*) comes from the word *kraska*, meaning "color" and refers to an egg dyed a single brilliant hue. Believed to possess magickal powers, these eggs were usually eaten. People placed the shells under haystacks or stashed them in the thatched roofs of their homes as protective charms against high winds. *Krashanky* were also used for healing physical ailments. A sick person might wear a whole *krashanka* on a string around his neck, or place the egg on the infected part of the body as a cure.

Pysanky (plural of *pysanka*), which comes from the word *pysaty* meaning "to write," involves decorating the egg with a variety of symbols and a wide array of colors. Believed to provide protection against fire and lightning, these eggs were displayed in the home, carried as talismans, and exchanged as gifts. An old folk legend claimed that *pysanky* ruled the very fate of the world. Only *pysanky* could stem the flood of evil that threatened the earth, and if people ever gave up the custom a vicious monster would consume the world.

You can create your own magick *krashanky* by hard-boiling some eggs. Make natural vegetable dyes from red cabbage (for red dye), beets (purple), yellow onion skins (yellow), carrots (orange), and spinach (green). Combine chopped dye material with a quart of water and boil. Strain the liquid into a jar and add 2 tablespoons of white vinegar to set the dye.

Soak the eggs in the color of your choice, making sure that the liquid covers the eggs completely. The longer the eggs soak, the deeper the color will be; however, they will not be nearly as dark as the dye liquid itself. For the most intense color, allow the eggs to soak overnight in the refrigerator. Be careful when handling freshly dyed eggs, as some of the dye will rub off.

After you eat the eggs, burn the shells in a ritual fire or cast them into flowing water—it's bad luck to just toss them in the trash.

To make a *pysanka*, pierce both ends of the egg and carefully blow out the contents. With a wax crayon, draw magick symbols and images on the shell. Then immerse the egg in the dye—the wax will prevent the dye from adhering to the marked portions of the egg. The wax designs will be lighter and will stand out against the darker background. When you are satisfied with your work, allow the shell to dry completely. You can then remove the wax by warming the eggshell in an oven for a few minutes, then wiping the wax off with a paper towel.

BELTANE

Witches usually celebrate Beltane on May 1, although some prefer to mark it around May 5, when the sun reaches 15 degrees of Taurus. Flowers bloom and plants begin sprouting in the fields. Bees carry pollen from blossom to aromatic blossom. The sabbat is named for the god Baal or Bel, sometimes called "the bright one." In Scottish Gaelic, the

The Modern Guide to Witchcraft

word *bealtainn* means "fires of Belos" and refers to the bonfires Pagans light on this sabbat. This ancient holiday has been adopted as May Day, and some of Beltane's old rituals (*sans* the overt sexuality) are still enacted today.

The Holiday's Significance

The second fertility holiday in the Wheel of the Year, Beltane coincides with a period of fruitfulness. To ancient and modern Pagans alike, this holiday honors the earth and all of nature. In early agrarian cultures, farmers built fires on Beltane and led livestock between the flames to increase their fertility. The tradition of the Beltane fires survived in Wales until the 1840s; in Ireland, the practice continued into the mid-twentieth century; and in Scotland to this very day, the Beltane Fire Society holds an annual bonfire.

Sexuality is also celebrated on this sabbat—the Great Rite (the sacred union of God and Goddess) has traditionally been part of the holiday's festivities. In pre-Christian days, Beltane celebrants engaged in sexual intercourse in the fields as a form of symbolic magick to encourage fertility and a bountiful harvest. Children who were conceived at this time were said to belong to the Goddess.

Ways to Celebrate Beltane

It's best to celebrate Beltane outside in order to appreciate nature's fullness. Because Beltane is a fertility holiday, many of its rituals contain sexual symbolism. The Maypole, around which young females dance, is an obvious phallic symbol. Witches often decorate the Maypole with flowers in recognition of the earth's beauty and fruitfulness. Sometimes a woman who seeks a partner will toss a circular garland over the top of the pole, signifying the sex act, as a way of asking the Goddess to send her a lover. You may also choose to write wishes on colorful ribbons and tie them on a tree.

Another fertility ritual utilizes the cauldron, symbol of the womb. Women who wish to become pregnant build a small fire in the cauldron, then jump over it. If you prefer, you can leap over the cauldron to spark creativity in the mind instead of the body.

Beltane's connection with the earth and fullness makes this sabbat an ideal time to perform prosperity magick. Incorporate peppermint, parsley, lavender, alfalfa, cedar, or money plant into your spells. This is also a good time to make offerings of food and wine to Mother Earth and the nature spirits.

SUMMER SOLSTICE OR MIDSUMMER

In the Northern Hemisphere, the summer solstice is the longest day of the year. The Sun King has now reached the highest point in his journey through the heavens. Witches generally celebrate Midsummer around June 21, when the sun enters 0 degrees of the zodiac sign Cancer. This is a time of abundance, when the earth puts forth her bounty.

The Holiday's Significance

In early agrarian cultures, Midsummer marked a period of plenty when food was abundant and life was easy. Our ancestors celebrated this joyful holiday with feasting and revelry. At this point, however, the sun has reached its pinnacle and begins its descent once again.

Folklore says that at Midsummer earth spirits abound—this belief inspired Shakespeare's delightful play *A Midsummer Night's Dream*. If you wish, you can commune with the elementals and fairies at this time. Our ancestors regarded Midsummer's Eve as a time of intense magick, especially for casting love spells. Any herbs gathered at midnight on Midsummer's Eve were believed to have unparalleled potency.

Ways to Celebrate Midsummer

Just as they've done for centuries, witches today celebrate the summer solstice with feasting, music, dancing, and thanksgiving. Remember to share your bounty with the animals, too, and to return something to Mother Earth as a sign of gratitude.

Midsummer is also a good time to collect herbs, flowers, and other plants to use in magick spells. Some say that if you wish to become invisible, you must wear an amulet that includes seeds from forest ferns gathered on Midsummer's Eve. Spells for success, recognition, and fulfillment are best done on the summer solstice, too.

Candle Spell to Mark Midsummer
Candles represent the sun and the fire element, so burning them at the sun's peak is a common way to mark the holiday.

INGREDIENTS/TOOLS:
- 3 candles: 1 red, 1 orange, and 1 yellow
- Cinnamon or sandalwood essential oil
- 3 candleholders
- The Sun card from a tarot deck
- Matches or a lighter

On Midsummer's Eve, dress the candles with the essential oil and fit them in their holders. Arrange the candles in a triangle pattern with the point facing you, on your altar or another place where they can burn safely. Lay the Sun card face up in the center of the triangle. Light the candles. The Sun card represents fulfillment, abundance, recognition and respect, creative energy, and all the good things in life.

As you stand in front of your altar, feel the message of this card being directed toward you and visualize yourself absorbing all that it symbolizes. Sense the candle flames illuminating you and increasing your power on every level. Imagine yourself radiating with the sun's bright light. Stand this way for as long as you like, allowing the fiery force to fill you. When you feel ready, snuff out the candles and pick up the tarot card. Slip it in your pocket. Wherever you go, whatever you do the next day, you'll shine like the sun and enjoy the fullness of Midsummer.

LUGHNASSADH OR LAMMAS
Named for the Irish Celtic god Lugh (Lew in Wales), this holiday is celebrated either on August 1 or around August 5, when the sun reaches 15 degrees of Leo. This cross-quarter day falls halfway between the summer solstice and the fall equinox. According to Celtic mythology, Lugh

is an older and wiser personification of the god Baal or Bel (for whom Beltane is named). Lughnassadh (pronounced LOO-na-saad) is the first of the harvest festivals. The early Christians dubbed the holiday Lammas, meaning "loaf-mass," because the grain was cut at this time of the year and made into bread.

The Holiday's Significance

Corn, wheat, and other grains are typically harvested around Lughnassadh. In agrarian cultures, this was the time to begin preparing for the barren winter months that lay ahead. Our ancestors cut, ground, and stored grain, canned fruit and vegetables, and brewed wine and beer in late summer. The old English song "John Barleycorn Must Die" describes the seasonal ritual of rendering grain into ale.

Early Pagans sold their wares at harvest fairs and held athletic competitions at this time of the year. You can see this age-old tradition carried on today at country fairs throughout rural parts of the United States.

Ways to Celebrate Lughnassadh

Today, witches enjoy sharing bread and beer with friends on Lughnassadh, just as they've done for centuries. You might like to bake fresh bread from scratch or even brew your own beer as part of the celebration. While you're kneading the bread, add a dried bean to the dough. When you serve the bread, whoever gets the bean in his piece will be granted a wish.

If you like, you can fashion a doll from corn, wheat, or straw to represent the Sun King. To symbolize the time of year when his powers are waning, burn the effigy in a ritual fire as an offering to Mother Earth. The custom of decorating your home with dried corncobs, gourds, nuts, and other fruits of the harvest is also connected to Lughnassadh.

AUTUMN EQUINOX OR MABON

The autumn equinox usually occurs on or about September 22, when the sun reaches 0 degrees of Libra. Once again, day and night are of equal length, signifying a time of balance, equality, and harmony. Mabon is also a harvest festival, and witches consider it a time for giving thanks for the abundance Mother Earth has provided.

The Holiday's Significance

This sabbat marks the last spoke in the Wheel of the Year. From this day until the winter solstice, the Sun King's path arcs downward toward earth. As the days grow shorter and the cold, barren winter approaches, witches reflect on the joys and sorrows, successes and failures of the year that is nearing its conclusion. Like all harvest festivals, this is also a time to give thanks for the year's bounty and to recognize the fruits of your labors.

Mabon is a good time to do magick spells that involve decrease or endings. Do you want to let go of self-destructive beliefs or behaviors? Lose weight? End an unfulfilling relationship? Now is the time to break old habits and patterns that have been limiting you. Anything you wish to eliminate from your life can now be released safely, before the New Year begins with Samhain.

Ways to Celebrate Mabon

Because the equinox is a time of balance, try to balance yin and yang, active and passive on this day. Seek rest and activity, solitude and socializing in equal portions. Mabon marks the sun's entrance into the zodiac sign Libra, which astrologers connect with peace, diplomacy, harmony, and balance. Are you at odds with someone? If so, this is a good time to make peace. Is something causing you stress? Use the energy of this special day to find ways—magickal and/or practical—to ease that stress and restore balance in your life.

As our planet continues revolving in a great wheel around the sun, the seasons of the witch keep you attuned to the earth and the sky—even if you live in a high-rise in the middle of a city. They also link you to the past, the traditions of your ancestors, and the ongoing circle of birth, death, and rebirth.

Chapter 22

WHERE DO YOU GO FROM HERE?

As you can see from what we've touched upon in this book, the world of magick is vast and complex. Countless books have been written about magick, and more are published every day. Movies and television shows, no matter how silly, reflect a growing interest in magick. Now that witchcraft and wizardry have come out of the closet and people around the world are sharing their wisdom openly, the field will continue to grow ever richer. Everyone's experiences contribute to the development of the whole. Each witch is a torchbearer whose flame, when joined with others', lights up the world.

If you've managed to finish reading this book, you're surely ready for more. Maybe you're trying to decide which magickal path suits you best—the simplicity and earthiness of kitchen and hedge witchery, the drama of ceremonial magick, or something else? Maybe you're wondering if you should become part of a larger group or continue studying and practicing alone. The ever-expanding circle of witches worldwide provides opportunities to share your ideas with a supportive community and to align your abilities with other witches and magicians. You can even join an online coven. This chapter will help you decide what's best for you, at least for now.

SOLITARY WITCHCRAFT: IS IT RIGHT FOR YOU?

Some witches choose to work alone rather than with a group. Perhaps no coven is available in her community, or she may prefer to follow solitary practice because it suits her particular purposes, temperament, or lifestyle. Some people may work alone for a period, and then join a coven for a period, or vice versa. Witches who don't belong to a coven may still gather with "kindred spirits" to celebrate the sabbats or other events, in a sort of extended Circle.

For seasoned witches, a solitary path may be simply a matter of choice. For the beginner, however, working alone can be, well, lonely. It can also be more difficult to stumble along by yourself, instead of being guided by more experienced colleagues. Unfortunately, most of us didn't have the opportunity to learn from experts as children. On the other hand, a solitary pursuit enables you to develop your own style of magickal expression, rather than taking on the ideology or outward form of an established group.

As a solitary witch—especially if you're just starting out—some guidelines can help you proceed safely and successfully:

- Read lots of books by different authors, to gain a variety of insights and perspectives.
- Meditate regularly to improve your mental focus and your connection with your higher self.
- Set a schedule for yourself that makes magickal study and practice part of your everyday life, just like working out at the gym.
- Apply what you learn—study alone won't make you a witch.
- Start with simple rituals and spells, then work up to more complicated ones.
- Don't get discouraged if something doesn't turn out the way you'd planned; try to determine what went wrong and why, and learn from your mistakes.
- Practice, practice, practice. Magick is like every other skill—the more you do it, the better you get.
- Keep a grimoire of your experiences.

After you've spent time studying and practicing on your own, you'll have a better idea of what type of magick appeals to you and which path you want to follow. At some point, you may decide to find a teacher or a group of like-minded individuals to work with. Working with a teacher can help you advance more quickly and may steer you away from some pitfalls along the way. Good teachers tend to be selective about the students they take on. If you can show that you've done your homework through solitary study, you'll have a better chance of convincing a teacher to help you reach the next level. Remember the old saying, "When the student is ready, the teacher will appear."

Witchcraft tends to appeal to people who dislike hierarchy and rigid dogma. In the past, witches often lived apart from the community they served, and even if people valued their wisdom and healing powers, the witches never quite fit in. Many modern witches were raised in patriarchal religions that didn't encourage free thinking; they have chosen Wicca (or another Pagan path) because it allows them to follow their own truth.

WHAT'S THE SCOOP ON COVENS?

The word *coven* originated from the Latin term *coventus*, meaning "assembly" or "agreement." (Covenant comes from the same root.) The term first appeared in Scotland around the 1500s to denote a witches' meeting or a local group of practicing witches. However, the word was rarely used until the modern witchcraft movement became more public and popularized.

In her book *The Spiral Dance*, Starhawk describes a coven as "a Witch's support group, consciousness-raising group, psychic study center, clergy-training program, College of Mysteries, surrogate clan, and religious congregation all rolled into one." That about sums it up. In short, a coven is a spiritual family in which each member is committed to the principles of the Craft and to one another.

It's nice to have "kinfolk" with whom you can share information about magick and your spiritual beliefs. Covens provide an opportunity for learning on all levels. It's also fun to celebrate meaningful holidays and events with people who feel as you do. In a world that still doesn't completely accept witches and magick, a coven brings you into a community where you can feel safe, accepted, and valued. Furthermore, the power a group can raise when working together far exceeds what one witch could muster alone.

The Magick Number Thirteen

A traditional coven has thirteen members, although some groups may choose to include more or fewer. Keeping the group small enables intimacy to grow among members and reduces the likelihood of developing into a pack of disciples led by a guru. Why thirteen? A year contains thirteen lunar months. Witchcraft is closely aligned with the moon and its feminine energy.

As you can well imagine, a group of independent-minded witches will likely have lots of differing opinions, ideas, and objectives. At times things can get pretty complicated. Some covens split up over trivial matters; others work through problems and find solutions. If you decide to become part of a coven, you'll want to ask yourself if you are willing to devote the effort necessary to make the coven work. Being part of something greater than yourself requires cooperation, respect, and tolerance.

Benefits of Working with a Coven

You can learn a lot—about magick and life—through working with a coven, especially a well-established one. In particular, you will have the opportunity to:

- Learn what modern magick really is, versus popular ideas and misrepresentations
- Discover the history of a specific magickal tradition
- Receive instruction on how to meditate and focus your mind effectively (in a group setting)
- Learn how to raise and direct energy through group spells and rituals
- Develop a closer relationship with deities that the coven considers important to its purposes
- Receive guidance on how to select your magick tools and use them effectively

Unless the group is eclectic, these points will be explained to you before you get involved. Usually, you'll have a chance to get to know the witches in a group and to work with them for a while before you (and they) decide if you should become a member.

Coven Culture

The best covens are made up of individuals who take their responsibility to the group seriously. You want a group whose practices honor both the individual and the group.

Consider the coven's traditions. Some covens follow specific "lineages" and ideologies, such as Celtic or Egyptian, Dianic or Alexandrian. If a coven holds to a particular tradition that doesn't interest you or makes you feel uncomfortable, you're in the wrong place. Ask yourself the following questions:

- What kind of attendance and study requirements are expected of you?
- Do these mesh with your schedule and responsibilities?
- Does the group have a specific initiation ritual? What is it like? Is there anything in that ritual that doesn't fit your vision?
- Does the group require secrecy? If so, what's the reason behind it and how hush-hush is everything?

Ask to attend an open Circle, celebration, or other function before you consider membership. This will allow you to observe how the coven operates and how the people involved interact.

Only you can determine whether joining a coven is right for you, and if it is, which coven best suits your objectives. Take your time. Bear in mind that every group will have its strengths, weaknesses, and idiosyncrasies—that's part of being human. Find a group with whom you feel a common bond and focus on the big picture; the nitpicky stuff you can work on over time.

FINDING A COVEN THAT'S RIGHT FOR YOU

After you've carefully considered the pros and cons of joining a coven, and decide to take the next step, how do you go about finding a group to join? It's not as if covens are listed in the Yellow Pages! You can, how-ever, discover a wealth of resources and information online. The first place to look is *www.witchvox.com*. Since 1997, "The Witches' Voice" has provided a forum for Neopagans around the world, including news, information, services, festivals, and a list of covens.

You may find a coven in your own hometown, or at least in your state. Get in touch with a group's contact person—she should be able to give you more information about groups and gatherings. If none exists in your area, you could connect with one of the many online covens and Pagan groups.

Also check bulletin boards at bookstores, health food cooperatives, yoga centers, and New Age shops. A nearby Unity or Unitarian Univer-salist Church could steer you in the right direction—it may even provide space for Circles and other spiritual events.

Leaders and Members

If you're lucky, you'll find several groups to choose from. Pay par-ticular attention to two key points: the aptitude of the leaders and the cohesiveness of the membership. These two factors can make or break a coven.

The best leaders don't seem to need titles. They are skilled facilita-tors, communicators, and diplomats. They remain sensitive to the indi-viduals and to the greater whole. They teach, inspire, and motivate the members of the coven. When deciding between covens, ask yourself whether the leaders have these qualities and whether they have earned the respect of the coven for their wisdom, responsibility, openness, and consistency.

The best members are those who work together for the greater good, placing their individual preferences and desires second to the group's. They are dedicated to the group's goals and the magickal tradition to which they belong. They support and encourage one another, and refrain from gossiping, criticizing, or bickering among themselves.

The witches you want to work with will welcome you into the collec-tive and respect you, without judging or trying to control you. They'll willingly share information with you and seek your input.

Cautions and Caveats

You'll want to keep in mind these things when considering a coven. If you see any of these warning signs, don't get near 'em with a ten-foot pole!

1. Any group that says you *must* do something in a particular way, even if it goes against your personal taboos or moral guidelines, is not for you.
2. Seeing members grovel before the coven's leader should raise a red flag. A leader needs help and assistance, but should not order members around like servants.
3. Be wary of any coven that charges dues for membership, unless there is a valid reason for fees, such as renting a place to gather (and proper accounting is in place). Most witches believe that learning should be free. It's okay to ask for help with the gas, or munchies for a meeting, but there's a huge difference between this and making a fast buck off someone's spiritual thirst.
4. A group whose members brag about their numbers, consider themselves all-powerful, or claim a 100-percent success rate in their magick isn't worth your time.

Many spiritual groups have been guilty of these problems—not just witches. Spiritual hubris is one of the most seductive and destructive forms of arrogance. Of course, witches aren't ego free, nor are they enlightened beings. They are humans, trying their best to become better people every day in every way.

Joining a Coven

If you have found your ideal coven and would like to join, the next step is to have an old-fashioned chat with the group's leader. Tell him or her of your interest and what attracted you to this particular coven. Ask if the coven is open to new members and how to go about getting more involved. Find out when they hold initiations. The initiation process will vary from group to group, but in any case you'll probably have some studying ahead of you and some things to learn before an actual initiation occurs.

Start thinking ahead. What role do you see for yourself in this group? Do you seek a specific function that utilizes your skills and talents? If, for example, you're a musician you might enjoy playing at rituals. Or, if you're a good writer, perhaps you could create some specialized spells, incantations, or rituals for the group.

This attitude will show your sincerity—and that you're thinking in terms of the group and not just about yourself. Also, it will help you define your place in the coven if and when you choose to take the next step (initiation).

Initiation Into a Coven

The initiation is a very important moment of bonding. At this stage, coven members extend their Circle, in all its quirky intimacy, to another person. Every person in the group should be present for this activity.

Each coven will enact its own, unique initiation ritual, even though there may be similarities from group to group. The ritual reflects the philosophy, traditions, objectives, and orientation of the group.

Welcoming Ceremony

One nice welcoming ritual involves braiding or knotting yarn to symbolize that the new member's path is tied in with the rest of the coven. The initiate brings a length of yarn, which is tied into the bundle created by the current members. In some cases, the coven's priest or priestess will keep the bundle or wear it as a belt as a sign of office.

At the time of initiation, new members can choose the magickal names they wish to use in sacred space. They then go to each person present, introduce themselves by that name, and greet them as brothers or sisters in the Craft (perhaps with a kiss on the cheek or a hug). Some covens have degrees of initiation and you may progress to higher levels in time.

If, down the road, you find you've made the wrong choice, there's nothing to prevent you from leaving a coven. Although covens would like people to stay for a while for the sake of continuity, witches recognize that each individual's path changes over time. Try to part on good terms. As witches say: "Merry meet, merry part, and merry meet again!"

The Modern Guide to Witchcraft

FORMING YOUR OWN COVEN

Sometimes you can't find an existing coven that meets your needs. Or you may have belonged to a coven, but over time things have changed and it's time to try something else. If you don't wish to be solitary, you might consider forming your own group.

Remember, this isn't a social club, it's a spiritually mindful group and establishing it should be done with sincerity. Sometimes people form covens for the wrong reasons (for instance, to show off to friends or weird out their parents). Do some preliminary soul-searching—you really need to know yourself and be honest about your intentions.

Getting Down to Details

If you've determined this is the right move for you, decide how many people you want to be involved. Thirteen is the traditional number of witches in a coven, but you don't have to follow that custom. Set a reasonable limit on membership. Quantity is less important than quality—in fact, a large quantity may diminish quality.

Next, ask yourself what kind of coven you want. Do you intend to focus on a specific magickal tradition? Do you want your group to be religious or secular? Do you want a rotating leadership or one defined leader? How will you choose the leader(s)? In other words, consider all the factors that will define and flesh out your group. These guidelines will make it easier for others to decide whether your coven is right for them.

Here are some other things to consider:

- How will authority and responsibility be handled?
- Will your coven work magick for magick's sake, or will you bring religious aspects into your group?
- Where and when will you meet?
- Will you have requirements about how many meetings a year a person must attend to remain a member?
- Will you have study requirements?
- Will members participate in activities together outside the coven setting?

- Do you plan to keep a book of shadows for your group (and if so, how and where will it be maintained)?
- Will you need to have specific tools or clothing for your coven meetings?
- What festivals will you observe?
- What other types of gatherings do you want to hold (for instance, to respond to a member's personal needs)?
- What types of members' personal problems should the coven avoid getting involved in?
- How will someone attain the role of priest or priestess in your group?
- Who will make the decisions? Will you run your coven democratically, or will the leader's word be the final authority in matters?

After you've ironed out these details, politely approach individuals you think might be interested. Talk over what you envision and listen carefully to the way each person responds. It's okay for them to ask questions. If they don't, you should be worried. Nonetheless, somewhere at the bottom line, their vision of the group has to mesh with yours, or there are going to be problems.

Moving Forward with Your Group

Once you've found a core group, the next stage is the "shake 'n' bake" period. Consider setting a time period (for example, a year and a day) before anyone is considered a full, formal member of the coven (and before she's initiated into the group). This trial period gives everyone a chance to see if the relationships between the members work. It also allows time to learn the skills necessary for working magick together. Rome wasn't built in a day, and neither is a good coven.

During this growing stage, try out a variety of rituals, spells, and meditations together, keeping notes in your book of shadows about each event. Find out what sensual cues work best for everyone. Note what goes really wrong, and what goes really right. Review these notes regularly.

At the end of the trial period, everyone should sit down together and powwow. Discuss your accomplishments. Talk about what has and

The Modern Guide to Witchcraft

has not worked. Ask each person if he or she would like to continue in a more formalized manner. If the answer is yes, great! If not, separate as friends and spiritual helpmates. Just because you're not working magick together doesn't mean your friendship will end.

Those who decide to move forward now have an even greater task ahead, that of keeping things going. Establish a line of authority and really start organizing. And, of course, it's time to start formally meeting as a coven.

LIVING A MAGICKAL LIFE

As Donald Michael Kraig writes in his book *Modern Magick*, "Magick is not something you do, magick is something you are." Once you shift your way of thinking from mundane to magickal, you'll never see the world as you did before. Now, when you walk into a building, you'll sense its vibrations. Gemstones won't be just pretty baubles; instead, you'll see them as life forms that can aid you in your spellwork. Dreams will no longer be nightly happenstances, but messages from your inner self.

Magickal awareness brings you into intimate connection with all life on earth and with the cosmos beyond. You become conscious of how your thoughts produce results. You notice how your emotions and actions influence others and how they create the circumstances you experience. You sense the presence of nonphysical beings in your environment and allow yourself to be guided by your spiritual guardians. You recognize coincidences as meaningful events and learn from them.

Magick Isn't a Spectator Sport

At some point in your magickal process, you'll have to decide why you've chosen this path. Many people, especially teens and young adults, initially get interested in witchcraft and magick because they feel weak and seek to gain power over others. If you stick with it, however, you'll soon discover that witchcraft is really about gaining power over yourself and your ego.

When people ask me to do magick spells for them, I usually encourage them to get involved themselves. I'm happy to share spells with them, as I've done in this and other books. But often spells you do for yourself can be more effective, if only because the outcome is more important to you than to another person. You can pour your emotions into the spell. You feel a strong connection to any other people who may be involved in the spell. You know the outcome you desire.

Everyone possesses magickal ability. But magick isn't for couch potatoes. It's for people who genuinely want to take charge of their lives and their realities. Magick involves study, discipline, and practice. You'll have to build your mental muscles. It requires you to shift your old habit patterns and beliefs, which is easier said than done. It demands that you "clean up your act" and examine your motives. Most importantly, magick forces you to delve deep within yourself to discover who you truly are.

Setting Up Shop

You don't need to purchase a warehouse full of supplies in the beginning. Start with a few basics: candles, incense, ribbons, and kitchen herbs. As you progress, add some quartz crystals and gemstones. Later on, you may wish to invest in a wand, chalice, athame, and pentagram. Tarot cards, a crystal ball, and pendulum might follow at some point. Build your collection as your need or interest dictates.

Sometimes magick items find you. A friend gives you a tarot deck. You spot a crystal lying on the side of the road. In time, you might decide to grow your own magickal herbs. Some witches like to fashion their own candles or even distill their own scents. Others fabricate special ritual clothing or jewelry. Apply your talents however the muse guides you.

A Lifelong Pursuit

No matter how long you study and practice witchcraft, you'll never know it all. You could be at it your entire adult life and still barely scratch the surface. It's like any other subject: The deeper you dig, the more you discover.

Some people begin studying one type of magick and then move on to learn about another. In the course of your studies, you'll undoubtedly find yourself drawn to certain schools of thought and not others. Your heritage, temperament, interests, locale, companions, and many other factors will influence your decisions about which path to follow.

As you explore different types of magick, you'll discover that despite their outer forms of expression, they contain many common denominators. Gaining knowledge about one school of thought can increase your skill in another. Although some purists might disagree, many people think it's fine to combine features from different magickal traditions and schools of thought.

Magick transforms you. It becomes an integral part of your life and your worldview. You might study intensely at one period and then ease off temporarily. You may do lots of rituals for a time, then not perform any for a while. But once you assume the magician's mantle, you'll wear it forever.

Magick exists everywhere, all the time. You are part of the magick. Blessed be.

INDEX

The Modern Guide to Witchcraft

The Modern Guide to Witchcraft

ABOUT THE AUTHOR

Skye Alexander is the award-winning author of more than thirty fiction and nonfiction books, including *The Everything® Wicca & Witchcraft Book, 2nd Edition; The Everything® Spells & Charms Book, 2nd Edition; Naughty Spells/Nice Spells; Good Spells for Bad Days; The Secret Power of Spirit Animals;* and *The Everything® Tarot Book, 2nd Edition.* Her stories have been published in anthologies internationally, and her work has been translated into more than a dozen languages. The Discovery Channel featured her in the TV special *Secret Stonehenge.* She divides her time between Texas and Massachusetts.